THE POWER OF HIS PRESENCE

The Power of His Presence

✧

Adrian Rogers

CROSSWAY BOOKS • WHEATON, ILLINOIS
A DIVISION OF GOOD NEWS PUBLISHERS

The Power of His Presence

This edition is revised and expanded from Dr. Rogers' earlier book, *The Secret of Supernatural Living.*

Published by Crossway Books
a division of Good News Publishers
1300 Crescent Street
Wheaton, Illinois 60187

Cover design and digital imagery: Pixel Graphics

Author Photo: ©Ramsey Photography

First printing, 1995

Printed in the United States of America

Unless otherwise indicated, Bible quotations are taken from the King James Version.

Library of Congress Cataloging-in-Publication Data
Rogers, Adrian.
The power of his presence / Adrian Rogers
p. cm.
1. Christian life. 2. Presence of God. I. Title.
BV4501.2R6296 1995 248'.4—dc20 94-24968
ISBN 0-89107-841-X

03 02 01 00 99 98 97 96 95
15 14 13 12 11 10 9 8 7 6 5 4 3 2

To Joyce

godly wife and mother,
cherished sweetheart,
wise counselor,
and
best friend

Grateful appreciation is given by the author to the staff at Good News Publishers/Crossway Books, the loving congregation of Bellevue Baptist Church, and especially to Phil Rawley for his editorial assistance and encouragement.

Contents

Preface

Real salvation is not getting man out of earth into heaven, but getting God out of heaven into man. That seems like a simple truth. So why did it take me so long to know it?

It is not that God has willingly hidden these things. Yet, as a young Christian I was evidently blinded to a discoverable secret that literally saturates the Word of God.

I came to Christ for salvation as a teenager. I meant every word of it when I gave my heart to Christ. My young heart was filled with zeal and a love for the things of God. At that time I gave all I knew of me to all I knew of Him.

Yet there was little victory in my daily walk. My small blips of overcoming and victorious living were rare moments in my continuing struggle. Raging hormones, a combative personality, and an untamed tongue were tools I placed in Satan's hand to build a prison house of failure for me. It seemed that I lived there most of my days.

By the grace of God I managed to hold on, to keep myself sexually pure and away from the more vile and open sins; but my life could not be described as victory.

Every so often I would venture from my prison house of failure. I would rededicate my life and make promises.

Now I had a fresh start. I would do better. But resolve, resolution, and repentance were not enough.

I was sincere when I said I wanted to do better. I promised I would try harder. I had learned determination on the football field, and I thought perhaps I could "gut it out" in my Christian life. But before many days or even hours had passed, I had failed again. Back to the dungeon!

If I had only learned then what I know now. There is only One who has ever lived the Christian life. His name is Jesus. If the Christian life is being lived through you, it indeed is not you but Christ who lives in you:

> I am crucified with Christ: nevertheless I live; yet not I, but Christ liveth in me: and the life which I now live in the flesh I live by the faith of the Son of God, who loved me, and gave himself for me. (Galatians 2:20)

Indeed, of all of the truths that I have finally learned, I do not know of one that is more encouraging and life-changing than the marvelous and vital truth that God is alive and well in me through His Son, Jesus Christ.

Yet it is possible to be a Christian like I was and not be aware of this. Paul had to remind the believers at Corinth, "What? know ye not that your body is the temple of the Holy Ghost which is in you, which ye have of God, and ye are not your own?" (1 Corinthians 6:19). He reminded them again in 2 Corinthians 6:16, "Ye are the temple of the living God; as God hath said, 'I will dwell in them, and walk in them; and I will be their God, and they shall be my people.'"

It may take us this lifetime and into eternity to finally understand and grasp all that this means, but I know this: God meant it to be a bright, living reality in our daily lives!

God wants to change the mundane into the momentous and drudgery into delight. He wants to turn struggle into victory.

So in these pages I want to explore with you some implications, applications, and, yes, some common misunderstandings of what it means to have God inhabit your humanity and make you a dwelling-place with a Royal Resident.

I have not arrived, but these truths are helping me move on to maturity and victory. And I am eager to share with you what the Holy Spirit is teaching me.

In our journey together we will touch on theology and some very important doctrines, but I want to give you a word of caution. I have learned that one can know theology and still not experience the power of God.

And I also know beyond a doubt that one can experience Christ without a full understanding of Christian theology. Thankfully, we don't have to choose between the two. Sound doctrine and holy living make up the norm for a victorious Christian.

One of God's great ways of communicating spiritual truth so it is easily understood is by use of illustrations. The Bible abounds with these. Jesus used illustrations over and over as He taught. The vine and the branches, a farmer's field, and a pearl are but a few examples.

One of the clearest illustrations and object lessons of spiritual truth is the Old Testament temple. This magnificent building, constructed according to a precise pattern, was given by the Master Teacher to help us grasp spiritual truth. Therefore, as we consider our experience of Christ we will begin with the truths taught by the Old Testament temple.

Not to worry. We are not going to embark on a complicated study of the intricate details of the temple. Nor will we go down long and come up dry theologically. As you will see, our study is really about you and the victory that God has provided for you.

In the Old Testament God had a temple for His people. In the New Testament He had a people for His temple. Our very bodies are holy temples. And the Lord Himself is the Royal Resident who lives within us. What a staggering thought!

This truth of the fullness of the indwelling God is so very vital and valuable to each one of us. There is no greater truth than to discover that the great God of glory has condescended to indwell mortals such as we. No wonder Paul wrote, "Christ in you, the hope of glory" (Colossians 1:27).

I pray that these words will become a bright, living reality in you, and that you will discover the key that unlocks the treasure house of a thousand other spiritual riches. Drabness and discouragement can be a thing of the past. You are a residence of the living God! Living supernaturally is the most natural thing a Christian can do.

CHAPTER ONE

✧

Where on Earth Does God Live?

In order to understand and apply all of the benefits of Christ's indwelling presence, I want to begin where God began revealing the truth that He would dwell among His people. That beginning point is God's instructions to Moses. The Lord came to Moses and told him to have the children of Israel bring Him an offering for the building of the tabernacle, "that I may dwell among them" (Exodus 25:8).

Don't miss the importance of what God said. The great God of creation, the God who inhabits eternity, wanted a place to dwell among His people! No, the tabernacle could not contain the infinite God, any more than the temple could. But this sanctuary, which was later made permanent in the temple, was the one place on earth where God would meet with His people for instruction, worship, blessing, and atonement for sin.

You can really see the importance of this dwelling in Exodus 29:45, where God said, "I will dwell among the children of Israel, and will be their God." But wait a minute. Was He not Israel's God before this? Yes, He was;

but the construction of the tabernacle/temple would mark a new day in God's relationship with His people. This structure would be a visible, daily reminder of His presence—and, more importantly, of His rightful place in the people's lives.

Calling out a people to be His dwelling-place on earth was God's purpose from the beginning. He made that clear in Exodus 29:46:

> And they shall know that I am the LORD their God, that brought them forth out of the land of Egypt, *that I may dwell among them*: I am the LORD their God. (italics mine)

As the late Bible scholar and professor Dr. Merrill Unger observed, "The tabernacle and all that pertained to it was typical of the presence of God with His people."[1]

Since the tabernacle was a prototype for the temple that would come later, it is important to remember God's command to Moses concerning the building of the tabernacle:

> According to all that I shew thee, after the pattern of the tabernacle, and the pattern of all the instruments thereof, even so shall ye make it. (Exodus 25:9)

A House for God

Many centuries after Moses, when Israel was safe and secure in the land, God put the desire in King David's heart to replace the tabernacle with a more permanent building in Jerusalem, a place where God would continue to dwell among His people. As we know, David was prohibited from actually building the structure, an honor that fell to his son Solomon.

This new building was called "the temple," but it is interesting that it was often referred to as God's "house," a place of settled habitation.[2] Don't miss the point: *each stage of God's habitation among His people was more permanent than the one that preceded it.*

Since Paul called you and me temples of the Holy Spirit, let's look more closely at the Old Testament temple. I said this would not be an intricate study of the temple's details, because that is not our purpose here. Rather, I want to take you on a brief walk around and through the temple.

When God designed the Old Testament temple, He designed it with the same three major parts or sections that the tabernacle contained. It is here that we get to the heart of our study, because the three-fold pattern of the temple teaches us something very important about the nature of our God and about us as His temples in this age.

If we could walk up to that great temple of Solomon's, we would see the first section, the outer court, which was visible to all and visited by all. It was here in the outer court that external worship took place.

Next, and further in, was the holy place. This was a more restricted place where only the priests could go for worship and service to God.

Last, there was the holy of holies. This was the innermost court, absolutely off-limits except for the high priest, who was a prefiguring of Jesus. The high priest would enter the holy of holies once a year to make atonement for the people. It was here that God dwelt in His *shekinah* glory between the cherubim that covered the mercy seat of the ark of the covenant.

A House of Three Rooms

This house of three rooms conformed to a precise pattern. We have already seen that God commanded Moses to be very precise about the original design for the tabernacle. Note also the detailed directions given by David to Solomon for the construction of the temple:

> Then David gave to Solomon his son the pattern of the porch, and of the houses thereof, and of the treasuries thereof, and of the upper chambers thereof, and of the inner parlours thereof, and of the place of the mercy seat. And the pattern of all that he had by the spirit, of the courts of the house of the LORD, and of all the chambers round about, of the treasuries of the house of God, and of the treasuries of the dedicated things. (1 Chronicles 28:11-12)

Then the Bible says, "All this, said David, the LORD made me understand in writing by his hand upon me, even all the works of this pattern" (v. 19). The reason for all this precision is that the tabernacle and the temple were to be grand object lessons. They were to teach us something of the nature of God and the nature of man.

One reason for this grouping into three areas is that the God we know and worship is a triune Being, one God in three distinct Persons—Father, Son, and Holy Spirit.

In fact, as we look at the world around us, we can see how all that God has created reflects the Holy Trinity in some way. For example, all space is triune in dimension: height, width, and depth. Each dimension is distinct from the other two, and yet all three are a part of the same, and no part exists without the other.

The same thing is true of time. Time is triune: past, present, and future. We cannot even imagine one element of time without the other two, and yet the three are always distinct from each other. Together these three components make up one basic entity—time.

Obviously, no illustration can adequately explain the Holy Trinity. Scholars have raced their theological motors to try and find an adequate, rational illustration of the Trinity. But all examples break down somewhere, and I am glad they do! The one true God—Father, Son, and Holy Spirit—is unique. Therefore, God cannot be truly compared to, or illustrated by, anything. We can only know the truth of the Trinity by revelation. "To whom then will ye liken me, or shall I be equal? saith the Holy One" (Isaiah 40:25).

Man: A Royal Residence

The truth of the Holy Trinity is certainly one of the mysteries of the faith. However, it is important to remind ourselves of God's triune nature because as the highest expression of His creation, we reflect His nature. If we are going to appreciate and appropriate all that it means to be the temples of the living God, we need to understand more about man's makeup.

The threefold nature of man is seen in 1 Thessalonians 5:23, where Paul wrote: "And the very God of peace sanctify you wholly; and I pray God your whole *spirit and soul and body* be preserved blameless unto the coming of our Lord Jesus Christ" (italics mine).

Since we know from 1 Corinthians 6:19 that the Christian is God's temple, God's house, we can see how the Old Testament temple—with its three distinct but related parts—illustrates the New Testament truth of man's triune nature. Borrowing the imagery of the temple as God's house, it could be said that we are a house of three rooms.

I am aware that some theologians prefer to think of man as a dichotomy, as having only two parts to his nature: the body as the material part, and the soul and the spirit lumped together as the immaterial part. There is some truth to this approach, because we are definitely both material and immaterial. But the Bible still speaks clearly of spirit, soul, and body. The spirit and soul may never be separated, and they do not operate independently of each other, but they certainly may be differentiated.

I believe that human nature consists of three parts because we are created to know three worlds: the spiritual world, the psychological world, and the material or physical world. Roughly speaking, we can think of these as the world above us, the world within us, and the world beneath us.

These three worlds are related to the three parts of our human nature—spirit, soul, and body. Understand this and many wonderful truths will come into focus. When a man is rightly related to the material world with his body, he is healthy. When he is rightly related to the psychological world with his soul, he is happy. When he is properly related to the spiritual world with his spirit, he is holy.

God's aim is that ultimately we are to experience all three realities: health, happiness, and holiness.

The Outer Man and the Material World

The body is what the Bible calls the "outward man" (2 Corinthians 4:16). The human body corresponds to the outer part of the Old Testament temple. That outer court of the temple was the place of sacrifice; and interestingly, our bodies are also the place of sacrifice. Paul commanded us to present our bodies as "a living sacrifice" (Romans 12:1).

It is not, by the way, true Christian thought to view the body as sinful or evil. The body is God's creation and should be presented to Him as a holy temple. Most of us need to realize this and do a better job of temple maintenance!

Yet, we do not need to buy into this fitness and fashion craze that overestimates the importance of the body. It is not your body, as we will see shortly, that gives you supreme value. Animals also have bodies, and so do vegetables. But man is much more than a toad or a turnip.

The Inner Man and the Psychological World

The soul is a bit more difficult for us to understand, if for no other reason than that it is invisible. Generally speaking we could say that the soul is the psychological part of our nature or human personality that lives in our body or "earthly house."

The Greek word for *soul* is *psyche*. This is the word from which we get *psychic, psychology,* and related words. The Bible seems to indicate that the soul consists primarily of our mind, emotions, and will. God's Word illustrates and catalogs the activities of the soul quite carefully.

For example, the soul is centered in the mind. "So shall the knowledge of wisdom be unto thy soul: when thou hast found it, then there shall be a reward, and thy expectation shall not be cut off" (Proverbs 24:14).

The soul is also the center of our emotions. "And it came to pass, when he had made an end of speaking unto Saul, that the soul of Jonathan was knit with the soul of David, and Jonathan loved him as his own soul" (1 Samuel 18:1).

Finally, the soul is the center of the will. "The things that my soul refused to touch are as my sorrowful meat" (Job 6:7).

We must not think of the soul as being inherently evil or irredeemable. Mind, emotion, and will are only evil as they have been corrupted through sin. The soul itself was created by God that through it we might understand Him, love Him, and serve Him. Thus, when we turn to the Lord, we are never called to crush or suppress our minds or wills or even our emotions. Instead, our souls (as do our bodies and spirits) come into union with Christ. As David says of the Lord, "He restoreth my soul" (Psalm 23:3).

The soul is also that part of our nature through which we relate to ourselves and others. My soul is the real me living inside my "earthly house." When you look at me, all you can really see is the "house" or body that I live in. This truth reminds me of former president Woodrow Wilson's favorite limerick, which went like this:

I know how ugly I are,
I know my face ain't no star,
But I don't mind it,
'Cause I'm behind it;
It's the fellow in front
Who gets the jar.

The Innermost Man and the Spiritual World

The human spirit, in the biblical sense of the word, is a mystery. What I mean is that it could never be discovered by human ingenuity. We know that man has a spirit only through the revelation of God's two-edged Sword. There is no surgeon's scalpel sharp enough to separate the human spirit from the soul; only the living Word of God can do that.

> For the word of God is quick, and powerful, and sharper than any twoedged sword, piercing even to the dividing asunder of soul and spirit, and of the joints and marrow, and is a discerner of the thoughts and intents of the heart. (Hebrews 4:12)

The uniqueness of man is seen in that he has a spirit. Animals certainly have bodies, and they can be said to have a soulish life, but they are void of spirit.

The Bible describes the creation of the animals in this way:

> And God said, Let the earth bring forth the living creature after his kind, cattle, and creeping thing, and beast of the earth after his kind: and it was so. (Genesis 1:24)

The Hebrew word translated "creature" in this verse is *nephesh*, which is usually translated "soul." It means self-conscious life, as opposed to plant life, which is without soul or spirit.

Plants and animals have bodies. Animals also have souls. But when God made man, He breathed into him "the breath of life" (Genesis 2:7). This "breath of life" became the human spirit, for the words *breath* and *spirit* are used interchangeably in the Bible. Man was endowed with a spiritual nature and thus the glorious ability to know and worship God. God did not breathe this special breath of life into any other of His creatures.

So note again, this is why the apostle wrote as he did in 1 Thessalonians 5:23, mentioning the three distinct parts of human nature as he prayed for believers.

If the human spirit is unique in all of creation, we need to ask, what is its function? We have already said it is the part of our nature that enables us to know and worship God. Mary said, "My spirit hath rejoiced in God my Saviour" (Luke 1:47).

Jesus told the woman at the well, "But the hour cometh, and now is, when the true worshippers shall worship the Father in spirit and in truth: for the Father seeketh such to worship him" (John 4:23). And Paul wrote, "The Spirit itself beareth witness with our spirit, that we are the children of God" (Romans 8:16).

Can Dogs Pray?

Animals will never pray, never seek God, never worship, because they have no spirit. That which keeps man from being more than a clever animal, with the ability to talk and walk upright, is his spirit. That which brings dignity to the soul of man—making it worth more than the whole wide world—is that it is inseparably linked to his spirit.

The soul of an animal will perish, but man's soul, eternally linked with his spirit, will live forever. It is endless, timeless, and dateless. One man or woman is worth more than all of the world because man, through his spirit, can know and worship and enjoy God.

How to Function with Unction

Understanding the human spirit is crucial to understanding what it means to have Christ living in us. The Bible describes the human spirit as a lamp. "The spirit of man is the candle of the LORD, searching all the inward parts of the belly" (Proverbs 20:27).

The word "candle" here is better translated as "lamp." A candle burns its own substance, but a lamp must be fed with oil. The oil that feeds the lamp of the human spirit is the Holy Spirit. Thus, we are given illumination through the power of the Holy Spirit working in our human spirit.

God the Father's intention for you and me is that we be joined to Christ so that the Holy Spirit can illuminate or enlighten our human spirit. Then our human spirit is meant to communicate God's divine will to our soul (the mind, emotions, and will), and the soul is meant to motivate the body to navigate out into the world with the purpose of accomplishing God's will.

We can see once again how the working of our spirit correlates with the Old Testament temple. Just as in the temple God's presence was most directly manifest in the innermost room, the holy of holies, so in our human temples the innermost room, the spirit, is where the very presence of God should dwell with all of His fullness.

But the holy of holies did not stand alone. Neither does our spirit exist alone. It takes body, soul, and spirit working together to make us what the New Testament calls a temple of the living God, a place where He dwells.

When we yield to Christ, the will and the power of the invisible God will be made visible through our bodies, we will be at peace in our souls, and we will know the fullness of God's indwelling presence in our spirits. Then our invisible God will receive the glory due His name.

Jesus put it this way: "Let your light so shine before men, that they may see your good works, and glorify your Father which is in heaven" (Matthew 5:16).

At this point I need to remind you that it is possible to misuse God's temple. The Jews were doing it in Jesus' day. They had taken charge of the temple, using it as a marketplace to make a profit. Jesus had to drive out the moneychangers and take control of His temple once again. We can make the same error when we try to take back control of our lives. But instead of fashioning a whip, Jesus uses the prodding of the Holy Spirit to call us back to yieldedness before Him.

Is He There?

As a house of three rooms, the Old Testament temple illustrates the fact that man also is a house of three rooms. Does the great God live in your house? If He does, you have this promise: "For thus saith the high and lofty One that inhabiteth eternity, whose name is Holy; I dwell in the high and holy place, with him also that is of a contrite and humble spirit, to revive the spirit of the humble, and to revive the heart of the contrite ones" (Isaiah 57:15).

Ian Thomas has put it so well:

> To be in Christ—that is redemption; but for Christ to be in you—that is sanctification! To be in Christ—that makes you fit for heaven; but for Christ to be in you—that makes you fit for earth! To be in Christ—that changes your destination; but for Christ to be in you—that changes your destiny! The one makes heaven your home—the other makes this world His workshop.[3]

CHAPTER TWO

✧

Supernaturally Natural, Naturally Supernatural

One of the curses of twentieth-century Christianity is Sunday-morning religion:

They're praising God on Sunday,
They'll be all right on Monday,
It's just a little habit they've acquired.

This is the problem of a house and a heart divided.

Have you ever been in a church service where people act "spiritual"? They get a stained-glass look on their faces and speak in funeral-home tones. Even the minister, who seems normal enough at the church picnic, stands in the pulpit and intones "dearly beloved" as if he'd just swallowed the Communion rail.

Yet, when the service is over and this sanctified throng reaches the cafeteria line over at the shopping center, they seem to be amazingly normal people. They have changed from the spiritual mode to the secular mode like someone has thrown a switch. The entire idea seems artificial, does it not?

The Sacred and the Secular

How do people acquire this "little habit" of worshiping God in church on Sunday and then reverting to their normal behavior when they pass through the doors? It's because they have bought the common idea that life is divided into the sacred and the secular. We leave the secular world outside when we go into a church to worship. Then, because we are in church, we suddenly begin acting like someone we're not. We keep the mask on for the worship hour, then lay it aside and head to the cafeteria line as if nothing had happened.

Let me pose an interesting question. What would happen to people like this if they had to spend all of their time in church? Working in the church, eating there, raising their families there, living there. Do you think their behavior would change? Would they act pious all the time because they were suddenly aware of being in God's presence in His house?

Yes, I know it's impossible to live at church. But as temples of the Holy Spirit, we do live in God's presence in His house. We *are* His house! We're not meant to be victims of "Sunday-morning religion." We are meant to be living sixty minutes an hour, twenty-four hours a day, three hundred and sixty-five days a year in the Spirit, worshiping and serving the Lord.

The sign over the church door where I attended as a boy said, "The Lord is in His holy temple. Let all of the earth keep silence." I mistakenly took that to mean that I had just entered the holy temple and had better start acting religious. How I wish that someone had taught me that the wonderful place I loved was not a temple of God, but that we, His people, are. Of course, we are to be reverent in a church service and should respect the place where we are meeting, but that is not the point at all.

The point is that as a Christian I needed to learn that I could not neatly divide my life into two divisions—the secular and the sacred. But when we restrict God's presence to a locality—the church on the corner, for example—that's what happens. And so we hear people say things like, "Politics and religion don't mix." "Faith is a private matter." "You don't understand . . . This is business!"

Well, it may be business, but it isn't biblical! Because we are indwelt by the Holy Spirit, the line between the secular and the sacred in our lives is erased. We do not need to "act" spiritual. We *are* spiritual. We are the temples of God on a full-time basis. Therefore, responding to life spiritually should be the most natural thing for us! Because the sign over our hearts reads "A temple of God," everything is to be done in His name.

That's exactly what the Apostle Paul said in Colossians 3:16-17. Notice these important verses, which give us the key to bringing all of life under the rule of Christ:

> Let the word of Christ dwell in you richly in all wisdom; teaching and admonishing one another in psalms and hymns and spiritual songs, singing with grace in your hearts to the Lord. And whatsoever ye do in word or deed, do all in the name of the Lord Jesus, giving thanks to God and the Father by him.

Look particularly at verse 17. "Whatsoever ye do" means everything, and therefore everything is to be done in the name of Jesus. That includes all of life. The scope of this exhortation is so wide that there's no room for the strictly secular. Even the so-called secular areas of life are to be sanctified, so that Jesus will be glorified in everything. Because He now lives in me, every day is a holy day, every time is a sacred time, and every task is a sacred task. The spiritual life is seven days a week.

What does it mean to do everything "in the name of the Lord Jesus"? One commentator says it means to live "in harmony with his revealed will, in subjection to his authority, in dependence on his power."[1] I think he has the idea. Jesus' revealed will is that which meets with His *approval.* Doing everything in His name certainly implies His *authority*. And when we act in dependence on Him, He wins the *acclaim* or glory.

Let's look at each of these in turn as we continue exploring what it means to be full-time temples of God.

The Approval of Jesus

In the Bible, as well as in life today, a man's name and his character are linked. So if we are to do everything in the name of Jesus, we must do only those things He can approve of.

One of the techniques that Madison Avenue uses in merchandising is to have a well-known personality endorse a product—that is, to lend his name and reputation to the product. This is frequently done by having the celebrity's picture or autograph inscribed upon some piece of merchandise. Many a little boy has wanted a specific baseball bat because his big-league hero had his name stamped on it.

That superstar was saying in effect, "I approve of this bat. It is consistent with the standards that I hold as a professional athlete, and it's just like the one I use."

In a similar way, to do everything in the name of Jesus means to do only that which He could endorse or approve. All that we do should be consistent with His character. We ought to do or say nothing that we could not sign Jesus' name to!

Rules Are for Kids

If *name* means character, then the character of Jesus, and not some set of rules, is the standard for our Christian life. The Bible is not primarily a rule book with a list of do's and don'ts.

Rules are for kids. The more immature a child is, the more rules his parents must lay down for him. "Don't play with matches." "Come straight home from school." "Practice your music every day for forty-five minutes." The more mature child does not need rules like this. "The son who has come to years of responsibility knows his father's will without having to be provided with a long list of 'Do's' and 'Don'ts.'"[2] The greater the maturity, the fewer the rules.

What a joy it was to me as a father when one of my children faced a situation about which we had not specifically talked and no rules had been laid down, and yet he came through with flying colors. "Daddy, I just did what I thought you would have wanted me to do. I knew you would approve." He did what he felt was consistent with my character.

This is a higher plane of living. One can find loopholes in rules. A lawyer reported to his client in a divorce case, "Mrs. Blake, I've succeeded in making a settlement with your husband that is eminently fair to both of you."

"Fair to both!" exploded Mrs. Blake. "I could have done that myself! What do you think I hired a lawyer for?"

One may twist the law, but he will never find a loophole in the character of Jesus. Therefore, the Bible is not primarily a book of minute laws, but of great principles. And chief among them is to do all in the name of Jesus. We ought to be able to sign His name to our every action.

The Authority of Jesus

Not only does *name* stand for approval, but it also confers authority. The signature on a check gives the banker the authority to pay certain funds out of that account, as long as the check bears the name of a person who has money in that bank.

A policeman who weighs 140 pounds can stand before an 18-wheeler and with uplifted hand say, "Stop, in the name of the law." He is appealing to an authority higher than himself. The truck stops because of that name or authority. The policeman certainly did not and could not stop the truck with physical force. His badge and uniform carry the authority of the government he represents.

We need to learn a lesson right here. Our authority over Satan does not rest in the fact that we are stronger than he is. We indeed are not. Yet when Jesus sent out His disciples He said to them, "Behold, I give unto you power to tread on serpents and scorpions, and over all the power of the enemy: and nothing shall by any means hurt you" (Luke 10:19). What Jesus literally said was, "Behold, I have given you *authority* . . . over all the power of the enemy."

Note the difference between power and authority. The policeman stops the truck with authority, not with power. Likewise, we overcome Satan not with power, but with authority.

Knowing that *name* confers authority, we can understand more fully what it means to pray in the name of Jesus. To pray in His name does not necessarily mean that we close our prayers with the familiar formula, "In Jesus' name, Amen." I cannot find any prayer in the Bible that ends that way. I am not saying it's wrong to close a prayer in that manner, but that is not what Jesus meant when He taught us to pray in His name.

Spiritual Forgery

Prayer in Jesus' name is prayer that has His authority behind it. And remember, name means approval as well as authority. Therefore, I can guarantee you that no prayer will have Jesus' authority if it does not first of all have His approval. There are too many spiritual forgers signing Jesus' name to their prayer checks, but those checks will not be honored at the bank of heaven. There is no authority because there is no approval.

Are you living every day with the conscious authority of Christ in your life? You ought to do your housework, rear your children, earn your salary, and enjoy your leisure time with the authority of His mighty name. Every effort ought to be crowned with the power of heaven.

Let me say here that we can never have authority from Jesus to live as we ought until we are first of all submitted to Him. One of the greatest lessons I have ever learned—and I'm still learning—is that I cannot be over until I'm willing to be under. I cannot have authority until I'm first of all submitted to authority.

We find an amazing example of this truth in Luke 7. A Roman army officer had a servant who was gravely ill. He sent some Jewish friends to ask Jesus to heal the servant, but as Jesus was coming to the house the centurion sent Him this message:

> Lord, trouble not thyself: for I am not worthy that thou shouldest enter under my roof: Wherefore neither thought I myself worthy to come unto thee: but say in a word, and my servant shall be healed. For I also am a man set under authority, having under me soldiers, and I say unto one, Go, and he goeth; and to another, Come, and he cometh; and to my servant, Do this, and he doeth it. When Jesus heard these things, he marvelled at him, and turned him about, and said unto the people that followed him, I say unto you, I have not found so great faith, no, not in Israel. And they that were sent, returning to the house, found the servant whole that had been sick. (vv. 6-10)

This man was a Gentile, but he had such an understanding of authority that Jesus marveled at him. He could command the soldiers under him, and they would go and come. This would continue to be true as long as he stayed under those who were over him. But should he step out from under this authority, he would lose the authority that was his to exercise over those under him.

The centurion then applied this principle to the work of Jesus. He said, in effect, "Jesus, because of Your submission to the Father over You, You have authority over this sickness. Just speak a word and my servant will be healed." The principle is clear. We cannot be over unless we are willing to be under.

What a tragedy when we live without the authority of God. There are pathetic preachers who preach without authority because they will not submit to the authority of the Word of God. They are the "bland leading the bland."

There are failing fathers who have no spiritual authority in the home because they have not submitted to the Lordship of Christ and to their elders in the church. Multitudes of mothers have no authority over their children because they will not submit to their own husbands as unto the Lord.

Think of the Christian young people who have no victory over the sins of the world, the flesh, and the devil because they are rebelling against their parents.

Many Christians, who ought to be victorious in their prayer life and have victory over the devil, are in a state of disarray because they are rebelling against the spiritual leadership that God has set up in the church.

Did you ever teach a youngster to drive a car? Suppose he says, "Dad, show me how to make it go! I've been wanting to get my hands on this baby for a long time."

You say, "Just a minute. Let me show you the brake first of all. You need to learn how to make it stop first."

"Oh, Dad," he replies, "I'm not interested in that. Show me how to make it go."

At that moment the driving lesson is put on hold. So it is with the power of the Spirit. If we are not interested in the *restraint* of the Spirit, we have little hope of knowing the *release* of the Spirit. "In the name of Jesus" means with His authority because I am submitted to it.

The Acclaim of Jesus

Finally, doing everything in the name of Jesus means doing it for His acclaim or honor. Occasionally I receive a note telling me that a gift has been given to a certain cause in my name. That was the donor's way of saying that the gift was given in my honor or for my acclaim. I have learned to pass such honors on to Jesus, because He's the only One who is worthy of acclaim.

You see, as the temple of God my life must be lived for only one purpose—that He will be glorified. This was Peter's goal. "If any man speak, let him speak as the oracles of God; if any man minister, let him do it as of the ability which God giveth: *that God in all things may be glorified through Jesus Christ*, to whom be praise and dominion for ever and ever. Amen" (1 Peter 4:11, italics added). Paul echoed the same desire: "Whether therefore ye eat, or drink, or whatsoever ye do, *do all to the glory of God*" (1 Corinthians 10:31, italics mine).

As one who is indwelt by the Holy Spirit, you carry a tremendous responsibility to God and to man. If, indeed, the sign on your house says "Under New Management," you are *de facto* on display.

It is only the life that is lived with the approval of Jesus and in the authority of Jesus that will bring acclaim to Jesus. To live in the Spirit and to do everything in the name of Jesus means that we will do nothing to dishonor His name.

Just think what would happen if Christians started living this kind of a life every day and in every place. When God's people realize that they are to live what Oswald Chambers has called "naturally supernatural and supernaturally natural" lives, the world will begin to take notice. The best argument for Christianity, and sometimes the best argument *against* Christianity, is the life of a Christian. Not only are we to be His witnesses—we ought to be a part of the evidence!

CHAPTER THREE

✧

Never Home Alone

A little girl was supposed to take her birth certificate to school. Her mother had solemnly warned her not to lose it because of its tremendous importance. But lose it she did. Later she was sitting on the steps of the schoolhouse, crying. The janitor asked her what was wrong. She replied, "I lost my excuse for being born."

Anybody who has not discovered the joy of salvation in Christ and the blessedness of being a temple of the Holy Spirit has indeed lost his excuse, his reason, for being born. Since salvation is the act by which the Spirit takes up His residence in us, we need to understand the importance and necessity of salvation and how man's house came to be empty. In the last chapter we surveyed the house. Here we will look at the work of the Builder and Designer.

I like the word *saved*. Sophisticated theologians may want to steer away from that word because they think it sounds too common, language that belongs under the revival tent. But *saved* is a good word. Furthermore, it is a biblical word, just like its opposite, *lost*.

Saved and *lost* are important words because they describe two conditions of the human heart. They draw a clear line down the middle of the race. Everyone is either saved or lost. In the language of our analogy, whether you are saved or lost determines whether God dwells in your spiritual house or not. We know that no lost person can possibly be a temple of the Holy Spirit, because a lost person does not possess the Spirit. "If any man have not the Spirit of Christ, he is none of his" (Romans 8:9).

I praise God that the Lord Jesus found me when I was a teen-aged boy. I had never been in serious trouble, but I am sure I gave my parents a fair share of heartaches. My folks were good, hard-working, salt-of-the-earth kind of people. Dad earned his living in the automobile and furniture business. I had my share of whippings. Dad always said it was because he loved me. I have often thought that if that was so, I must have been his favorite child, for I received far more of this love than the rest of the kids!

But, like all of us, I needed something more in life than parental example and discipline. At an old-fashioned revival crusade in our hometown of West Palm Beach, Florida, my dad stepped out to give his heart and life to Christ. I followed right behind him. I believe that an eternal change took place in those moments, and that night I became a new creature in Christ. I was lost, but I got saved!

When God Moved Out

Before we can understand and appreciate fully what it means to be saved, we first have to understand what it means to be lost. The gospel has to be bad news before it can be good news.

Very simply, to be lost is to be in a state of spiritual death.

This spiritual death is best illustrated in the experience of Adam. His death and our deaths are linked. "In Adam all die" (1 Corinthians 15:22). But if we died in Adam, just how did Adam die?

You will recall that God had placed Adam and Eve in the Garden of Eden, where He had given them all that they needed to be healthy, happy, and holy. He had made ample provision for Adam—body, soul, and spirit. At that time God Himself lived as a Royal Resident in His first temple, named Adam.

But in order for man to have the ability to truly love God, he had to have the opportunity to choose not to love God. A choice had to be given. God described the basis of that choice to Adam:

> And the LORD God took the man, and put him into the garden of Eden to dress it and to keep it. And the LORD God commanded the man, saying, Of every tree of the garden thou mayest freely eat: but of the tree of the knowledge of good and evil, thou shalt not eat of it: for in the day that thou eatest thereof thou shalt surely die. (Genesis 2:15-17)

When God spoke of death, He was not giving a threat but a warning. Parents are not threatening their children when they warn them about a hot stove. If Adam chose not to love God enough to obey Him, he would die.

What is the record? What did Adam do? "When the woman saw that the tree was good for food, and that it was pleasant to the eyes, and a tree to be desired to make one wise, she took of the fruit thereof, and did eat, and gave also unto her husband with her; and he did eat" (Genesis 3:6).

When Adam disobeyed God, he insulted his Royal Guest. He didn't commit murder or adultery, but he failed to love and obey God. This was his great sin. Adam was no longer a clean and holy house. He was now defiled by sin.

The sure and swift result of Adam's sin was death. We just read it. God had said, "In the day that thou eateth thereof thou shalt surely die" (Genesis 2:17). But wait a minute! Did Adam "surely die"? The Bible records that he went on to live for many hundreds of years! There has been endless discussion and controversy about how, and even if, Adam died on the day he sinned. Indeed he died, but it is so important to understand just *how* he died.

First, Adam died *immediately* in his spirit. Death in the biblical sense is not primarily the separation of the soul from the body, as we think of death. For example, if I were to drop this pen and get very still and stay that way for a long time, some doctor might take my vital signs and say, "He is dead."

But biblically speaking that would be inaccurate. I would simply have moved out of this earthly "house" and gone on to heaven. Jesus said, "Whosoever liveth and believeth in me shall never die" (John 11:26). So how could I be dead? I would be more alive than ever. And while you attended my funeral, I would be "kicking up gold-dust on the streets of Glory," as one writer has put it. For "to be absent from the body [is] to be present with the Lord" (2 Corinthians 5:8).

What I am saying is that spiritual death is far different than physical death. Spiritual death is not the separation of the soul from the body, but the separation of the spirit from God. Adam died spiritually that very day, even though he was left standing on his feet. What happened was that

God's Holy Spirit moved out. God will not live in a dirty house. Adam came under what the Scripture calls the condemnation of sin and death.

A group of college boys wanted to keep the football team mascot, a goat; so they made intricate plans to smuggle the animal into their dormitory room.

"But what about the smell?" someone asked.

"The goat will just have to get used to it," the others replied.

College boys may be content to live in a dirty place, but a holy God will not do so. It is against His very nature.

What was the result of God's moving out of Adam? God's Spirit is to the human spirit as blood is to the body. He is the life-giving power of the human spirit. John said, "In him was life; and the life was the light of men" (John 1:4). These words are speaking of Christ, but what is true of Christ is true of the Spirit as well. God is the light and the life of man.

So when Adam sinned, *the Lord went out*. And when the Lord went out, *the life went out*. And when the life went out, *the light went out*. Adam was now spiritually depraved—no Lord. He was spiritually dead—no life. He was spiritually darkened—no light. It was not until centuries later that the death, burial, and resurrection of Jesus Christ would deal with all three of these problems.

Adam not only died immediately in his spirit. He died *progressively* in his soul. His spirit was supposed to receive directions from God's Spirit. "For as many as are led by the Spirit of God, they are the sons of God" (Romans 8:14). Adam's spirit was, in turn, to give directions to his soul (mind, emotions, and will), which would then motivate and direct his body.

Man was not given the sense of instinct that most animals have. The reason for this is that God made His Holy Spirit available to man. In one sense, the Spirit should be to man what instinct is to the other creatures. Can you imagine the confusion if instinct were removed from bees? Or from birds as they prepare to head south? Or from a guard dog as he senses danger? Take a look at what we call "civilization" and you will have some idea of the result when God's Spirit moved out of man!

So Adam was minus God in his spirit. God no longer lived in him and walked with him. Adam was no longer a *spiritual* man. He was now a *natural* man. That is, sin had reduced him to operating by his soul alone. His spiritual transmitter was jammed. His *mind* became a garden of weeds. His *emotions* began to churn with fear. His *will* was corrupt and paralyzed. He was free to do what he wanted, but not free to do as he ought.

Rather than becoming the master over his house, Adam became the household slave when he rebelled against God. When God moved out, Adam's soul (mind, emotions, and will) took over the control center. Now Adam would operate not as a God-centered man, but as a self-centered man, dominated by sin.

Ever notice how a natural man operates? His mind says, "I think I want to do thus-and-so." His emotions say, "I feel like doing it." His will says, "All right, I'll do it."

Do you know anybody who lives like that? The world is filled with such people. They are the living dead! It sounds like a horror movie, doesn't it? Well, it is horrible, but sadly it's not a movie! All you have to do is watch the evening news to realize that we are living in a chamber of horrors where everyone does exactly whatever he pleases.

Even Christians operate this way all too often. But what does the Bible say? "She that liveth in pleasure is dead while she liveth" (1 Timothy 5:6).

Adam died immediately in his spirit and progressively in his soul. He also died *ultimately* in his body. "And all the days that Adam lived were nine hundred and thirty years: and he died" (Genesis 5:5).

Now, at last, his body had ceased to function. Adam, however, had been dead long before this. He was like a Christmas tree, cut off from the root (the transmitter of life) and brought into your living room. It looks good in your house with all of its colorful ornaments and lights. That is, it looks good until about New Year's Day! By then, what happened to the tree when it was cut off has gradually become obvious by outward signs of deadness.

Similarly, many people who are severed from God through sin decorate themselves and even come to church on Sunday morning and try to worship. They may look very good, but there's no life there. They may even try to please God, but they cannot pull it off. Their temples are adorned but empty. Their houses are brightly decorated, but there's no one home.

Many are aware that something is wrong, and they are miserable. They are cut off from the Source of true life and are dead spiritually. Ultimately they will die physically as well. It has been well said that the heartbeat in your chest is but "a muffled drum beating a funeral march to the grave."

So God's first temple was Adam, but God moved out of Adam. And when God moved out, Adam died. And Adam's death has been passed on to each of us. "Wherefore, as by one man sin entered into the world, and death by sin; and so death passed upon all men, for that all have sinned"

(Romans 5:12). The Bible teaches that we all died in Adam, the result of what theologians call "original sin."

When God Moves Back In

But now comes the good part. Salvation is not merely about getting man out of earth into heaven. It is also about getting God out of heaven and back into man! Here's something exciting: when a person receives Christ and is born again, God reverses the effects of sin!

Adam died immediately in his spirit, progressively in his soul, and ultimately in his body. But when one becomes a child of God, he is *justified immediately in his spirit, sanctified progressively in his soul, and glorified ultimately in his body!*

Nearly 2,000 years ago God the Father made His final move to gain back His dwelling-place among men. By the work of His Holy Spirit in the womb of a godly peasant woman named Mary, the eternal Son of God—the Second Person of the Trinity—assumed human flesh, became man, and was born on earth.

Jesus Christ, from that miracle on, was and is fully God and fully man. They called His name Immanuel—"God with us!" As the firstborn of a whole new race, those with whom God dwells, Jesus proved to us that God could inhabit humanity.

But this was not all. God's justice demands that our sin be dealt with. Jesus died to remove the sin barrier so that God can once more dwell in man. It was sin that caused God to move out, and He cannot return until that sin is properly dealt with. This is why the cross was necessary.

If we were to choose one word to describe the character of God, it might be *love,* because "God is love" (1 John 4:8).

In fact, He is perfect love. But let me suggest a word that perhaps best epitomizes the character of God: *holy*. He is the thrice-holy God, for Isaiah tells us, "Holy, holy, holy, is the LORD of hosts" (Isaiah 6:3).

God's holiness demands that sin be properly judged. If God were to merely overlook our sin, He would cease to be holy. In a court of law, it is said that when a guilty man is acquitted, the judge is condemned. God "will not at all acquit the wicked" (Nahum 1:3).

But through faith in Christ's finished work at Calvary, we who believe are immediately justified in the spirit:

> Now to him that worketh is the reward not reckoned of grace, but of debt. But to him that worketh not, but believeth on him that justifieth the ungodly, his faith is counted for righteousness. Even as David also describeth the blessedness of the man, unto whom God imputeth righteousness without works, saying, Blessed are they whose iniquities are forgiven, and whose sins are covered. Blessed is the man to whom the Lord will not impute sin. (Romans 4:4-8)

God is now free to move into the cleansed temple of our bodies and to dwell in us, because the barrier of sin has been taken away.

But not only are we justified immediately in the spirit—we can also be sanctified progressively in the soul. Our minds, emotions, and wills can be taken captive by the Holy Spirit within the human spirit, and we can begin to live like the people we have become.

Remember that while justification is immediate, sanctification is a process that will not be finished until we are with Jesus. "Being confident of this very thing, that he which hath begun a good work in you will perform it until the day of Jesus Christ" (Philippians 1:6).

After my salvation, I discovered that old habits and ways die hard. The cheating in class, the school-yard fights, truancy, bad language, and disobedience still pulled at me. I was up and down in my Christian life for over a year, and I was miserable.

One night after I had walked my girlfriend home from church, I stopped and prayed. I was tired of the struggle, the doubt, the failure. Also, I had by this time learned more of the truth of God. "Lord Jesus," I prayed, "right now, with all of my heart, once and for all, now and forever, I trust You and You alone to save me according to the promise of Your Word.

"If I have never really trusted You, I do so now. If I am already saved, then I reaffirm it. But one thing I know is that I am driving down a spiritual peg tonight. I do not ask for feeling. I stand upon Your promise, Lord Jesus, and I know that settles it!"

At that moment a wonderful river of God's peace and assurance began to flow through my heart. And, praise His name, it has never stopped flowing.

As a young man I had thought seriously about being a lawyer or an architect. But now I knew that God had a right to make these choices in my life. He would lead me into His will, and He would decide for the best. "Lord, whatever You want me to do, I'll do it. Just let me know," I prayed.

I am not sure exactly how the seed-thought that God might want me to preach got into my heart. But I found it there. "Lord, do You really want me to preach?" I would ask Him. As a high-school football player I was not afraid of much that moved on the gridiron, but the thought of being a public speaker was disturbing. More candidly, it scared me to death.

Yet, this little seed of a thought would not go away. For weeks I would pray like this: "Lord, I think You want me to preach." Then for days I would pray, "Lord, if You don't want me to preach, You had better let me know." Finally it was, "Lord, You are calling me, and I know it."

I finally made a public commitment, and it was settled. From that point on I did not look back. I was thrilled—and still am—that God would call me to serve Him in this way. Joyce, my high-school sweetheart who is now my wife, was also thrilled. In her heart she sensed God calling her into His full-time service as well. This was all a part of the process of sanctification in our lives, and God is still working with us!

But someday the process will be complete. Ultimately we will also be glorified in our bodies. Every Christian should be looking for the coming of the Lord Jesus, "who shall change our vile body, that it may be fashioned like unto his glorious body, according to the working whereby he is able even to subdue all things under himself" (Philippians 3:21).

Therefore, it is not until we receive our glorified bodies at the resurrection that our salvation will be complete. It unfolds in three stages:

Past tense: I have been justified in my spirit and have been saved from the penalty of sin.

Present tense: I am being sanctified in my soul and am being saved from the power of sin.

Future tense: I will be glorified in my body and will be saved from the possibility of sin.

But until the time of my glorification, I have a Royal Resident who lives within me and has promised He will never leave or forsake me (Hebrews 13:5). Is anybody home in your house today?

CHAPTER FOUR

◇

When Glory Fills the House

When King Solomon dedicated that magnificent temple on Mount Moriah, it was among other things an object lesson, an illustration of every believer in the Lord Jesus Christ. For now, after Pentecost, at the moment of our salvation we become temples of the Holy Spirit. God through His Holy Spirit indwells us, just as His Spirit came and filled the holy of holies of Solomon's temple with *shekinah* glory when it was fully dedicated to Him: "And it came to pass, when the priests were come out of the holy place, that the cloud filled the house of the LORD, so that the priests could not stand to minister because of the cloud: for the glory of the LORD had filled the house of the LORD" (1 Kings 8:10-11).

Yet, some Christians appear not to be filled with the Holy Spirit. Glory does not fill their house. They have allowed the self-life and the cares of this world to move the Lord Jesus from that place of preeminence that is rightfully His. They are no longer Spirit-filled but are what the Bible calls "carnal" or fleshly. Therefore, we have this admonition of the Apostle Paul: "Be not drunk with wine, wherein is excess; but be filled with the Spirit" (Ephesians 5:18).

In this chapter I want to address this matter of the Spirit-filled life. I need to emphasize here that a Spirit-filled Christian is not some super-edition of a Christian. He is not a regular believer raised to the highest power! When the God of the universe moves into our lives, He won't be relegated to a back room. He wants to fill the whole house!

Thus *all* Christians ought to be experiencing the Spirit-filled life. It is the normal Christian life. The fullness of the Spirit is not some special touch for the evangelist or minister but is a provision for every blood-bought child of God. "The promise is unto you, and to your children, and to all that are afar off, even as many as the Lord our God shall call" (Acts 2:39).

Since all of this is true, we had better find out what's involved in letting God the Holy Spirit fill every corner of our houses. In Ephesians 5 and 6 Paul gave the reasons, the requirements, and the results of the Spirit-filled life.

Reasons for the Spirit-filled Life

I see at least three reasons why Christians need to live Spirit-filled lives.

OBEDIENCE

The first reason for any Christian to be Spirit-filled is simple obedience. God has told us, "Be filled with the Spirit" (Ephesians 5:18). This is not a suggestion or a request but a command. The Christian who is not Spirit-filled is actually living in rebellion. His disobedience to God is not weakness but wickedness.

Any congregation would be scandalized should the

minister attempt to preach a sermon while drunk. His thick tongue, bleary eyes, and foolish thoughts would cause a quick meeting of the elders, deacons, or other official bodies within the church. What a disgraceful thing it would be. How tongues would wag!

Yet, I sincerely believe it would be a greater sin for any man of God to fail to be filled with the Spirit when preaching than to be drunk. The same verse that commands us not to be "drunk with wine" commands us to be "filled with the Spirit."

The Scripture also teaches that sins of omission are just as offensive to God as sins of commission (James 4:17). In a sense, it is a greater sin to fail to do what we ought than to do what we ought not. As a matter of fact, if we are doing what we ought to do, we cannot be doing what we ought not to do.

Now I am not minimizing the sin of drunkenness or any other sin. But in my estimation the cause of Christ has been hurt far more by Christians who are carnal and not Spirit-filled than by Christians who are drunk. I have known of churches torn apart by carnal leadership. Many people who are at the forefront of church splits are teetotalers. The devil would rather start a fuss in the body of Christ than sell a barrel of whiskey any day.

It is important for us to understand that the Spirit-filled life is not an option. It is not merely a blessing to enjoy; it is a command to obey. To fail to obey is a sin worse than being drunk.

OBLIGATION

A second reason Paul gave for being filled with the Spirit is that it is our obligation. As Christians, we have tremendous responsibilities to fulfill.

Look at the obligation of our *worship life*. "Speaking to yourselves in psalms and hymns and spiritual songs, singing and making melody in your heart to the Lord" (Ephesians 5:19). Our worship life is to be alive with joy and the reality of Christ. This kind of worship is the overflow of the Spirit-filled life. It is what Jesus called "worship in spirit" (John 4:24, NIV).

Yet, many Christians would confess that for them, worship could be more aptly described by the words of the hymn, "How Tedious and Tasteless the Hours."

Look at the obligation of our *wedded life*. "Wives, submit yourselves unto your own husbands, as unto the Lord" (Ephesians 5:22). In this day of radical feminism, the role of the submitted wife is doubly difficult. Many, even in the church, teach that verses like this are simply tools of a male-dominated establishment that seeks to oppress women. To put it mildly, submission is not popular. But the fact of the matter is, this has never been done in any age apart from the power of the Holy Spirit.

Further, submission does not mean the woman is inferior. Everyone knows that a woman is infinitely superior to a man—at being a woman! And the man is infinitely superior to a woman—at being a man! God made us different so He could make us one.

It is Satan's lie that submission means inferiority. I like to think of what happened in the Garden of Eden as a three-act tragedy: Adam's rib, Satan's fib, and a wrong sort of women's lib. A woman is truly liberated by the Spirit of God when she is freed not only to do what she wants, but to do what she ought. And God says she will find her freedom in obeying her husband.

Paul's command is not one-sided. "Husbands, love

your wives, even as Christ also loved the church, and gave himself for it" (Ephesians 5:25). How does Jesus love the church? He loves it sacrificially and completely. A husband should be willing to die for his wife, but he need not die physically in order to live sacrificially for her.

Note that far more is required of the husband than of the wife. The wife's model is the church, but the husband's is Christ Himself. How is any mortal man going to do anything as Jesus does it? There is no way apart from the Spirit-filled life. I am encouraged by the emerging movement in the body of Christ to call men to faithfulness as husbands and fathers.

Look at the obligation of our *work life*. "Servants, be obedient to them that are your masters according to the flesh, with fear and trembling, in singleness of your heart, as unto Christ; not with eyeservice, as men-pleasers; but as the servants of Christ, doing the will of God from the heart" (Ephesians 6:5-6). Work for our employers as though they were the Lord Jesus Christ? That's what Paul said!

When an employer calls an employment agency looking for new workers, he ought to say (if Christians were generally what they are meant to be in this area), "If you have any Christians, please give them the first opportunity. I don't understand it, but they are different from my other workers. They are on time; they do not gossip, cheat, or steal. They work hard. You would think that they think I am the Lord." I am convinced that if more employees began to live like that on Monday, far more employers would believe what is preached on Sunday.

Look at the obligation of our *war life*. "For we wrestle not against flesh and blood, but against principalities, against powers, against the rulers of the darkness of this world, against spiritual wickedness in high places" (Ephesians 6:12). The Christian is at war! Ours is a fight to the finish with a sinister foe, and there are no holds barred. Satan is our adversary who has let loose with all the artillery of hell.

We will never defeat him with the weak efforts of our human flesh. If the battle were against mere humanity, then flesh might defeat flesh. But this is a spiritual war. Satan laughs at our organizations and mocks our schemes, but he trembles before the mighty power of God released through a Spirit-filled saint. I pity the Christian soldier who fights Satan with his own puny human strength.

OPPORTUNITIES

A third reason for being filled with the Spirit is our opportunities. "Redeeming the time, because the days are evil. Wherefore be ye not unwise, but understanding what the will of the Lord is" (Ephesians 5:16-17). These verses come just before the command to be filled with the Spirit. It is God's reminder that we are to use our time and opportunities wisely.

Any day that is not crowned with the Christian being consciously and conspicuously filled with the Holy Spirit is a wasted day. It will be lost for all eternity. At the judgment seat of Christ it will at best be counted as wood, hay, and stubble (1 Corinthians 3:12).

What golden opportunities we let slip through our fingers because the Spirit is not in control. There has never been a greater day or age to witness for Christ than ours. There is such a need and such a hunger everywhere. There are even efforts afoot to share the gospel with the whole world by the year 2000.

But I have noticed a subtle yet deadly thing happening

in the lives of some Christians. They see the Spirit-filled life simply as a source of enjoyment rather than a force of employment. They are interested in spiritual gifts—but as toys rather than tools. Consider, for example, the "health and wealth" gospel that is preached so fervently today by what I call the "happiness boys."

A woman was giving a word of appreciation to her first-aid class. She said, "There was a terrible accident in front of my house. A man was lying there with bones splintered, rolling around in pools of blood. His arteries were severed. He was in a state of shock. But I remembered my first-aid instructions that if I would put my head between my knees, I wouldn't faint. It worked, and I didn't faint. I am so grateful that I took this class."

Some Christians are like that. We need to get our heads from between our knees and realize that Jesus said, "Ye shall receive power, after that the Holy Ghost is come upon you: and ye shall be witnesses unto me both in Jerusalem, and in all Judaea, and in Samaria, and unto the uttermost part of the earth" (Acts 1:8).

We are filled with the Holy Spirit in order to "Rescue the perishing / Care for the dying . . . / Tell them of Jesus, the mighty to save." Our opportunities give us good reason to be Spirit-filled.

Requirements for the Spirit-filled Life

How does the Holy Spirit fill us? In answering this question, it should be noted that the Holy Spirit is a Person, just as God the Father and God the Son are Persons. The Spirit acts, wills, and loves, and He may be grieved or insulted. I say this because some people think of the Holy Spirit merely as some kind of impersonal force or power emanating from God.

The Holy Spirit does indeed have force and power, but He is a Person. So the concept of being filled with the Holy Spirit is not that of a vessel being filled by some substance or a machine being supercharged with power, but of a human house being completely occupied by a divine Person. We are not co-mingled with God. We are still human, and He is forever divine. But we are empowered by Him, used by Him.

With that concept in mind, let us consider three requirements for the Spirit-filled life.

TOTAL COMMITMENT

First, there must be a *complete commitment to the Spirit*. All of us have had guests in our homes. We double up the kids in one room and make a place for the newcomers. We clear a space in the closet for their clothes. "Here's your room." we tell them. "Here's the bath. Here are the extra towels. Here's the refrigerator and a key to the house. Make yourself at home. Our house is your house," we say.

But suppose you come home one day to find your guest in your own bedroom going through your personal records. He is reading your old love letters, your tax reports, and your will. You clear your throat and try to be calm as you ask, "Are you looking for something I can help you with?" But by the tone of your voice you are really asking, "What are you doing in here? You have no business in my personal papers!"

Your guest replies, "No, thank you. I don't need any help. I was just curious about your personal affairs and thought these things would be interesting reading."

By this time you cannot control your anger. "You have no business prying into my personal papers. That desk should not concern you. Please close it immediately."

Your guest responds, "I don't understand you. You said that I was to make myself at home, that your house was my house."

"Well, I didn't mean that you are free to pry into my personal affairs." And a friendship begins to unravel.

Have you ever been guilty of doing something like that to the Holy Spirit? "Dear Holy Spirit, come and live in the temple of my body. My heart is Your abode. Make Yourself completely at home." But the searching question is: have you given Him the key to every room, every closet, every desk? Is there any part of your life that is off-limits to your Heavenly Guest?

If so, you are not filled with the Spirit. Remember, we said it is impossible for the great God of the universe to be relegated to a back room of His own temple.

The Holy Spirit must have the key to your business life, your social life, your thought life, *everything*. The Holy Spirit deserves and demands access to every corner of the temple that Christ purchased with His blood. "What? know ye not that your body is the temple of the Holy Ghost which is in you, which ye have of God, and ye are not your own?" (1 Corinthians 6:19). He will not settle for one room—even a prominent one. He demands preeminence.

In the last century some ministers were planning a united crusade. They met to select an evangelist. The majority wanted Dwight L. Moody, the great preacher who was filled with the Spirit and anointed with God's mighty power, to preach His Word.

One minister on the committee, however, was holding

out for another evangelist. In exasperation he finally said, "Moody, Moody, Moody . . . That is the only name you seem to know. Does Moody have a monopoly on the Holy Spirit?"

One of the others answered, "No, but it seems that the Holy Spirit has a monopoly on Moody."

Moody himself said, "I know perfectly well that, wherever I go to preach, there are many better preachers known and heard than I am; all that I can say about it is that the Lord uses me."[1]

That's what I'm talking about. Does the Holy Spirit have a monopoly on you? Have you given Him the key to every room? Is He merely a resident, or is He president? Have you made a complete commitment to Him?

TOTAL POSSESSION

The second requirement for the Spirit-filled life is *continual control by the Spirit*. Ephesians 5:18 may be translated, "Be ye being filled with the Spirit." This matter of the Spirit-filled life is not a once-for-all matter. To be sure, there may be a crisis experience when we yield our all to Him, but this crisis is followed by a process. The Holy Spirit's control must be recognized day by day as we yield to Him.

We saw that the command is, "Be not drunk with wine . . . but be filled with the Spirit." Why didn't the Lord say, "Don't commit adultery, but be filled with the Spirit"? Or why didn't He name lying, stealing, pride, or some other sin in contrast to being Spirit-filled?

The answer is that He was speaking both by way of contrast and comparison. There is a sense in which the result of being Spirit-filled may be compared to being intoxicated. The disciples were accused of being drunk with new wine when they were filled with the Spirit on the Day of

Pentecost. But Peter answered, "These are not drunken, as ye suppose" (Acts 2:15). The people who were watching the disciples automatically assumed that no one would act like that unless he was drunk.

When a man is drunk, he is brought under the control of another power. Liquor has been called "the devil in liquid form." Satan uses it to take over a man's life. His walk, his talk, his thoughts, his courage, and his morals all change for the worse. But when a man is Spirit-filled, they are changed for the better.

Here is the point. How does a man get drunk? By drinking! But how does he stay drunk? He must keep on drinking. I believe I know some Christians who were once Spirit-filled, but they've "sobered up." As Christians, we must keep drinking from that fountain that never shall run dry.

In order for there to be continual control, there must be continual appropriation of the dear Holy Spirit in all of His fullness. Remember that He is a Person and not a substance like wine. But as a drunkard yields totally to alcohol and is thoroughly affected by it, so as we yield to the Spirit totally He affects our whole personality.

DELIBERATE ACCEPTANCE

The third requirement of the Spirit-filled life is that of a *conscious claiming of the Spirit*. Remember that when the Holy Spirit came to live within you, He came in as a divine Person. It is so easy to miss what Paul is saying. He does not say to be filled *by* the Spirit but *with* the Spirit. We must not get the idea that the Holy Spirit is waiting outside of us to place into us what we need.

If that were so, we might say, "I need more love," and He would fill us with love. Or, "I need more patience," and

He would pour in the patience. But that is not the idea at all. That would be being filled *by* the Spirit. We are to be filled *with* the Spirit Himself. He floods every area of our lives with His blessed self.

Therefore, when He is present in our lives, we have all the love, patience, or anything else that we could ever need. In Him we are complete.

A country pastor's wife was at her wit's end. She was left alone with two active children while her husband commuted to the seminary for his weekday studies. The pressures upon her were terrific, and she cried out to God for help. "Give me more patience, Lord. Give me more strength. Give me more love." Yet she had no victory.

One day it dawned upon her that through the Holy Spirit, Jesus was alive and well and living within the temple of her body. Her prayers began to change. She no longer prayed, "Give me more patience, Lord." Now her prayer was, "Thy patience, Lord."

She made a conscious claiming of that which was already hers. All that she needed, she already had. She recognized the presence and gracious sufficiency of the Holy Spirit in her. The supply of her every need was just waiting to be claimed by faith.

Immediately there was a new release of power in her life as God's Holy Spirit expressed His love, patience, and strength through her. The difference was dramatic.

Results of the Spirit-filled Life

The verses that follow the command to be filled with the Spirit in Ephesians 5 speak of the results that are sure to manifest themselves when the Lord Jesus Christ is enthroned in the holy temple of our bodies, when His glory fills our house. All of us live in relationship to God, circumstances, and others. The Spirit-filled life affects each of these.

AN ATTITUDE OF WORSHIP

In our relationship to God, there will be a *spirit of adoration.* We quoted Ephesians 5:19 above. As we have already noted, it is the holy obligation and blessed privilege of the people of God to worship the Lord in the Spirit.

As our means of adoration, Paul spoke of "psalms and hymns and spiritual songs." The Old Testament "psalms" were the songbook both of Israel and of the early church. "Hymns" and songs of praise issue forth adoration directly to God. "Spiritual songs" seem to mean joyful and spontaneous music that overflows from the heart.

The whole idea is that Spirit-filled worship, whether congregational or personal, is to come joyfully from the heart and is to be unto the Lord.

It seems almost a truism to say that songs of worship should be sung "to the Lord." Yet this definitely needs to be said. Much of the music in our churches today is not real worship at all but is merely flesh on parade. Just as we may pray to be "seen of men" (Matthew 6:5), we can sing the same way. We are often singing one to another rather than to the Lord.

Perhaps the worst thing that could be said about some music is not that it is off-key, but rather that it is sung to the wrong audience. I have observed that when music is truly sung to the Lord, it speaks to the congregation also.

I am also convinced that God is not all that impressed with musical perfection. None of us should ever do less than his best musically, but for some of us our best is not so great. One minister of music called me a "prisoner-singer."

He said, "You are always behind a few bars and can't find the right key."

Be that as it may, God would just as soon hear a blackbird sing as a nightingale, and I am convinced that He is pleased when I make melody in my heart. Actually, the phrase "making melody" means to strum an instrument. Therefore, I am to make music not *in* my heart, but *with* my heart. My heart is to be the instrument of praise for God's glory.

AN ATTITUDE OF THANKSGIVING

In our relationship to circumstances, the result of the Spirit-filled life will be a *spirit of appreciation*—"giving thanks always for all things unto God and the Father in the name of our Lord Jesus Christ" (Ephesians 5:20).

Perhaps the most common but often-transgressed command in the Bible is the command to be thankful. A carnal Christian is often grumbly hateful. The Spirit-filled Christian is humbly grateful.

This command to be thankful would not be such a difficult one had the Lord not said "always" and "all things."

We thank Him for sun,
Do we thank Him for rain?
We thank Him for joy,
Do we thank Him for pain?
We thank Him for gains,
Do we thank Him for losses?
We thank Him for blessings,
Do we thank Him for crosses?

To give thanks when there is personal hurt, cancer, divorce, financial reverse, or heartbreaking disappointment seems to be unnatural. But when we give thanks, we are not necessarily expressing approval of those things for which we give thanks. We are rather announcing our confidence that our God is greater than any of these things.

Allow me to give you a very personal and painful example of a time when I learned this truth firsthand. After our seminary days, Joyce and I were called back to Florida to a fine little church in Fort Pierce. By this time we had three children—Stephen, Gayle, and Phillip. Phillip was only two months old when we got settled in the new parsonage, nestled right next door to the little white cement-block church.

It happened on a beautiful Mother's Day. I had just preached a Mother's Day message on the blessings of a Christian home. Joyce was out in the kitchen of our small house preparing lunch after the service. I was in the living room reading.

Suddenly I heard her distraught voice. "Adrian," she cried, "come here quickly! Something is wrong with Phillip!"

I leaped to my feet. She had our baby boy in her arms. He was not breathing. His face had a blue cast upon it.

"What's wrong?" she cried.

"I don't know. You call the hospital and tell them I'm coming."

I took our little boy and put him inside my coat to keep him warm. With eyes blinded by tears, I screeched out of our driveway and sped to the emergency room. "Please help me!" I cried to a waiting nurse as I burst through the heavy double doors to the hospital. Kind hands took Phillip and rushed him into a nearby room. I kneeled outside that emergency-room door and prayed for God's mercy, not caring who saw me or what they might think.

After a while an attending doctor came out of the room, without Phillip, and walked over to me. "He's gone," he said as he laid his hand on my shoulder and shook his head. "There was nothing we could do. We tried."

It was one of those sudden "crib deaths."

Joyce was standing in the doorway of our house when I returned alone. The look on my face told the story. Mother's Day had turned into a day of incredible grief and confusion for us. We had not known death in either of our families. It was so sudden, so stark. We did the only thing we knew to do. We kneeled and called out to the Lord for help.

Then we turned to the Word of God. I wasn't sure where to begin reading. But the Lord led us to the message we so sorely needed. This is what God said:

> Grace be to you and peace from God our Father, and from the Lord Jesus Christ. Blessed be God, even the Father of our Lord Jesus Christ, the Father of mercies, and the God of all comfort; who comforteth us in all our tribulation, that we may be able to comfort them which are in any trouble, by the comfort wherewith we ourselves are comforted of God. (2 Corinthians 1:2-4)

I did not understand all that God was allowing to happen to us. But He had already made one thing abundantly clear: the Father of mercies was going to use our sorrow to help us be a blessing to other broken hearts. We gave our brokenness and confusion to the God of all comfort.

That Sunday afternoon we drove to our parents' homes. The church had gotten someone to fill the pulpit for me for the evening service. The services were just beginning as we backed out of the driveway. I can still hear the congregation today as they were singing, "No, never alone / no, never alone / He promised never to leave me / Never to leave me alone."

Joyce and I willed to worship the Lord together, and we sang every praise song we knew as we drove those sixty miles back to our hometown. And it was so very true. *We were not alone!* God's presence was never more real.

In the days and months that followed, we sought the Lord in a new way. Then, by God's grace, a friend and fellow pastor came to our church and preached a message on the Spirit-filled life. Our hungry hearts reached up and received the truth, and the transformation took place. The Lord Jesus truly was alive in us and was just waiting to take over.

You see, since God is love and God is sovereign, there is no area where He does not lovingly rule or overrule—even in tragedy. Nothing comes to us unless He allows it. Not a blade of grass moves without His permission. Romans 8:28 is always true: "And we know that all things work together for good to them that love God, to them who are the called according to his purpose." Therefore, we can give thanks.

AN ATTITUDE OF ACCOMMODATION

In our relationship to others, a Spirit-filled life will result in a *spirit of accommodation*: "submitting yourselves one to another in the fear of God" (Ephesians 5:21).

When a person consistently insists on standing up for his rights, he may know little of the Spirit-filled life. We have been crucified with Christ. What rights does a dead man have? What did Paul say about our rights? "Ye are not your own"!

In earthly relationships submission is one equal willingly and lovingly placing himself or herself under another equal so that Jesus will be glorified. "We preach not ourselves, but Christ Jesus the Lord; and ourselves your servants for Jesus' sake" (2 Corinthians 4:5).

We do not submit to one another because of one another as such, but because of the Lord Jesus Christ. Submission, therefore, is not only for wives. It is for Christians!

The Spirit-filled life is for all of us who know Jesus Christ. Why settle for anything less than God's best for you? Why invite the Spirit of God to take up residence in your house and then try to shut Him up in the closet?

Remember, it is not your job to persuade Him to fill you, but to *permit* Him to do so when you give Him the key to every room in your house. You do not need anything more and should never be content with anything less.

CHAPTER FIVE

✧

Supernatural or Superficial?

A noted Southern Baptist preacher, the late Dr. Robert G. Lee, once preached an excoriating sermon against sin. He didn't pull any punches. A lady whose feathers had been ruffled met him at the door and said, "I didn't appreciate that sermon one little bit."

Dr. Lee reportedly replied, "The devil didn't either. So classify yourself."

Classification is not always flattering, but it is always needed in spiritual matters. The Bible teaches that in the broad sense there are three categories or classes of people living on Planet Earth. In 1 Corinthians 2–3 the Apostle Paul called them the natural man, the carnal man, and the spiritual man. For our purposes we might also think of them as three kinds of houses or dwellings.

Classification is important because it is the starting point in our understanding of the life of faith. Just as no one really grasps his need to be saved until he realizes he is lost, so we cannot get to where we ought to be in our spiritual pilgrimage until we recognize where we are.

We need to know into which of Paul's three classifications we fit. Armed with this insight, we can then lay a proper spiritual foundation as we build a home for Christ in our hearts. As we study the characteristics of the natural man, the carnal man, and the spiritual man, may God show us where our house is out of line with His blueprint and help set our spiritual house in order.

Doing What Comes Naturally

Let's look at these categories in 1 Corinthians 2–3. Meet first the natural man. Here's how he looks to God: "The natural man receiveth not the things of the Spirit of God: for they are foolishness unto him: neither can he know them, because they are spiritually discerned" (2:14).

Why do we call the natural man by such a term? Because he is just that—natural. He is the sum total of all that he has received by nature from his first birth . . . and nothing more.

He is born into the natural world. He may have been born well physically, receiving many admirable traits through his natural birth. He may be witty, charming, cultured, outwardly moral, and educated. Why, he may even be religious! But because the natural man has had no second birth, he is dead to the spiritual world. Having been born only once, he is spiritually dead. Naturally!

How do we know the natural man is spiritually dead? Because as we saw earlier, the Scripture says, "In Adam all die" (1 Corinthians 15:22). What does that mean? Let us do a quick review.

Remember that Adam was designed to be a house inhabited by the Lord. God's Holy Spirit was to indwell and give life to Adam's human spirit. But when Adam sinned, he died. He did not die an immediate physical death, but he did die spiritually at that moment. We said that spiritual death is the separation of the Spirit of God from the spirit of man. God moved out of Adam's spirit; Adam became devoid of God in his spirit.

Concerning our Lord Jesus, God says by way of contrast, "In him was life; and the life was the light of men" (John 1:4). So when the Lord went out of Adam, the life went out, and the light went out.

How does this apply to us? Every person born since that time has inherited Adam's nature. We are born minus God in the spirit—dead, depraved, and darkened like our father Adam.

Thus, when we say that man was made in the image of God, we need to remember it is Adam to whom we are referring. But that image was marred and defaced by sin. The Bible says concerning Adam's children, "Adam lived an hundred and thirty years, and begat a son in his own likeness, after his image; and called his name Seth" (Genesis 5:3).

We are born, therefore, in the image of Adam rather than in the image of God. Incidentally, that's a comforting thought to me. I would hate to look around at humanity as it is and think we are all in the image of God. Surely God is in better shape than that!

This deadness to spiritual things that we inherited from Adam does not mean that every person is outwardly vile or inwardly cruel. One person's lifestyle may not be as corrupt as that of someone who seems more wicked. But both are just as dead.

When a body is dead, there may be degrees of corruption and decay, but there are not degrees of deadness. Dead is dead! All people in Adam are from the same mold, though I will agree that some may be moldier than others.

The natural man is blind to the spiritual world. Because of this deadness and blindness, the natural man has no appreciation of spiritual things. Look again at Paul's words: "But the natural man receiveth not the things of the Spirit of God: for they are foolishness unto him" (2:14). The word "receiveth" here means to welcome as one would welcome a house guest. The natural man, therefore, has no welcome for Christ or for the things of God.

We need to be clear in our understanding here. This does not necessarily mean that the natural man may not enjoy coming to a religious service. He may thrill at the great music. His aesthetic nature can appreciate sunlight streaming through a stained-glass window. He can be stirred by the oratory of a gifted pastor. He may receive great comfort from the warm handshake of friendly people who congregate together.

Yet he does not truly welcome the message of God in his spirit. He does not surrender to Christ. Satan knows this and therefore is not against religion as such. He would just as soon send a man to hell from the pew as from the gutter.

Paul amplified the natural man's lack of appreciation for spiritual things when he wrote, "For the preaching of the cross is to them that perish foolishness; but unto us which are saved it is the power of God" (1 Corinthians 1:18). The natural man does not know the real meaning of the cross, which is at the heart of our faith.

Even if he could get there in his natural state, heaven would be a form of hell for the natural man. Some people who think they want to live forever don't even know what to do on a rainy afternoon! What would a person with no appreciation for the things of God do in heaven for all eternity?

Not only does the natural man have no appreciation for spiritual things, he has no comprehension of them: "Neither can he know them, because they are spiritually discerned" (2:14).

What good is a television set if the tuner is broken? No program can be received. The natural man has no spiritual apparatus, as it were, to receive divine impulses. He may hear the words, but he never really gets the message.

Nicodemus was an educated man, a ruler in Israel. But Jesus told him one night that he had to be born again before he could see or perceive the kingdom of heaven (John 3:3).

When I talk with a natural man about Jesus Christ and he says, "I just don't see it that way," I do not argue with him. Why scold a blind man for not seeing? Our job is to bear witness to Christ, then pray that God in His mercy will turn the light of His revelation onto the darkened spirit of the person involved.

A person in this condition is bound to this material world, which compounds the tragedy of life without God. Because the natural man has no appreciation for the spiritual world, he lives basically for the same things that an animal lives for—a self-gratifying, materialistic level of living without the miracle of a birth from above.

Whenever I meet a natural man, my heart yearns to say, "There is more—so much more!"

Doing What Comes Supernaturally

The second category of humanity that Paul described is the spiritual man. What are the marks of the spiritual man, the person who is living a supernatural life?

First, as the name implies, *the spiritual man lives by the Spirit.* "We have received, not the spirit of the world, but the spirit which is of God; that we might know the things that are freely given to us of God" (2:12).

He that is spiritual is simply the one who has received the Spirit of God. Because of this, he has received life. He has been born from above. He is not merely a natural man who has been improved. Rather than a tadpole who has finally turned into a frog, he is more like a frog who has been transformed into a prince by the kiss of God's grace. Christians are not merely nice characters. They are *new* creatures.

We must remember, too, that salvation is a matter of receiving Christ through His Spirit into our hearts. It is not merely getting our sins forgiven. Forgiveness is necessary, but it just sets the stage for salvation—the entrance of Christ into our lives. Nor does salvation merely mean going to heaven when we die. That is wonderful, but heaven is the by-product of salvation. Salvation begins with getting the Lord, the life, and the light back into our deadened spirits.

Second, *the spiritual man learns from the Spirit*. He is given supernatural insight into the things we have been freely given by God. Paul continued, "which things also we speak, not in the words which man's wisdom teacheth, but which the Holy Ghost teacheth; comparing spiritual things with spiritual" (2:13).

"We have received . . . the Spirit . . . that we might know," Paul said. There are some things that can only be known through the illumination of the Holy Spirit. The human spirit becomes the organ of spiritual knowledge. The Lord reveals spiritual truth to the human spirit. Of course, the mind and the emotions come into play, but they depend on the revelation that the human spirit has received from the Lord.

The One who reveals God's truth to the human spirit is

the Holy Spirit. I must always keep this in my mind and heart when I preach. How important it is that I depend upon Him. For while I can *preach* truth, only the Holy Spirit can *impart* truth. An intellectual pursuit of the Bible is important. But remember, the mind can only help us understand what God has revealed to us by His Spirit.

When God wants to illumine man, the lamp He uses is the human spirit. But the oil that feeds that lamp is the Holy Spirit. How wise we would be if we would learn to burn the oil of divine illumination rather than the wick of human intuition, which quickly burns out and leaves only so much smoke.

Third, *the spiritual man is liberated through the Spirit*. "But he that is spiritual judgeth all things, yet he himself is judged of no man. For who hath known the mind of the Lord, that he may instruct him? But we have the mind of Christ" (2:15-16).

How is the spiritual man liberated? He is no longer chained in the prison of this world's system. He sees right through it. He judges, or discerns, all things. The word "judgeth" is a legal word that implies an examination made upon the basis of illuminated insight and knowledge.

Because of the Holy Spirit, the value system of the spiritual man is operating aright. He is set free from the bondage that enslaves the thinking of the natural man. This truth sets the spiritual man free.

The last half of verse 15 makes it clear that the spiritual man will forever be a puzzle to the world. The things that motivate the natural man do not motivate the spiritual man. He marches to the beat of a different drummer. "Wherein they think it strange that ye run not with them to the same excess of riot, speaking evil of you" (1 Peter 4:4).

Don't feel, however, that the spiritual man is an oddity. He is not odd, just different. Whatever is odd about a Christian was probably odd about him before he got converted. Yet there will be an exciting distinctiveness that marks the liberated saint. The world will be puzzled at the victory that is ours.

Doing What Comes *Un*naturally

There is yet a third kind of person that Paul mentioned. This person was once spiritual but is now known as carnal or fleshly. I call him unnatural. Why? Because he is a strange mixture. He is neither fish nor fowl. He has truly been saved, for Paul called the carnal believers at Corinth his brethren. But this strange creature looks and acts much like an unsaved person. What are the marks of a carnal Christian?

The carnal Christian is deformed. "And I, brethren, could not speak unto you as unto spiritual, but as unto carnal, even as unto babes in Christ" (3:1).

Paul said the carnal Christian is like a baby who has never grown up. There is a legitimate babyhood—who doesn't love a baby? What a delight came into our home when God sent each of our children. It was a thrill when they first said, "Dada." But if my grown son were to speak that way to me today, I would not be amused at all.

In the physical realm when a child fails to develop, the parents do not judge or condemn that child if there are physical reasons. They only pour more love and care into that precious life.

But it is quite another matter when for no reason at all we do not develop and grow spiritually. How sad it is when we have all that we need to grow and yet, because of stubbornness, ignorance, laziness, or sin, we are the spiritual counterpart of a gray-headed baby. We are spiritually deformed. It is one thing to be *childlike;* it is quite another thing to be *childish.*

The carnal Christian is not only deformed but dependent. "I have fed you with milk, and not with meat: for hitherto ye were not able to bear it, neither yet now are ye able" (3:2).

Paul said that, like a little baby, the carnal Christian must be fed a milk diet. There is nothing wrong with milk for the newborn, but there are so many more good things to taste and enjoy for the adult!

Technically, milk is predigested food. Carnal Christians expect a pastor to bottle-feed them on Sundays and then burp them on their way out of the sanctuary.

Because of his weak digestion and his spiritual dependency, the carnal Christian never grows in his theology much beyond "Hell is hot, heaven is sweet, and Jesus saves." Thank God that these things are true, but there is so much more to know and enjoy about the Lord Jesus Christ. While the spiritual man is sitting down to a juicy, spiritual steak with all the trimmings, the carnal Christian never gets beyond his milk, pabulum, and strained beets. And he even needs someone to feed him those.

The carnal Christian is also divisive. "For ye are yet carnal: for whereas there is among you envying, and strife, and divisions, are ye not carnal, and walk as men?" (3:3).

Like a spoiled brat, the carnal Christian is often the center of division and controversy in the church. I have noticed that little children are hardly ever concerned about the great issues of life. They are more apt to pout if the toast is cut straight across rather than diagonally (they want it to look like a little sailboat). In the church there are big babies who are not really concerned about the greater matters of our faith but who can become absolutely unbending over where the organ should be placed.

The Corinthian church had gotten into petty squabbles over personalities. They had the "favorite preacher" syndrome. Some were in the Paul camp. "He is such a great theologian." Some were in the Peter camp. "He tells it like it is." Others were followers of Apollos. "Did you ever hear such oratory?"

Here are Paul's words to these big babies: "Therefore let no man glory in men. For all things are yours; whether Paul, or Apollos, or Cephas, or the world, or life, or death, or things present, or things to come; all are yours; and ye are Christ's; and Christ is God's" (3:21-23).

Thus we have God's three classifications of people, three kinds of human houses. These truths are not meant to put us down but to urge us on. When we know where we are, by God's grace we can begin to move to where we ought to be.

May the natural man repent of his sins and trust Christ. May the carnal man repent of his sins and enthrone Christ. May the spiritual man keep on repenting when he sins and so grow into greater maturity and an increasing enjoyment of Christ.

CHAPTER SIX

Inhabited or Inhibited?

May I ask you a few questions about yourself? Are you a Phi Beta Kappa, an All-American, Miss America, listed in *Who's Who*, voted "Most Likely to Succeed," or in the bluebook of society? If you answered yes to any or all of these questions, I have good news for you. God can still use you, though He is going to have a little more difficulty doing it.

But if, on the other hand, you have done or achieved none of the things the world prizes so highly, God delights to use you. If you have never won anything but the booby prize, God desires to get glory through you. As a matter of fact, He prefers to use ordinary people.

You'll understand why I say all of this when you read the following verses, which are crucial to our study of what it means to be a temple of the living God:

> For ye see your calling, brethren, how that not many wise men after the flesh, not many mighty, not many noble, are called: but God hath chosen the foolish things of the world to confound the wise; and God hath chosen the weak things of the world to confound the things which are mighty; and base things of the

> world, and things which are despised, hath God chosen, yea, and things which are not, to bring to nought things that are. (1 Corinthians 1:26-28)

Before we look at why God has chosen to do things this way, we need to deal with a practical matter. Is it humility to say you are not capable of being used of God? No; that is an insult to the mighty God who inhabits your heart! Believers sometimes stand with drooping shoulders and with apologetic voice declare, "I just serve God in my poor, little, weak way."

Whenever I hear that I want to say, "Well, quit it! God does not want you to serve Him that way. He wants you to serve Him in His mighty, dynamic way. You are a temple of God. He lives within you. He wants to display His glory in you!" What some people call humility, I call poor posture. My question to people like this is, why should we be so inhibited when we are so inhabited?

You see, God has a wonderful plan. He is in the business of getting glory to Himself, and here is how He does it: He uses what the world calls a foolish message. "For the preaching of the cross is to them that perish foolishness; but unto us which are saved it is the power of God" (1:18).

He then chooses what the world considers to be a weak and unworthy messenger and compounds the two in the crucible of His mighty power and wisdom. He does this so that "no flesh should glory in his presence" (1:29). This way the God who lives in the house gets all the glory, not the house!

Embarrassing Qualifications

To serve God in this mighty army of the ordinary, there are

some downright embarrassing qualifications. Let's see how close we come to being admissible.

First are *the "foolish" ones.* The word *foolish* that Paul used comes from the Greek word *moros*. It is the word from which our word *moron* comes. It denotes someone who is dull, sluggish, or perhaps even somewhat silly.

So you were not at the top of your class? You hold no Ph.D. degree? Does this mean you cannot be used? To the contrary, God is looking for someone just like you. Relationship is more important than scholarship.

Next are *the "weak" ones.* This word means physical weakness, even infirmity. Are you feeling weak and sickly? Congratulations! God is willing to do mighty things with and through your frail body. His strength will be made perfect in your weakness.

Then come *the "base" ones.* This word means of lowly birth, ignoble, without pedigree. Perhaps you are not from the aristocracy. You were not born with a silver spoon in your mouth. You may be like a seminary classmate of mine who said, "I wasn't born in a log cabin like some of the great men of our country, but I want you to know that just as soon as our family could afford one, we bought it and moved in!"

Praise God, He delights to use those who were born on the wrong side of the tracks. Don't let what the world may consider your social inferiority keep you from serving Him.

God also delights to use *the "despised" ones.* This word means those whom the world writes off as of no account. It means those who are treated with contempt and scorn. Do others look down on you and say you will never amount to anything? That is terrific! That means that when God does use you, it will be obvious to all around that He is the One who is doing it and He, therefore, will get the glory.

Last of all, there are *the ones who "are not."* This refers to people who are completely overlooked. They do not even get to be despised. They are not considered good enough to be despised. They are not listed in *Who's Who*. They're not even listed in *Who's Not*!

Am I by any chance talking about you? Your name is never listed in the church bulletin. When people talk, your name is not discussed, either for good or evil. Do you consider yourself a nobody? Well, with God everybody is a somebody. He is looking for someone like you. Your name may not be mentioned much down here, but God wants you to make headlines in heaven.

These are the kinds of ordinary people God delights to use. Now let me make three things clear concerning God's plan to use His people.

God's Mighty Plan

First, God does not say that no one who is mighty or noble are called. He just says that not many of the world's elite will submit themselves to Him. I thank God for those wealthy, those gifted, those intellectuals who know and serve the Lord Jesus Christ.

Paul himself was one of these, in fact. This gifted religious aristocrat had one of the most scintillating minds of all time. He was sought after, flattered, and praised by his peers. He had achieved the highest positions in the religious world and had an impeccable academic pedigree. Yet, Paul said concerning these achievements, "[I] do count them but dung, that I may win Christ" (Philippians 3:8).

A British noblewoman once told the great preacher John

Wesley that she was saved by an *m*. Wesley was puzzled and asked what she meant. "God said not many noble were called. He didn't say not any," she explained.

The second thing I want to emphasize about spiritual qualifications is this: Paul is not encouraging half-heartedness, laziness, or mediocrity.

If you are a preacher or teacher with only an average IQ, you must study all the more. A preacher in Pennsylvania was noted as an expert fox hunter. An old Quaker said to him one day, "If I were a fox, I would hide me where thee could not find me."

"And where is that?" inquired the preacher.

"In thy study!" the Quaker replied.

You may be a singer with less than a great voice, but still it ought to be your ambition to make that voice sing the sweetest note it can sing for the glory of the Lord Jesus Christ.

You may not have great strength, but the important thing is that every nerve, fiber, bone, and sinew in your body be given over completely to the Lord Jesus. Let Him have every ounce and every inch. It has well been said, "It doesn't take much of a man to be a Christian—just all there is of him."

Third, remember that Paul is not talking about relying upon our own strength anyway. The secret of the whole matter is that God gives to ordinary people extraordinary power. He gave Himself *for* us in order that He might give Himself *to* us and therefore live His life *through* us. The issue is not so much our responsibility as it is our response to His ability.

God's Mighty Weak Ones

When I think of God using "foolish" things, I think of Billy Sunday. He was the best-known evangelist of his day, in many ways his era's counterpart to Billy Graham.

Sunday certainly could not be classed as an intellectual. He was a former baseball player who had only a high school education. He used slang and had some laughable ideas. His antics on the platform scandalized some of the more refined church members of that era. One biographer called him "God's laugh at the preachers." Sunday used to say that he didn't know any more about theology than a jackrabbit knows about Ping-Pong.

One of my older seminary professors told me of going to hear Billy Sunday preach when the evangelist was in his heyday. He said that Billy carried on and performed in his usual way, but then God moved on him and he struck fire. He began to preach "hell hot, heaven sweet, judgment sure, and Jesus saves!" He then gave the invitation to "hit the sawdust trail," and multitudes came to trust Christ.

My professor said that among those who came forward was an old man with a long, white beard. For some reason Billy Sunday became fascinated with that man's beard. He couldn't take his eyes from it. Finally temptation overcame him, and the unpredictable evangelist went to the edge of the platform, bent over, grasped the man's beard, and pulled it several times saying, "Honk, honk!" Can you imagine that?

You and I might raise our eyebrows and say God couldn't use a man like that. But He did. Now, God did not use Billy Sunday because of these foolish things. And I do not suggest that any would-be preacher go and do likewise.

But here is the point: many a well-trained minister with all of the ecclesiastical accouterments (Dr. Sounding Brass or Dr. Tinkling Cymbal, for example) who trusts in his worldly knowledge and ability has been passed by. God in His wisdom chooses instead to use a Billy Sunday to bring glory to Himself. And how God used Billy Sunday! Literally hundreds of thousands came to Christ through his ministry.

When I consider God using the "weak" things, I remember an episode that took place in a church I once pastored. We were having what we called a "Week of Champions" to reach the young people in that area for Christ. We invited many great professional and amateur athletes to come and share their testimonies for Christ. The affair took place at the high school gymnasium. Among those who came was the late Paul Anderson, who at that time was reputed to be the strongest man in the world. What a specimen he was. He had biceps like coconuts.

He was asked, "Were you ever a ninety-seven-pound weakling?"

He said, "Yes, when I was four years old!"

Anderson's testimony was clear and strong. He said, in effect, "If the strongest man in the world needs Jesus, so do you."

The next Sunday a young man came forward in our church service to confess Christ publicly as Lord and Savior. After visiting with him, I found that he was converted the night Paul Anderson was present.

"What was it Mr. Anderson said that touched your heart?" I asked.

"Oh, it wasn't what Paul Anderson said. It was what George Wilson said that reached me."

George Wilson? I couldn't remember which athlete he was. Then I recalled that George was a paraplegic in a wheelchair who gave his testimony during a time of open sharing afterwards. He was not even a part of the official program. But he spoke of the joy of the Lord with a face shining like the noonday sun. That student said to me,

"When I saw the happy expression on the face of George Wilson, I thought that if God could do that for a man in a wheelchair, perhaps He could do something for me."

I have never forgotten that episode. On a night when the strongest man in the world was present, God used a man in a wheelchair to bring a college student to Christ.

God's Noble Base Ones

And what about the "base" things? Do you remember the story of Gideon? He was about as ignoble and base as a man could be. He lived in a time of great trouble in Israel. The Midianites had overrun the land with their fierce warriors.

Gideon was threshing wheat one day when the angel of the Lord appeared and said to him, "The LORD is with thee, thou mighty man of valour . . . thou shalt save Israel from the hand of the Midianites" (Judges 6:12, 14).

Gideon must have looked over his shoulder to see whom the angel was talking to. When it dawned on Gideon that he was being called a "mighty man of valour," he quickly protested, "Oh my Lord, wherewith shall I save Israel? behold, my family is poor in Manasseh, and I am the least in my father's house" (v. 15).

What Gideon was saying was something like this: "Of all the tribes in Israel, Manasseh is the worst; of all the families in Manasseh, my family is the poorest; and of all the kids in my family, I am the runt of the litter."

But this is just what God wanted—a man base enough that God could display His glory through him. And if you remember the story, you know that God made Gideon reduce the size of his army to only 300 soldiers. It was then that God took a nobody general and a nothing army, defeated the Midianites, and got the glory. God has again and again chosen the base things of this world for His use.

Here is one more illustration of this exciting principle: when I think of despised things that God has chosen, I think of young David who later became the king over all Israel. The episode I have in mind is David's historic battle with Goliath of Gath.

The valley of Leah, about fifteen miles due west of Bethlehem, was the scene of the confrontation. The armies of Israel and the forces of the Philistines had been joined in battle for almost six weeks. Goliath, a monstrous giant almost ten feel tall and covered with brass armor, stepped forward and delivered his challenge to fight single-handedly with a Hebrew. He would raise his ham-like fists to heaven, blaspheme the God of Israel, and ridicule and taunt God's children. Who would want to take that challenge? Even mighty Saul was quaking in his boots.

David was there that day. He was just a lad, a teenage boy with fuzz on his chin. But there was something in David that was stirred to white-hot indignation when he heard the name of his thrice-holy God being mocked.

In the face of derision and certain scorn, David went forth to meet Goliath. He was armed with but a sling and five smooth stones.

There was a fundamental difference between David and everyone else that day. All the others were mumbling, "Look how much bigger Goliath is than we are." But David was thinking, "Look how much smaller than God Goliath is." The others were saying, "He's too big to hit." David was thinking, "He's too big to miss!"

At this point let's consider the scriptural account. It thrills me every time I read it:

> And the Philistine came on and drew near unto David; and the man that bare the shield went before him. And when the Philistine looked about, and saw David, he disdained him: for he was but a youth, and ruddy, and of a fair countenance. And the Philistine said unto David, Am I a dog, that thou comest to me with staves? And the Philistine cursed David by his gods. And the Philistine said to David, Come to me, and I will give thy flesh unto the fowls of the air, and to the beasts of the field. Then said David to the Philistine, Thou comest to me with a sword, and with a spear, and with a shield: but I come to thee in the name of the LORD of hosts, the God of the armies of Israel, whom thou hast defied. This day will the LORD deliver thee into mine hand; and I will smite thee, and take thine head from thee; and I will give the carcasses of the host of the Philistines this day unto the fowls of the air, and to the wild beasts of the earth; that all the earth may know that there is a God in Israel. (1 Samuel 17:41-46)

Clearly, David was not intimidated by Goliath's threats. He knew that the battle was the Lord's.

The key to me is the last part of verse 46, where David declared that victory would be his and then gave us the reason: so God's glory would be made known in all the earth. Don't miss that point.

What would it have meant for God's glory that day if both the Philistines and Israel had put forth a giant, and the Israeli giant had defeated the Philistine giant? Not a thing in the world! It would have been just a good fight, that's all.

But when a despised, unheralded teenage boy with faith in God wins such a victory, everyone is forced to confess that there is a God in Israel. Do you see why God enjoys using despised things so that He will get the glory?

Because He Lives in Me

In the light of all this, let us as temples of the living God make a threefold application to our lives:

First of all, *there is a rebuke to our pride*—"that no flesh should glory in his presence" (1 Corinthians 1:29). God will not share His glory with another. How God hates the sin of spiritual pride! I have observed that God will keep using a person as long as that person keeps giving Him the glory.

Don't ever be like the woodpecker who while pecking away on a pine tree was stunned by a bolt of lightning that struck the tree and split it from top to bottom. Hardly able to believe his eyes, the woodpecker backed off and looked at the damage for a few moments. Then he flew away and came back leading nine other woodpeckers. With a great deal of swagger he said, "There it is, gentlemen, right over there!"

When we start to take the credit for what God does, He stops doing it!

Second, *there is a reckoning of our power.* "But of him are ye in Christ Jesus, who of God is made unto us wisdom, and righteousness, and sanctification, and redemption" (v. 30).

Don't ever insult God by saying He cannot use you. That is not humility—it is blasphemy! Christ is alive and well and lives in you if you have been saved. You are His temple. Therefore, do not say, "Lord, help me to use my love, my strength, my wisdom." Instead, rely on His! Remember that God gives extraordinary power to ordinary people.

Third, *there is a response in our praise.* ". . . that, according as it is written, He that glorieth, let him glory in the Lord" (v. 31). How we ought to praise Him! What a wonderful plan it all is. The great God, who is big enough to fill His mighty universe, is small enough to live within my heart. *I am the temple of God.* He literally dwells in me. Hallelujah!

CHAPTER SEVEN

◇

Like a River Glorious

We have already gazed at several important applications of the truth that our bodies are temples of the Holy Spirit. One is that when God truly possesses a temple, He possesses *all* of it. He cannot be relegated to a back room in His own temple.

We also saw that the overflowing, Spirit-filled life is the normal Christian life God wills for each believer, not a deluxe edition reserved for the choice few.

We have studied these and other truths from several standpoints. Since the Bible often teaches us by way of an illustration or picture, I want to take a close look at what I believe is one of the most thrilling Old Testament pictures—that of the Christian who has a river of revival flowing out of his life.

This great picture is found in Ezekiel 47:1-12, where the prophet had a vision of a river flowing out from the temple of God that will be built during the Millennium. Since we are considering temple truth, let's examine these marvelous verses to see how Ezekiel's vision of the future can help us as we serve the Lord in the present.

To say the least, the writings of Ezekiel are difficult to understand. But of this I am certain: every temple designed by God in the Old Testament is in some way a preview and an illustration of the Christian believer, whose body is a temple of the Holy Spirit. With that in mind, let's turn to this great text and mine its truths.

A Mysterious Source

Ezekiel saw a river flowing out of the "house"—that is, out of the temple of God.

> Afterward he brought me again unto the door of the house; and, behold, waters issued out from under the threshold of the house eastward: for the forefront of the house stood toward the east, and the waters came down from under from the right side of the house, at the south side of the altar. (v. 1)

Right away our minds should go to a startling event that took place in the ministry of Jesus, which may explain what Ezekiel was speaking about. The Feast of Tabernacles, the zenith of Israel's holy days, was coming to a climax in Jerusalem. It was a time of joyous thanksgiving at the end of the harvest season.

During the feast there were ceremonies each day at the time of the morning sacrifice, when the priests would bring a golden flask of water from the fountain of Siloam and pour the contents into a basin near the altar. This ritual symbolized God's bountiful provision for His people.[1] Jewish tradition says, "He who has not seen the rejoicing at the place of the water drawing has never seen rejoicing in his life" (*The Talmud*, Sukkah 5:1).

Imagine yourself there on the last day of the feast at the height of the ceremony. The city is filled with rapturous shouts as the white-robed priest pours out the sparkling water. At that very moment you hear Jesus cry out with a loud voice:

> If any man thirst, let him come unto me, and drink. He that believeth on me, as the scripture hath said, out of his belly shall flow rivers of living water. (But this spake he of the Spirit, which they that believe on him should receive: for the Holy Ghost was not yet given; because that Jesus was not yet glorified.) (John 7:37-39)

What a startling moment that must have been. Jesus could no longer be silent. He saw the hilarity, the joy, the shouting. He heard the sounding trumpets. But He knew how hollow it all was. His soul was stirred because He knew it was a passing moment of religious fervor and excitement. Before long the people would go back to their same old fears, habits, and lethargy. The excitement would soon evaporate, just as the pitiful amount of water in that golden pitcher would soon be less than a vapor.

But at that moment Jesus Christ proclaimed Himself to be the fulfillment of the symbol, offering the water of life right in the midst of the ceremony. But the people did not recognize Him—even though it was not ceremony but Christ, not ritual but reality, they thirsted for. It will be a great day in any land when people stop enduring religion and start enjoying salvation!

So Jesus, with a heart full of compassion and urgency, shouted out His great promise. John's parenthetical comment made it clear that this river of which Jesus spoke was the Holy Spirit, who would soon come to indwell God's people permanently.

Every Christian, therefore, is to have a river of refreshment and blessing flowing out of him as God's dear Holy Spirit expresses Himself through that Christian. Jesus pictured that river flowing out of a person's innermost being. Ezekiel pictured it flowing out under the threshold of the temple. The two pictures fit together beautifully. As we have seen, our innermost being is our spirit where we commune with God, just as the temple was the place of communion with God in the Old Testament.

The ones to whom Jesus spoke—and still speaks—are the thirsty ones. Jesus prefaced His great promise with an "if." Thirst is the only prerequisite for the blessing. How thirsty are you? Those who are filled with the stagnant waters of carnality and self-love are seldom thirsty for the things of God. Even Christians who know they are empty may not be genuinely thirsty. The gasoline tank in my car has often been empty, but never once has it been thirsty.

But thank God for those who have a burning and blistering thirst and are willing to pay any price to satisfy it. We should be like the little girl who asked her mother for a drink of water three times in one night. Finally the mother said in an exasperated tone, "If you ask for water one more time, I am going to spank you."

A while later the girl said, "Mama, when you get up to spank me, will you please bring me a drink of water?"

I believe that one reason we are unwilling to let go of the cheap toys of this world and drink of Jesus' fullness is that we have never really been that thirsty. Let a man have a burning, blistering thirst and he will pay almost any price for water.

How wonderful that in Christ we can have an everlasting supply of deep spiritual blessing and life. Jesus told the Samaritan woman of water that would quench her thirst forever (see John 4:14). Christians are going from conferences to seminars to weekend retreats to get their cups filled. That will no longer be necessary when there is a river flowing from within us.

Ezekiel seemed to be foretelling the same thing that Jesus spoke of—a river of revival as God's flood of spiritual power flows from the cleansed temple of the believer in Christ.

Let's return to the prophet's vision in Ezekiel 47. Notice that the river Ezekiel saw had *a humble source*. It flowed from under the temple's threshold (v. 1). That is a lowly beginning. Genuine revival begins when God's people are on their faces before Him.

Next, it had *a holy source*. It flowed past the altar. Every temple had an altar, and we as God's temples are no exception. There can be no revival that does not flow past the altar. The altar speaks of sacrifice and cleansing, and we have these abundantly in Christ. When we meet God at the altar, the river begins to flow.

So often we cry out to God for revival as though we must persuade Him to send it. It is not our duty to persuade God to send revival, however. All we need to do is permit Him to send it when we come to the precious blood of Jesus for cleansing. There is no way we can bypass the altar and still receive the blessing.

This river flowing from the temple also had *a heated source*. Ezekiel noted that the river flowed from the east door of the temple. That was the door facing the sunrise. Also, it flowed from the south side of the altar. That was the sunny side. What a picture of the warmth of God's blessing. How our cold and frigid lives need to be warmed by God's love and power. Our coldness is one reason we are missing the blessings of God's revival power.

Robert Burns, the great Scottish poet, once went into a church hoping to find some spiritual warmth for the depression and chill that had settled upon him. But the church service was more like a funeral dirge held in a mausoleum. He failed to find any comfort in the congregation's coldness. So he took a hymnal and scribbled these words in it:

As cold a wind as ever blew,
As cold a church as in it but few.
As cold a minister as ever spak.
Ye'll all be hot ere I come back.

A Marked Course

As Ezekiel was led into the river, this sparkling and bubbling trickle that came from under the temple threshold grew as it cascaded down the mountainside:

> Then brought he me out of the way of the gate northward, and led me about the way without unto the utter gate by the way that looketh eastward; and, behold, there ran out waters on the right side. And when the man that had the line in his hand went forth eastward, he measured a thousand cubits, and he brought me through the waters; the waters were to the ankles. Again he measured a thousand, and brought me through the waters; the waters were to the knees. Again he measured a thousand, and brought me through; the waters were to the loins. Afterward he measured a thousand; and it was a river that I could not pass over: for the waters were risen, waters to swim in, a river that could not be passed over. (vv. 2-5)

The water was now surging in an ever-deepening and widening course. It was a supernatural river because it grew without any tributaries. Who can add anything to the all-sufficiency of God's Spirit?

Note that the water was measured in thousand-cubit increments. Ezekiel watched it go from ankle-deep to knee-deep, from knee-deep to waist-deep, and finally from waist-deep to a river that was over their heads—water deep enough to swim in.

Here is a deepening work of God. The ankle-deep water may speak of walking in the Spirit. The knee-deep water may speak of praying in the Spirit. Water to the loins may speak of being strong in the Spirit. The water to swim in may speak of the mighty reviving force of the Spirit that picks us up and sweeps us along in its fullness as it overwhelms us completely. What a glorious thought!

Now God asked Ezekiel a question. "Son of man, hast thou seen this? Then he brought me, and caused me to return to the brink of the river" (v. 6). I want to see it, don't you? How I long for an ever deeper work of the Spirit of God in my own life. How I long for that mighty river to flow from my life into my world.

This has been my prayer and desire for many years. As a young would-be preacher, I knew I needed God's might and power in my life. I also knew I was totally inadequate. I had not heard much about the power of God available to the Christian, but I knew I needed something.

Our home in Florida was near the field where we practiced football. I went alone to that field one night to seek the Lord. It was a beautiful South Florida summer night. I walked and prayed, "Lord Jesus, I want You to use me." Then I knelt down and repeated, "Lord Jesus, I want You to use me." Then, wanting to humble myself before Him, I stretched out prostrate, facedown on the grass, and said, "Lord Jesus, I am Yours. Please use me."

That still did not seem low enough, so I made a hole in the dirt and placed my nose into it. "Lord Jesus, I am as low as I know how to get. Please use me." (I did not know it then, but I learned later that the English word *humble* comes from a Latin root *humus*, meaning "ground" or "earth.")

Something happened in my life that night. I didn't have ecstasies or a vision of any kind, but there was a transformation. At that time I knew very little theology. But I would be less than honest to deny that God graciously released His power into my young heart and life. There was a great joy and a desire to share Christ with everyone.

Shortly after that, I entered college and was asked to serve as pastor of a small country church. I was nineteen years of age and utterly untrained. I am sure my preaching was greatly lacking in form and content, but God graciously and visibly worked. I was often surprised at His power. There were commitments for repentance and tears of joy from the start in that little congregation. People were brought to Christ in unusual numbers for such a small church and town. There was no mistaking the mighty hand of God.

How I thank God for answering my prayer for His fullness and power, not only back then but many times since. I am burdened, though, that so many are not seeing the deeper work of God. We are so satisfied with the status quo. The late Vance Havner said it well: "We have sacrificed depth for width. So rather than having a mighty power dam, we have a stagnant swamp."

Where does this river flow? According to Ezekiel's

vision, *it flows into the depressed places*. "Then said he unto me, These waters issue out toward the east country, and go down into the desert, and go into the sea: which being brought forth into the sea, the waters shall be healed" (v. 8).

The waters flowed from the temple mount downward. "These waters . . . go down." Those who have traveled in Israel know that the area where the waters were headed is 1,300 feet below sea level—the lowest spot on the face of the earth. But just as gravity causes water to seek the deep places, grace leads to the Spirit's seeking the depressed places in men's hearts.

And what depression there is in this world around us. It affects the up-and-outs as well as the down-and-outs. Many thought the collapse of communism in Eastern Europe and the former Soviet Union would rid the world of the threat of war and usher in a "new world order" of peace and prosperity. Did that happen? For most people it did not, and now even in America we are being told that the abundance we have enjoyed for generations is in dire jeopardy.

No wonder people whose hopes are pinned on this world are depressed! Some college students who entered a contest were asked to write a definition of life for the college newspaper. Here are some entries that won honorable mention: "Life is a joke that isn't even funny." "Life is a jail sentence that we get for the crime of being born." "Life is a disease for which the only cure is death."

These were not the deprived and the underprivileged. These were young people who seem to have everything—except Jesus.

A glorious river of revival needs to flow into depressed lives like these. This river needs to touch the college student without Christ, the businessman with his problems, the homemaker who is reduced to tears because of the depressing situation in which she may find herself. Oh, that this river of love and power might flow from temples like you and me into the depressed places.

It also flows into desert places. "These waters . . . go down into the desert." Ezekiel spoke of the Arabah, or the Judean desert. Those who have seen it know how parched and barren it is. This desert speaks of dry and fruitless lives that need the bubbling waters of revival.

This barrenness is not only in the lives of the unsaved, but in the lives of some of those who name the name of Jesus. The curse of modern Christianity is the desert of dry mediocrity in which so many Christians are living. Jesus has chosen and ordained us to a life of fruitfulness and fullness. Yet the average Christian is living a life of dry devotions, fruitless faith, and barren evangelism. He needs the refreshing and reviving touch of the river of life that will cause his desert to blossom and bloom.

This river flows into the deadly places. "These waters . . . go into the sea." The sea that Ezekiel spoke of is the Dead Sea, which I referred to above. Because the Dead Sea receives but does not give, except by evaporation, it has an extreme concentration of salt. It is 25 percent more salty than ocean water, and the magnesium bromine prevents organic life. The waters of the Dead Sea are leaden and poisonous.

Those who dwell in deadly places like this, those under the curse of death and judgment because of their sinfulness and selfishness, need the touch of the healing waters that flow from under the thresholds of God's temples—the hearts of His people.

There is indeed something deadly working in America. Americans, like the Dead Sea, have often taken in God's blessings, but we have not given. As a result many people are asking, "Is God going to judge America?"

I am convinced that God *is* judging America. Look at the unthinkable natural disasters that have struck us. I was in St. Louis during the terrible days of the Great Flood of 1993 and saw the unbelievable, unstoppable power of the mighty Mississippi River at peak flood stage.

I met with a large group of believers there, and the number one question on their minds was whether the flood was a judgment from God on America. I do not know how you can draw any other conclusion, which is not to say that the people of the Midwest were being singled out.

But no nation can mock, ignore, and thumb its nose at the sovereign God of the universe and expect to escape His wrath. All God has to do to bring His judgment is to withdraw His protection and we are in trouble.

As I see runaway crime, racial hatred, economic confusion, moral compromise and perversion, and America's continuing loss of face nationally and internationally, I cannot help but feel that all of these comprise the judgment of God upon a sinful and selfish society.

America and the world need revival! Only God's mighty river can flow into the deadly places and make them live again.

A Mighty Force

What a mighty force a river is. We all saw the television images of the raging Mississippi wiping out entire towns. A river seems to be unstoppable. You can build levees against it and pile sandbags to the skies, but it keeps on flowing. You can dam it up, but it just rises higher until it overflows its banks and spreads over the land.

The only way to stop a river is to cut it off at its source. Since the river Ezekiel saw flowed from the temple of God, that is the only place where it can be stopped. It would seem that the Christian himself is the only one who can stop this mighty flow of power. God forbid that we should be guilty of restricting the waters of His love and power that should flow from us.

What a life-giving force this water is. Water is so very common but so very priceless. One writer said, "Water is used to cool engines, produce electricity, regulate temperatures. To produce one loaf of bread takes three hundred gallons. Between cattle rancher, butcher, packager, and processor, four thousand gallons of water will be used to put a pound of beef in the supermarket. The building of one automobile requires ten thousand gallons. The human body is seventy percent water. We are constantly losing this precious liquid, and if it's not replaced quickly, we will die."[2]

Notice also that *where the waters flow, the trees will grow.* "When I had returned, behold, at the bank of the river were very many trees on the one side and on the other," Ezekiel said (v. 7). Where these life-giving waters flow, there will be life rather than a sterile desert of death.

A healthy saint is pictured in the Bible as "a tree planted by the rivers of water" (Psalm 1:3). Therefore, a Spirit-filled believer should be like a river whose life will strengthen fellow believers. We are not to be reservoirs of truth but rivers of blessings to those around us.

And *where the waters flow, the fish will go.*

> And it shall come to pass, that every thing that liveth, which moveth, whithersoever the rivers shall come, shall live: and there shall be a very great multitude of

> fish, because these waters shall come thither: for they shall be healed; and every thing shall live whither the river cometh. (v. 9)

Obviously God has more in mind in this majestic passage than mere fish. Jesus spoke of our becoming "fishers of men" (Matthew 4:19). He was speaking, of course, of winning the lost; but as we look at the modern church, we seem to be catching very few fish.

One reason our nets are empty is that despite all of our plans, propaganda, and paraphernalia we are fishing in stagnant seas and polluted pools. What a harvest of souls there will be when true revival comes and rivers of revival flow!

Think of the events that took place on the Day of Pentecost in Jerusalem. Because Pentecost was such a great festival, the city was wall to wall with people. Perhaps a million or more Jews were present at that time. How would the early church reach them? The believers were just 120 common people. They had no printing presses or radio or television stations. But they became the center of attention, and the "multitude came together" (Acts 2:6). What an opportunity to preach the gospel.

Why did the people come together? Because where the river flows, the fish will go. The river of God's Holy Spirit was flowing that day, and 3,000 fish were caught in the gospel net.

Next, *where the waters flow, the fruit will show.*

> And by the river upon the bank thereof, on this side and on that side, shall grow all trees for meat, whose leaf shall not fade, neither shall the fruit thereof be consumed: it shall bring forth new fruit according to his

> months, because their waters they issued out of the sanctuary: and the fruit thereof shall be for meat, and the leaf thereof for medicine. (v. 12)

What is this succulent fruit that hangs in clusters from the bending boughs of these ever-green saints? Is it not the fruit of the Spirit?

Listen to Paul: "The fruit of the Spirit is love, joy, peace, longsuffering, gentleness, goodness, faith, meekness, temperance" (Galatians 5:22-23).

The world is hungry for fruit like this! In reality Paul was describing the character of Jesus. Each of these characteristics is a facet of our dear Savior. We do not produce this fruit; He is "the true vine" (John 15:1). We merely bear the fruit when God's river is flowing from the temples of our bodies.

Finally, *where the waters flow, the health will glow*. Its "leaf" shall be "for medicine," the prophet recorded. Today the body of Christ is suffering from a sickness that is a dishonor to its Head, the Lord Jesus Christ. But where the river of revival flows in full power, weak and anemic saints will vibrate with spiritual vitality and health. What a day that will be!

It is sad indeed that there should be so many spiritually sick saints when our great God has provided such miracle-producing medicine.

Dear reader, is the river of revival flowing from the temple of your body? If not, remember that Jesus said when we come to Him and drink, a river of living water will begin to flow from our innermost being. But He also said we must be thirsty in order to come. Ask Him to increase your thirst for the things of God.

Like a river glorious,
Is God's perfect peace,
Over all victorious,
In its bright increase;
Perfect, yet it floweth,
fuller every day;
Perfect, yet it groweth,
Deeper all the way.

FRANCES R. HAVERGAL

CHAPTER EIGHT

✧

Keeping Your House Clean

Remember those college boys I told you about back in chapter 3, the ones who wanted to smuggle a goat into their foul-smelling dormitory room? I said then that college boys may be content to live in a dirty place, but a holy God will not.

If you want the Holy Spirit of God to be at home in the temple of your body, it must be clean. Keeping your spiritual house clean is one of the most important responsibilities you have as a Christian.

One of the marks of a true Christian is that he feels dirty when he has sinned. David was a man after God's own heart, and yet he sinned grievously with Bathsheba and against her husband, Uriah. In his prayer of repentance David cried out, "Wash me throughly from mine iniquity, and cleanse me from my sin" (Psalm 51:2).

Here was a king who lived a life of royalty, bathed in a marble tub, slept on silk sheets, and wore regal robes, and yet he felt dirty when he sinned. "Wash me . . . cleanse me," David prayed. He needed a spiritual housecleaning because of his sin.

The person who does not know the Lord will not be deeply affected by the grime of guilt. Sin may be so much a part of his nature that he's not even aware of its presence. A sow, for example, never feels dirty. To wallow is her way, even after she's been washed (2 Peter 2:22).

The difference between the saint and the sinner is not so much in whether they can sin. Any human being is capable of sinning. It is the basic attitude toward sin that makes the difference. The saint lapses into sin and loathes it. The sinner leaps into sin and loves it.

I know that in my life I have been made to feel dirty because of sin. But I came to Jesus, and just as He cleansed the temple in His days on earth, He cleansed and forgave me. He made the temple of my body and my life sparkling clean and fresh. And the ongoing efficacy of His shed and sprinkled blood is there to keep me clean.

In the first chapter of his first epistle, the Apostle John gave us a marvelous lesson on spiritual housekeeping. It has been a personal guide to me, and I want to share it with you.

The Consequences of a Christian's Sin

> That which we have seen and heard declare we unto you, that ye also may have fellowship with us: and truly our fellowship is with the Father, and with his Son Jesus Christ. And these things write we unto you, that your joy may be full. (1 John 1:3-4)

These verses speak of the joy of fellowship with the Father and with the Lord Jesus Christ. This fellowship brings a joy that is full and complete. The great and costly consequence of sin in the life of a saint is the loss of this joy. The lights start to go out in his house, and the warmth starts to go too.

We do not lose our salvation when we sin (an important truth we will study in chapter 13). But if we persist in sin, we most certainly will lose the joy of our salvation. Hear the prayer of the repentant David: "Restore unto me the *joy* of thy salvation" (Psalm 51:12, italics mine).

If you want to know whether you are backslidden and away from God, take the joy test. It's very simple. Is there in your heart this very moment "joy unspeakable and full of glory" (1 Peter 1:8)? If not, you are not in fellowship with the Father.

"Wait a minute!" you say. "No one can be happy all the time." I agree. But I did not speak of happiness. I spoke of joy. The two are not the same. Happiness depends on what happens. That's why we call it happiness. If your happenstances are good, then you are happy. If they are bad, you are unhappy.

But joy does not depend upon happenstance or circumstance. It comes from Jesus, and He does not change. "These things have I spoken unto you, that my joy might *remain* in you, and that your joy might be full" (John 15:11, italics mine). Therefore, a promise of constant joy awaits us.

Happiness is like a thermometer; it registers conditions. Joy is like a thermostat; it regulates conditions. Paul said, "Great is my boldness of speech toward you, great is my glorying of you: I am filled with comfort, I am exceeding joyful in all our tribulation" (2 Corinthians 7:4). Jesus also spoke of His joy even when He was facing the cross.

There is only one thing that can steal your joy—sin! And only one kind of sin can do that—yours! It is not what others do to you that takes away your joy. It is your reaction to what they do that takes away the joy. Neither your wife, your children, nor your boss can diminish your joy. They may grieve you or cause you sorrow, but they cannot lay hands upon your joy. Only your reaction to what they do can take away your joy.

By the way, it is our reactions, not our actions, that show what we really are. I can more or less plan and control my life. But if you really want to know what I am like, watch me when someone insults me or steals my parking place. If you want to know what is inside a man, wait until someone jostles him, then see what spills out.

The loss of joy in a saint is a terrible loss. The most miserable person on earth is not an unsaved person, but rather a saved person who is out of fellowship with the Lord. When He saves us, God does not fix us so we cannot sin anymore. If He did, we would be robots. But He does fix us so that we cannot sin and enjoy it.

If you know pain (the great saints often have), there is all the more reason to know joy. It helps you to bear it.

The Concealing of a Christian's Sin

To err is human—and to try to conceal it is too! Notice how often in 1 John 1:6-10 the apostle repeated the phrase, "If we say . . ." We are going to look at these verses below. But first I want you to realize how this points out the deceitfulness of sin. There is within the human heart an inborn desire to conceal rather than confess sin.

One act of deceitfulness builds upon another. The longer sin goes without confession, the worse it gets in its concealment and deception. We get to the point that we will lie to others, to ourselves, and even to God.

Lying to others. "If we say that we have fellowship with

him, and walk in darkness, we lie, and do not the truth" (v. 6). The Christian who is beginning to grow cold is tempted to put up a front. He pretends he is in fellowship with God. He wants others to think he is as spiritual as he has always been.

Moses had an encounter with God on the mountaintop. As a result, his face shone so brightly he wore a veil to hide the glory of God reflecting from his countenance.

Later, however, when the glory had faded, Moses still wore the veil. Only now he wore it not to hide the glory, but to hide the fact that the glory was no longer there. Many Christians in our churches are wearing a veil because the glory they once had from God has faded.

Lying to self. "If we say that we have no sin, we deceive ourselves, and the truth is not in us" (v. 8). Sin that is not quickly confessed is easily rationalized. "Maybe it is not sin after all." We might call it by other names—a mistake, an error in judgment, a glandular malfunction, or an environmental reaction.

The sad thing is that when we believe our own lies about our sin, we are doubly deceived. "If therefore the light that is in thee be darkness, how great is that darkness" (Matthew 6:23).

Lying to God. "If we say that we have not sinned, we make him a liar, and his word is not in us" (v. 10). If the Spirit of God says we have sinned, and we deny it, we are then lying to Him. And our lies to Him are a way of calling *Him* a liar. But for the grace of God, there would be no hope for a person who has gone this far in concealing his sin.

We need to learn to confess sin early. There is a deadly deception and an inevitable spread of sin when it is not confessed.

The Conviction of a Christian's Sin

"This then is the message which we have heard of him, and declare unto you, that God is light, and in him is no darkness at all" (v. 5). Thank God that He is light. Because of this, He turns the searchlight of His unspotted holiness onto every area of our lives. It is His light that reveals the dirt in His temple.

The wise Christian will open the doors and windows of his temple and let the Father flood him with light. Never be afraid of the light. More foolish than a child afraid of the darkness is a Christian afraid of the light. It is time for all of God's children to come out of the twilight zone and into the Sonlight.

But understand this: there is a vast difference between the Holy Spirit's conviction and satanic accusation. The nature of Satan is to accuse. The Holy Spirit does not accuse the saints; He convicts them. Many Christians are living lives of subsurface misery because they do not know the difference between the two. Just how does the Holy Spirit convict the child of God of his sin?

Legitimately. The Spirit will only convict you of unconfessed and uncleansed sin. Those sins that have been placed under the blood and have been forgiven have also been forgotten. God said, "I will remember their sin no more" (Jeremiah 31:34). Therefore, He never brings up our sin again.

The devil, however, loves to dredge up forgiven sin and accuse us with it over and over. He will repeat the saga of your past for you just as long as you're willing to listen to the replays.

One man was counseling with his pastor. He was being

tormented by the ghost of guilt; some sin from his former days was haunting him. The pastor said, "Have you confessed it to God?"

"Oh, yes," he said, "I've confessed it a thousand times."

The wise pastor said, "That is nine hundred and ninety-nine times too many. You should have confessed it once and thanked God nine hundred and ninety-nine times for forgiving you."

Specifically. If Satan cannot accuse you of cleansed sin, he will accuse you of imagined sin. Some Christians are going around feeling bad in no particular spot but all over. They are not certain what they have done wrong, but they feel like they surely must have done something.

The Holy Spirit, however, is like a doctor making an examination. If there is a sin in our lives, He will put His finger on the sore spot and press hard. There will be no doubt as to where the problem is. He will speak to us and say something like, "You lied to your wife" or "You were harsh to your son" or "You are filled with envy."

Incidentally, while I was working on this book one morning I spoke harshly to my wife. There was the pressure of a deadline, and I thought that my rudeness was acceptable. The Holy Spirit did not think so. "Adrian, go ask Joyce to forgive you."

"Lord, it was such a small thing."

"Ask her!"

"Yes, Lord." I did, and the joy came back.

When the Holy Spirit convicts, there will be no need for morbid introspection. We do not need to take ourselves apart a little piece at a time looking for sin. Just open your heart up to the light, and the Holy Spirit will do His work.

If He does not convict you of some sin by name, then it is probably the devil who is accusing you.

Redemptively. Satan accuses you in order to condemn you. But the Holy Spirit convicts you that you might be cleansed. Accusation leads to despair. Conviction leads to confession, cleansing, and victory.

The Confession of Sin

"If we confess our sins, he is faithful and just to forgive us our sins, and to cleanse us from all unrighteousness" (1 John 1:9).

After true conviction, there must be true confession. The word *confess* literally means "to agree with" or "to say the same thing." Therefore, a genuine confession of sin is not simply an admission of that sin. Nor is confession something you do simply because you got caught. Along with admission of wrong there must be an agreement with God concerning the seriousness of the sin and agreement that the blood of Christ cleanses you from it.

We must say about our sin what God says about it. We must take sides with Him against it. When we have done that, we have truly confessed it.

"Confess" is in the present tense, which means that it is to be the habitual practice of the saint. A Spirit-filled Christian is quick to confess sin when he becomes aware of it. It becomes a way of life. There is instantaneous and continual confession.

Not only should we confess *continually*, we should confess *completely*. Notice that verse 9 is plural: "our sins," not "our sin." Don't try to simplify your confession. Don't kneel and say, "I confess all my sins." When the Holy Spirit convicts you specifically, confess specifically.

Sometimes I get a pen and paper and write down those

areas where the Spirit of God has convicted me. I have to tell you, it really *hurts* to write those sins down and look at them. But it's been a good experience for me.

We sing the little song, "Count your many blessings / Name them one by one / And it will surprise you what the Lord hath done." Perhaps we should also sing, "List your many failures / State them one by one / And it will surprise you just what *you have done*."

But I never stop with making my list. I then confess my sins one by one. I claim victory and absolute cleansing by the blood of Christ, and I tear up the list. I am careful to put it where no one else will ever find it. At the same time, I know God forgives and forgets.

I am convinced that many of God's children never have the joy of full forgiveness because they sin retail and confess wholesale. Deal with sin completely.

Finally, confess *confidently*. Remember that our loving Heavenly Father is "faithful and just to forgive us . . . and to cleanse us." He can do that because every sin you have ever committed was totally paid for at Calvary—even those you did willfully and that have caused permanent damage. Do you find that difficult to believe? By the grace of God, Jesus Christ paid for "the sins of the whole world" (1 John 2:2). Certainly that covers *your* sins, including the very worst of them.

Because of Calvary

If God did not forgive and cleanse *everything* we confess, He would be a liar (unfaithful) and a crook (unjust). But our God is "faithful and just." This is not a matter of our own feelings but of His faithfulness.

Pay close attention to that big little word "*all*" in verse 9.

You'll also find it in verse 7: "The blood of Jesus Christ his Son cleanseth us from *all* sin" (italics mine). There are no sins that God will not cleanse.

Hallelujah! Every stain, every spot, every blur, every blot, every blemish in your life can be washed whiter than snow. And what God calls clean, let no man call unclean. Even you do not have the right to hold back God's forgiveness of you!

It makes no difference how many times you have failed; He will still forgive. We may fail over and over in the same area of our lives. We become ashamed to come and ask God for forgiveness again. "Surely His patience must be worn out," we think. "He keeps forgiving me, but I keep failing."

What I am about to say is not meant to minimize sin. The fact may be, if you are continually failing in an area, perhaps you need to seek counsel from your pastor in order to become more consistent and victorious in Christ. But that is not the point here. I now want to tell you with all my soul that *if you have honestly confessed, He will forgive you, no matter how many times He has forgiven you in that same area before.*

After all, it may seem like many times to you. But from God's marvelous point of view, it is really like the first time you ever came to Him with that sin. Why? Because He forgot all the other times! The Scriptures assure us that He does not remember our iniquities and holds them against us no more.

I heard of a little girl who had been put to bed for her afternoon nap. Her mother was in the kitchen, cleaning up the lunch dishes. But noises from the bedroom indicated that the child was jumping up and down on the mattress, not sleeping.

"Settle down," the mother told her daughter as she

peeked into the room through a slightly opened door. "You need your sleep. And besides, before you know it you'll break the lamp on the bedside table." It was a beautiful lamp, a prized possession in the family.

Minutes later the jumping resumed. Then came the predictable crash. "I'm really sorry," the little girl sobbed after her spanking as her mother cleaned up the broken glass.

When the mess had been taken out and dumped in the trash, the mother came back to the room, hugged her girl, and said, "I forgive you. And as far as the lamp is concerned, I'll never mention it to you again."

The very next day, as the mother was walking through the house, she inadvertently stepped on and crushed the daughter's favorite doll. The little girl ran over and picked up the broken form, held it close, and said, "Mommy, I forgive you, and I'll never mention it to you again."

Forgiveness is contagious. God not only cleanses you—He promises not to bring your sins up again . . . ever. When this assurance of sins forgiven becomes yours, you can forgive yourself, and others too, and never mention it again.

The message of God's Word is clear: "If we confess our sins, he is faithful and just to forgive us our sins, and to cleanse us from all unrighteousness." Confess your sins. Clean up your house. Take the broken pieces of your sins out to the trash and dump them there. Forget them. God has. Then move out in the confidence that your house is clean!

CHAPTER NINE

◈

Keeping Your Doors Locked

There's no doubt about it—God's provision for cleansing when His people sin is wonderful. But how much better it is if we can learn to nip evil thoughts and impulses in the bud *before* they become sin. Did you know that this is God's will for us? The same apostle who penned 1 John 1:9 also wrote, "My little children, these things write I unto you, that ye sin not" (1 John 2:1).

It is one thing to build a hospital at the bottom of a cliff in order to treat the people who plunge over the precipice. It is quite a different thing to build a guardrail up on the cliff! In this chapter we want to build guardrails around our spiritual lives, strengthening God's temple—specifically, our minds—that we might function effectively in spiritual conflict.

Your mind is a valued trophy over which a fierce battle is constantly being waged. Paul likened the human mind to a citadel or a stronghold that is the focal point of a strategic war.

> For though we walk in the flesh, we do not war after the flesh: (For the weapons of our warfare are not carnal, but mighty through God to the pulling down of

> strong holds;) casting down imaginations, and every high thing that exalteth itself against the knowledge of God, and bringing into captivity every thought to the obedience of Christ. (2 Corinthians 10:3-5)

Notice the terms Paul used to speak of warfare concerning the thought life: "imaginations," "knowledge," and "thought." Without question, the human mind is a battlefield in spiritual matters. Mighty forces are assaulting your temple, striving for the citadel of your mind!

God wants your mind because He wants you. You are His temple. You have been bought with a price. It is quite obvious that if He does not control your thoughts, He will not control His temple. The command to every Christian is to "love the Lord thy God . . . with all thy mind" (Matthew 22:37).

But why is the human mind so important? Simply because we become what we think about. (I sometimes think it's a wonder I didn't turn into a girl back in high school!) "For as [a person] thinketh in his heart, so is he" (Proverbs 23:7). This verse tells us that the thought is the father of the deed. An old proverb puts it this way: "Sow a thought and you reap a deed. Sow a deed and you reap a habit. Sow a habit and you reap a character. Sow a character and you reap a destiny."

The whole process starts in the area of thought—in the mind itself.

Satan's Desire

It goes without saying that Satan wants your mind. "But I fear, lest by any means, as the serpent beguiled Eve through his subtilty, so your minds should be corrupted from the simplicity that is in Christ" (2 Corinthians 11:3). A corrupted mind—what a horrible state! And this was written to the *saints* at Corinth! Satan wants to capture, control, and corrupt the thought life of the children of God, as well as that of the unsaved.

Further, the devil knows he can disgrace the testimony of a sincere Christian and bring heartache and ruin if he can first capture his control center—the mind. If Satan can get us to *think* a wrong thing, it is likely he will be able to push us to *do* a wrong thing.

The enemy is aware that God destroyed the entire civilization of Noah's day because of evil imaginations.

> And God saw that the wickedness of man was great in the earth, and that every imagination of the thoughts of his heart was only evil continually. And it repented the LORD that he had made man on the earth, and it grieved him at his heart. And the LORD said, I will destroy man whom I have created from the face of the earth; both man, and beast, and the creeping thing, and the fowls of the air; for it repenteth me that I have made them. (Genesis 6:5-7)

Indeed, Satan knows the awesome destructive power of the corrupted mind.

Satan's Devices

The devil has a well-laid plan—a strategy, if you will—to wreak havoc on our thought life. We need not guess what Satan's strategy is, for Paul has said, "We are not ignorant of his devices" (2 Corinthians 2:11). Paul had pulled the veil of darkness off of the enemy and exposed his methods.

These methods can be summarized under two major headings.

First, *Satan blinds the mind of the unsaved.* As the god of this age, Satan has "blinded the minds of them which believe not, lest the light of the glorious gospel of Christ, who is the image of God, should shine unto them" (2 Corinthians 4:4).

A spiritually blinded mind is one that cannot see or perceive spiritual truth. Someone who is in this condition needs to have his eyes opened to Christ. This explains why Jesus said, "Except a man be born again, he cannot *see* the kingdom of God" (John 3:3, italics mine).

A young man who was a gifted communicator wrote a newspaper in a Florida city to tell its readers why he was an atheist. It seemed he had dipped his pen in acid. He concluded his letter to the editor by saying, "When people finally stop praying to a non-existent God to save them from a non-existent hell, then maybe one more time the world will be populated by men rather than sheep."

Sometime later that young man was given the good news of Christ by a Spirit-filled Christian who had prayerfully asked God to open his friend's blinded eyes. God in mercy broke through the midnight darkness of this young atheist's mind with a shaft of gospel sunlight. He was born again and could finally see.

I spoke to him shortly after his conversion. He wanted to become a baptized member of our church. He said, "Pastor Rogers, it's so amazing what has happened to me. Before God opened my heart, I was so sure He did not even exist. But now all of that has changed, and I can hardly remember the argument I used for my atheism."

Don't scold a blind man for not seeing. Pray for him.

Bind the powers of darkness and loose the powers of light by your prayers of intercession. Claim this promise: "I will give unto thee the keys of the kingdom of heaven: and whatsoever thou shalt bind on earth shall be bound in heaven: and whatsoever thou shalt loose on earth shall be loosed in heaven" (Matthew 16:19).

Second, *Satan corrupts the minds of the saved.* Don't think that salvation means automatic immunity from satanic attack on your mental fortress. We have already noted Paul's deep apprehension concerning Satan's activity among the Corinthian believers (see 2 Corinthians 11:3 above).

Because Christians can have corrupted minds, there are saints across the world filled with anxieties and fears. Chilling inner doubts have come to hide the star of hope. Impurities—unclean pictures—are hung on the walls and corridors of the mind. Cares and worries wear away the health like sand wears away or paralyzes machinery. Deceptions and false doctrines neutralize and destroy the faith and testimony of the saints. This is the tragedy of corrupted minds!

Unguarded Doors

You might ask, "How does the devil gain entrance into a Christian's thought life?" He comes in through unguarded doors. The Great Wall of China did not keep out the enemy. All that was necessary was to bribe a gatekeeper and the enemy came in. I want to mention three unguarded doors through which Satan enters the citadels and corrupts the minds of God's children.

The perverse mind. Unconfessed, harbored sin in any life is the devil's open door.

> Be renewed in the spirit of your mind; and . . . put on the new man, which after God is created in righteousness and true holiness. Wherefore putting away lying, speak every man truth with his neighbour: for we are members one of another. Be ye angry, and sin not: let not the sun go down upon your wrath: neither give place to the devil. (Ephesians 4:23-27)

Look at that last phrase again. Paul's thought is this: when any Christian allows the sun to set on his sin, he has given the devil a place from which to work. It's like going to bed and leaving the back door of your house wide open with the light on!

The devil's place of entry is unconfessed sin, which in this case is anger. This becomes a foul nest from which Satan can hatch his hellish ideas and a stronghold from which he hurls his fiery darts of doubt. Unconfessed sin becomes Satan's legal ground from which he will not budge. By harboring unconfessed sin the Christian can give Satan access to his house, a place to bed down.

Look at the remaining verses of Ephesians 4 and you will see that this sin may be an attitude ("anger," "bitterness," "wrath," "malice") as well as an act. Have you given the enemy easy access to your mind? Unconfessed sin is a very dangerous matter for the child of God.

The passive mind. Another door many Christians have opened to Satan is a mind that is not aggressively controlled and kept by the believer. Our minds are to be actively guarded, never wandering or passively neglected. Solomon wisely warned, "Keep thy heart with all diligence; for out of it are the issues of life" (Proverbs 4:23).

What does it mean to "keep" your mind or heart? It

means to guard it, control it, and never release it to anyone or anything other than the Lord. If you become passive and fail to think for yourself, a foreign power will take up the slack. Ungodly thoughts will be planted in your heart and mind.

John made it clear that Judas was thinking Satan's thoughts when he betrayed Jesus: "supper being ended, the devil having now put into the heart of Judas Iscariot, Simon's son, to betray him . . ." (John 13:2).

It is true that Judas, the son of perdition, was void of spiritual life. But Satan also has the power to put suggestions into the minds of God's children. I am amazed at the willingness of so many people to throw open the doors of their minds by passivity. This is the technique of the New Age movement. If you want to make contact with the spiritual forces within and around you, say the New Agers, you must surrender your mind to these forces and welcome them. Anyone who does this will make contact with spiritual forces all right, but it will be contact with the powers of darkness.

You wouldn't open all the windows and doors of your house and then go to sleep at night, just to see what might come in, would you? Who in his right mind would welcome unscrutinized guests?

Christian friend, never turn your conscious mind over to anybody or anything except the Lord. Keep it with all diligence. Spiritism, hypnotism, yoga, channeling, and other New Age forms of phony spirituality are merely unlocked doors and opened windows. Do not be foolish enough to open yourself up to them.

Even amusement can lead to passivity. It is interesting to consider what the word *amuse* really means. "Muse" means to think, but when we add the negative prefix *a* (not), it means *not* to think. When we are being amused, we are not really thinking. Our minds are in neutral and are bypassed.

It's amazing how careless peopel are when it comes to what they allow their minds to be exposed to. For example, some viewers sit in front of the television for hours, undiscerning victims of garbage programming. According to some media experts, an eighteen-year-old has watched 25,000 hours of television—including literally thousands of murders.

Many of today's most popular television programs are situation comedies that make a mockery of sin. Harmless, you say? Not at all! The devil knows that once you have laughed at sin, it is difficult to think seriously about it anymore.

God has warned that His children should always have control of their minds, even when they worship Him. God does not work by putting the Christian into a blind trance or an unthinking stupor. His method is not to step outside of your mind or do an end-run around your intellect. He renews your mind and uses it.

We may meditate as Christians, but our meditation must be centered on Christ. We are to gird up the loins of our minds. "Thou wilt keep him in perfect peace, whose mind is *stayed* on thee" (Isaiah 26:3, italics mine).

The polluted mind. The use of drugs and intoxicants is the third unguarded door through which Satan slips to corrupt the thought life.

The Scriptures issue clear warnings against sorcery. The word itself is a translation of the Greek word *pharmakeia,* from which we get our word *pharmacy*. It means one who enchants with drugs. Drug abuse is a form of instant insanity that opens the door to mind control by the enemy.

Here I mean more than illegal drugs. Any beverage containing alcohol is probably the most dangerous drug in America. We are told that each year alcoholism is one of the leading causes of death in this country. According to one estimate, 18 million Americans are addicted to alcohol. A home resource on medical disorders lists twenty-four conditions that are either caused by or aggravated by the consumption of alcohol.[1]

That's bad enough, but of course this list does not include the most damaging effect of alcohol—the spiritual devastation it causes. And I am not just talking about the heavy drinker. Even the so-called social drinker can be prey to the evil effects of a drug that one former alcoholic called "dirty, vicious, and brutal." With alcohol so widely accepted, even within the church, the danger is that much greater.

One man bragged that he drank vodka so no one could smell liquor on his breath and know he was drinking. A friend said, "If I were you, I would drink something else. It would be better for them to know you are drunk than to think you are stupid."

Not only is it stupid to give our minds over to pollution, it is sad. Many Americans who claim to be Christians have opened the door to mind control by the devil through sorcery or the use of drugs. Beware of the polluted mind!

Satan's Defeat

Thank God that it is possible for His children to actively recapture the citadel of their minds. If you have misused your mind, I have good news and hope to offer. It is found in the verses I quoted at the outset of this chapter, 2 Corinthians 10:3-5.

Clearly, according to Paul, there is victory for the child of God. But please notice that "carnal" weapons are not sufficient for this spiritual battle. The battle for the mind will never be won by education, psychology, psychiatry, or positive thinking. These all have a proper place, but one might as well throw snowballs at a Stealth bomber as to try to dislodge Satan's thought patterns with such carnal weapons.

If "the weapons of our warfare are not carnal, but mighty through God to the pulling down of strong holds," what are those weapons? I want to mention three mighty weapons that will secure and guard the mind of the believer who has suffered invasion by the enemy.

For the perverse mind there is repentance. Don't ever think that only the unsaved need to repent. Jesus' last word to the church was not the Great Commission. It was, "Repent." Five of the seven churches of Asia Minor that the risen Lord addressed in Revelation 2–3 were commanded to repent.

The Greek word for repentance is *metanoia,* which literally means "a change of mind." There is no way to deal with the perverse mind but to change it. The sin that has become Satan's foul nest and legal territory must be uprooted and removed. It will not do you much good to try and keep your house in order if Satan occupies the rumpus room!

Repentance always leads to confession, confession leads to cleansing, and cleansing takes away the place given to the devil (Ephesians 4:27). How wonderful when the cleansing tides of Calvary wash over the soul and the fresh breeze of the Spirit sweeps through the mind.

Why is it that we modern Christians are willing to try almost everything today but good old-fashioned repentance? Are there areas of satanic stronghold in your mind right now over which you need to exercise mind-changing repentance? Is God the Holy Spirit telling you that you need to repent?

Turn from these things *now*. If not, I don't think there is much else I can say to you in this book that will help. Come to Christ with a soft heart, and repent of your sins—that is the only answer.

For the passive mind there is resistance. "Submit yourselves therefore to God. Resist the devil, and he will flee from you" (James 4:7). Why should you resist? Because Satan will not give up anything or anybody without a struggle.

And how can you resist? Do what you know is right. Say no to sin. Make certain that every sin is confessed. Make sure that you have, through God's power, taken back every stronghold you yielded. And then ask the Lord to rebuke Satan (see Jude 9). Remember, the devil now has no legal right. He *must* flee.

You may also need to say, "I resist the enemy in the name of Jesus. He has no right or authority in my life. My body is the temple of the Holy Spirit. I am bought with the price of the blood of Christ. The devil cannot trespass on my Father's property. Lord, rebuke him!"

For the polluted mind there is renewal. Minds that have been damaged and distorted can be made over. New thought patterns can and must be established. Listen to these marvelous promises:

> Be renewed in the spirit of your mind. (Ephesians 4:23)

> I beseech you therefore, brethren, by the mercies of God, that ye present your bodies a living sacrifice,

> holy, acceptable unto God, which is your reasonable service. And be not conformed to this world: but be ye transformed by the renewing of your mind, that ye may prove what is that good, and acceptable, and perfect, will of God. (Romans 12:1-2)

God will renew your mind after you repent and resist. This will be done as you change the focus of your attention. Remember that we become what we think about.

Now here's the exciting part: God has so engineered your mind that you cannot think two thoughts at one time. So if you are thinking what is right, you cannot be thinking what is wrong.

Paul stated this so beautifully:

> Brethren, whatsoever things are true, whatsoever things are honest, whatsoever things are just, whatsoever things are pure, whatsoever things are lovely, whatsoever things are of good report; if there be any virtue, and if there be any praise, think on these things. (Philippians 4:8)

Let me give you this word of advice about the renewed mind. Do not try to avoid thinking wrong thoughts. That never works. For example, for the next thirty seconds, whatever you do, don't think about an elephant. If my guess is right, that's about all you *will* think about for the next thirty seconds. Why? Because you are trying *not* to think about an elephant. Right?

Here's the way to do it. Just get up each morning and bathe your soul in the presence of Jesus. Talk with Him, first off, in prayer.

Then saturate your mind with His Word. "Let the word

of Christ dwell in you richly in all wisdom; teaching and admonishing one another in psalms and hymns and spiritual songs, singing with grace in your hearts to the Lord" (Colossians 3:16). Commit your day to Him. Before long, it will become evident that God is renewing your mind.

The doors of your temple can be shut to the enemy while its windows are open to the Lord!

CHAPTER TEN

✧

A House of Prayer— Not a Den of Thieves

As temples of the Holy Spirit, we should be houses of prayer.

The importance of prayer was uppermost in the Lord Jesus' mind as He cleansed the temple in Jerusalem. He then stood guard over the temple, not allowing anyone to defile it. And He had a message: "He taught, saying unto them, Is it not written, My house shall be called of all nations the house of prayer? but ye have made it a den of thieves" (Mark 11:17).

Anything that distracts us from vital prayer is a treacherous thief. It steals from us the blessings the Father longs to bestow, and it takes from the Father the glory He so richly deserves.

How foolish we are to allow ourselves to be so robbed. If we are to keep our temples clean and well-protected, we desperately need to learn the art and the discipline of prevailing prayer. Prayer is so fantastic because it links us with the Almighty God in a miraculous way. Prayer can do anything God can do, and God can do anything. That may sound astounding, but read on.

One day as I was meditating, one of the most electrifying thoughts I have ever had came into my heart. I cannot fully explain the impact that it made on me. Yet, this thought is so simple and presumably so well-known that I almost hesitate to tell you about it. But here it is: *God hears and answers prayer!*

Oh, you say, every Christian knows that. Yes, so did I—in my head. But somehow I suddenly saw the *truth* of that truth, if you will, and it shook me to my very foundations.

I thought, "If this is true, and it is, then the one thing above everything else I should learn to do is to pray." There can be no greater achievement than a vital prayer life. I challenge you to stop and consider the impact of this thought with me—that we as mortals can link our nothingness with God's almightiness through prayer. I say it again: what fools we are if we do not learn to pray!

Failure to pray is a tragedy, but it is more than a tragedy. It is a *sin*. God's Word says in 1 Samuel 12:23, "As for me, God forbid that I should sin against the LORD in ceasing to pray for you: but I will teach you the good and the right way."

With this in mind, I want us to see what Jesus taught about prevailing prayer. Do not let your familiarity with the following passage keep you from giving it the full attention of your heart and mind. What an amazing passage it is. The more we look at it, the more we see. It is sweet to the child, perplexing to the scholar, and beneficial for every one of us.

> After this manner therefore pray ye: Our Father which art in heaven, Hallowed be thy name. Thy kingdom come. Thy will be done in earth, as it is in heaven. Give us this day our daily bread. And forgive us our debts, as we forgive our debtors. And lead us not into temp-

tation, but deliver us from evil: For thine is the kingdom, and the power, and the glory, for ever. Amen. (Matthew 6:9-13)

Before Jesus gave this lesson on prayer, He had warned against praying only to be seen by men.

I heard of a young lawyer who had just opened up a brand-new office. He was seated behind his shiny new desk, eagerly awaiting his first client. Soon he heard footsteps in the hall and then a hand on the doorknob. Wanting to look important he pretended to be busy, so he picked up the telephone and carried on a fake conversation.

"Yes, yes, I'll have my secretary tend to that. I have a very heavy schedule. Call me back in a few days." He motioned toward the door as if to say, "Come in, come in." The stranger entered the office, listening to one end of the high-level conversation.

Finally the receiver was put back on the hook, and the lawyer turned to what he hoped was a prospective client. "Now, what may I do for you?"

The man answered calmly, "I'm from the phone company, and I came to connect your telephone."

So much of our praying is like that. We are praying to be seen by men, but no one is on the other end of the line. Wouldn't you like to quit playing games and get down to serious business in this matter of prayer? Let's allow the Lord Jesus, the Master Teacher, to show us how as we examine His wonderful model of prayer.

The Person of the Prayer

Our Father. Notice how Christ's model prayer begins. Right away we learn that vital prayer is not an empty repetition of words, but is rather a child talking with his Father. Because this is so, several other truths come quickly to mind.

First, we must be children of God in order to pray with effectiveness. Not everyone has the right to call God "Father." Only those who have been born into His family have that right.

Someone may protest, "Wait a minute. God created everybody, so God is the Father of everybody." I beg to differ. He is not the Father of everybody. God does not become Father by creation. He created cats and dogs, flies and frogs, but He is not their Father. He is only their Creator.

God has made it clear in the Scriptures that some human beings are not His children. Jesus said of the unconverted Pharisees, "Ye are of your father the devil" (John 8:44). We become children of God and can call Him "Father" only when by faith we receive Christ as our Lord and Savior and are born into God's family. The Apostle John made this clear when, concerning Jesus, he said, "He came unto his own, and his own received him not. But as many as received him, to them gave he power to become the sons of God, even to them that believe on his name" (John 1:11-12).

If God is your Father, how simple and natural it ought to be for you to pray. Some think that we have to use the language of Shakespeare in order to pray. This is not so! Nor do we need to repeat certain prayers over and over. Jesus said, "When ye pray, use not vain repetitions, as the heathen do: for they think that they shall be heard for their much speaking" (Matthew 6:7).

Suppose when my daughter was still at home she had met me when I came home one day and said, "Oh, hail thou eminent pastor of Bellevue Baptist Church. I beseech thee that thou wouldest grant to thy daughter, whom thou lovest, some financial assistance that she may sojourn to yon apothecary for some cosmetical necessities."

I think I would have said, "Huh?"

But my daughter wouldn't have done that. She would simply have said, "I love you, Daddy. I'm so glad you're home. By the way, I need five dollars to get some things at the drugstore."

Remember, God is your Father. The Holy Spirit has even taught you to pray, "Abba, Father" (Romans 8:15). *Abba* is an Aramaic word that is very close to our word *Daddy*. It is one of the first words formed upon the lips of a little baby. How thrilling to know that if you are God's dear child, you can come with such intimate confidence as to call Him "Abba, Father."

The Purpose of the Prayer

Thy will be done. This phrase tells us immediately that prayer has one major purpose: to seek and to secure the will of God. Prayer is answered only when it is offered in the will of God. "This is the confidence that we have in him, that, if we ask any thing according to his will, he heareth us" (1 John 5:14). Someone has wisely said, "Nothing lies beyond the reach of prayer except that which lies outside the will of God."

Someone may ask, "Do you mean that in my praying I am restricted to the will of God?" Yes . . . but do not be concerned about that! For us to worry about being restricted by the will of God is like a minnow worrying about being hemmed in by the Atlantic Ocean.

Praying in the will of God does not mean fewer blessings for us but more and greater blessings. God wants for us what we would want for ourselves if we only had enough sense to want it. We should never fear the will of God.

Remember that prayer is not some exercise whereby we try to bend God's will to fit our wills. Prayer is not talking God into doing something that He ordinarily would not want to do. Prayer is the thrilling experience of finding God's will and then asking Him for it.

That brings into focus a very key question: how do we know God's will? Obviously, God's will is made known in a general sense as we read the Bible, but there are so many specific things that the Scriptures do not touch upon. There is no Scripture that tells us what job to take, whom to marry (incidentally, proper prayer would help avoid many divorces—and quite a few marriages), or what school to attend.

The secret of knowing God's will in prayer is not only to know the Bible and let its truth abide in us, but to be very, very sensitive to the leading of the Holy Spirit. Because you are a temple of God and a house of prayer, God's Holy Spirit abides within you and *will help you pray* (Romans 8:26-27). The Bible calls this "praying in the Spirit."

> Praying always with all prayer and supplication in the Spirit, and watching thereunto with all perseverance and supplication for all saints. (Ephesians 6:18)

> But ye, beloved, building up yourselves on your most holy faith, praying in the Holy Ghost . . . (Jude 20)

When we pray we are to pray to the Father, through the Son, in the Spirit. What a glorious partnership there is between the Holy Spirit and the human spirit. He teaches us the will of God and helps us to pray as we ought. The Holy

Spirit, as our Helper, wants to think through our minds, feel through our hearts, speak through our lips, weep through our eyes, and express Himself through our spirits.

One of the greatest truths I have ever learned about prayer is this: the prayer that gets to heaven is the prayer that starts in heaven. All we do is close the circuit.

I once heard someone give this definition of prayer: "Prayer is the Holy Spirit finding a desire in the heart of the Father and then placing that desire into our hearts. The desire is then sent back to heaven in the power of the cross."

This is why we must learn to wait before the Father in meditation and openness when we pray. So often we simply rush into the presence of God and say, "Listen, Lord, your servant speaks" rather than saying, "Speak, Lord, your servant is listening."

Are you listening? Are you honestly seeking to know and do the will of God? Man's ruin began in the Garden of Eden, when the spirit of the first Adam said, "Not Thy will, but mine, be done."

Man's rescue came in another garden when the last Adam said, "Not my will, but thine, be done" (Luke 22:42).

The Spirit of the Lord Jesus is the Spirit that should characterize our praying.

The Provision of the Prayer

Give us this day our daily bread. Surely we may ask for what we need. While we are not to pray selfish prayers, we certainly may pray for personal needs. Our Father is concerned with every need we have.

Remember that this model prayer is but a guide for praying. I do not believe that Jesus meant we should ask only for bread. What He did mean was that we should bring all of our needs to the Father and ask Him specifically for what we need.

We can pray this way because the earlier petition for God's name to be "hallowed" is a guard against mere self-seeking in prayer. If you can sincerely pray, "Hallowed be thy name," which means to regard God as holy and to make His holy name known, then you are ready to pray for your needs.[1]

Paul reminded us, "My God shall supply all your need according to his riches in glory by Christ Jesus" (Philippians 4:19). I am so very glad he did not say, "out of his riches," but "according to his riches."

A millionaire may give you one dollar out of his riches, but that is not necessarily according to his riches. The gift does not reflect what he is capable of doing. Think of the vast riches of our Father, and realize that He is ready to meet our needs according to those riches.

I am also very glad Paul did not say, "all your wants." He said, "all your need." I have sometimes wanted things I did not need; and I have sometimes needed things I did not want. For example, my dad would say sometimes, "Adrian, you need a spanking." He was quite right, but of course I did not want one.

I believe many Christians have needs that are unmet simply because they do not pray. "Ye have not, because ye ask not" (James 4:2).

When I was a student pastor in Florida, I shepherded a small church in Indian River County. You may not know it, but the best citrus fruit in all of Florida grows there. One day as I was returning to college after serving my church on the weekend, a deacon gave me several bushels of delicious oranges.

I said, "Mr. Ingram, I cannot eat all of those oranges

before they spoil."

He said, "Well, take them back to college, Adrian, and give them away."

So I took the oranges back with me to college, lugged them upstairs to our tiny, second-story garage apartment, and put them in a closet.

One day shortly after that, I looked out into our backyard and saw a little fellow about seven years of age sneaking around in a suspicious manner. He was looking every way but up. (Does that remind you of anyone you know?)

I realized after a while that he was going to steal an orange from the lonely orange tree in our backyard. I decided I would let him, because he did not know that this was a sour-orange tree. In Florida these sour-orange trees are very beautiful ornamental shrubs, but the fruit is extremely bitter. As a matter of fact, it is not fit for man or beast.

I watched that little guy as he plucked his prize. Even though I was working my way through school, I believe I would have given a dollar to see him take that first bite.

Now the irony of the whole matter is this: had he only knocked on my door and asked, "Mister, may I have one of those oranges?" I would have said no. But then I would have loaded him down with more of the very best oranges than he could carry.

When we get to heaven, I wonder if the Heavenly Father will not bring us to some huge cosmic closet and say, "Look in there. Do you see all of those things? They are the blessings I longed to give you, but you never asked. You were enjoying the bitter fruit of your own scheming and wisdom rather than asking Me for what is best."

Let us learn to ask the Father for the things we need.

Remember, there is nothing big enough to concern us that is too small to concern Him. Ask Him for your needs.

The Pardon of the Prayer

Forgive us our debts. Powerful prayer must come from a clean heart. Jesus taught us to pray for daily forgiveness just as we pray for daily bread. Since we have already talked at length about confession and repentance, let me just highlight a few things by way of review.

The reason many of our prayers are not answered is that we are not including confession and repentance with our petitions. A prayer from a dirty heart is a prayer not answered.

We like to quote the Bible's prayer promises, don't we? Let me give you a prayer promise we are prone to forget: "If I regard iniquity in my heart, the Lord will not hear me" (Psalm 66:18).

Is there any iniquity that you have made peace with? Is there any sin, habit, or grudge that you have regard for? If so, for God to answer your prayer would merely be an encouragement for you to continue in that sin.

James warned all of us when he wrote, "Draw nigh to God, and he will draw nigh to you. Cleanse your hands, ye sinners; and purify your hearts, ye double minded" (James 4:8). We cannot pray effectively with dirty hands, defiled hearts, and double minds.

I am told that monkeys are captured in the South Sea Islands in an unusual way. The natives fasten a coconut with a hole in it to a tree. Some rice is then placed inside the coconut. A curious monkey will examine the coconut and see the rice inside.

He then puts his paw through the hole and grabs a fistful of rice. But with his hand now doubled up, it is too big to withdraw. The poor monkey will plead and scream as his captor approaches, but he will not release the rice so he can withdraw his hand.

One wise man prayed like this: "Oh, Lord, help me to cooperate with You so You won't have to operate on me." We should do the same. So many of us, it seems, would rather hold on to our sins than enjoy the freedom of a prayer life that knows no limits.

If there are sins that have made your temple a den of thieves rather than a house of prayer, pray, "Forgive me my debts." Then let go of your fistful of rice, so God can stop chastising you and start blessing you.

The Protection of the Prayer

Deliver us from evil. This phrase could be rendered, "Deliver us from the evil one." Satan is so very real. He has already made plans to sabotage your life and to hurt your loved ones. He has already dug a pit for your feet to fall into today.

His real war is with God, but he cannot get at God directly. He knows, as evil people have always known, that if you cannot harm someone, the next most effective thing is to harm someone whom that someone loves. God loves you, and therefore Satan has aimed all the artillery of hell at you. You need protection.

Your protection is provided through prayer. The prayer for deliverance from evil and temptation is preventive medicine, though we are prone to forget that. I feel certain that the reason we keep wearily asking for forgiveness for the same sins and making the same confessions is that we have not been claiming our protection from the enemy.

The reason we fall into this trap is that we remember to pray, "Forgive us," but we fail to pray, "Deliver us."

What happens is something like this: we wake up a little late. We hurry through our devotions—or have none at all. But it's a new day anyway, and nothing has happened yet to upset us. Things are running smoothly. We catch a snatch of the newspaper and gulp down a little breakfast and dash off to work. (Why do they call it "rush hour" when the traffic moves so slowly?)

But we get our day started, and everything seems to be going just fine. Then at an unsuspecting moment Satan tosses a bombshell into our laps, and spiritually we are blown to smithereens. (I've always wondered what a smithereen is.) We fail miserably!

At the end of the day we try to clean up the mess. We bow before God and pray, "Forgive me my debts." And He does.

But this model prayer Jesus has given us is not a prayer for the end of the day. This is a morning prayer. Can you imagine someone coming to the end of the day and praying, "Lord, give me today my daily bread"? And then off to sleep he goes. That would be foolish. Just as in the morning we ask for the day's provision, we are to ask for the day's protection too.

I have a friend, a former professional football player, who likes to tell this story: "When I graduated from college, my coach said, 'Mike, would you help me do some scouting?' (For the uninitiated, that means to look for some prospective football players to be enrolled in college!)

"I said, 'Sure, coach, what kind of player are you looking for?'

"He said, 'Well, there's the kind of guy that when you knock him down, he just stays down.'

"'We don't want him, do we, coach?'

"'No, we don't. But there's the kind of guy that when you knock him down, he gets up; knock him down, and he gets up; knock him down, and he gets up; knock him down again, and he just keeps getting up.'

"'That's the guy we want, right, coach?'

"'No, we don't want him either. What I want you to do is find the guy who's knocking all the other guys down. That's the guy I want.'"

I say Amen to that. I am glad God enables us by His grace to keep getting up every time Satan knocks us down. But I think it is time that God's people got off the defensive and went on the offensive. It's time Satan started fleeing from us. And he will flee when we begin the day by putting on the whole armor of God and bathing our souls in the presence and power of the Lord Jesus by claiming the protection of prayer.

The Praise of the Prayer

Thine is the glory. Notice that Jesus' prayer opens and closes on a note of praise. How appropriate. Prayer must be done in faith, and praise is the best expression of faith I know of. Praise is faith turned inside out.

When we ask God for things, that is petition. But petition without praise is unbelief. Praise without petition, however, is presumption. But when we link petition and praise together, that is power. When I ask God, and then praise God, I am believing God. Petition says, "Please." Praise says, "Thank You."

If your faith is strong, your prayer will be strong. Pray

and believe and you will receive. Pray and doubt and you will do without.

How important it is, therefore, that we learn to praise. I cannot overestimate the power of praise. If your prayer life seems useless and powerless, learn to praise God.

The Bible says that God inhabits the praises of His people. He is so very near when we praise Him. Billy Sunday was right when he said, "We need to jerk some of the groans out of our prayers and shove in a few hallelujahs."

Why shouldn't we offer praise? Our Father is a King! Just think about that. I have a Father who will hear me and a King who can answer me. I have the sympathy of a Father and the sovereignty of a King attuned to my prayer. Why shouldn't I offer God praise? You will discover victory when you make your temple a house of prayer and a house of praise!

CHAPTER ELEVEN

The Golden Key of Faith

Paul's prayer for the Ephesians was "that Christ may dwell in your hearts by faith" (Ephesians 3:17). The door through which Jesus enters the human heart—and thereby makes you His temple—swings upon the hinges of grace, and faith is the key that unlocks that door.

In this chapter I want to think with you about what I call the "golden key of faith," which opens the door of the heart to Jesus and also the door of heaven's riches to the believer. Faith is not only our house key, but the key to God's storehouse.

All of God's blessings come to us through faith. Jesus said, "According to your faith be it unto you" (Matthew 9:29). Therefore, the bench mark of blessing is not according to our feelings, friends, fame, or fortune, but according to our faith. The measure of accomplishment in the Christian life is always faith.

Conversely, most of the problems in a Christian's life are caused by lack of faith. *Worry,* for instance, is the opposite of faith and is an insult to God. Worrying is like saying,

"God, I don't think You can handle this one." *Loneliness* is the result of not believing in God's presence. Faith makes God's presence very real to us even when no one else is near. *Unbelief*, however, leaves us isolated even in a crowd.

Many other people are haunted by the ghost of *guilt* because they lack confidence in the full forgiveness of God's grace. Faith is our acceptance of God's acceptance of us. *Disobedience* results from lack of faith in what God has said.

It is human nature to touch the paint when the sign says, "Wet Paint." We are not quite sure it's wet, so we check for ourselves. If we truly believe the "wet paint" signs in God's Word, however, we will not so easily transgress.

The Description of Faith

The book of Hebrews contains a mighty message on this vital subject of faith, probably the most well-known description of faith in all of Scripture: "Faith is the substance of things hoped for, the evidence of things not seen. For by it the elders obtained a good report" (Hebrews 11:1-2).

To my knowledge, there is no precise definition of faith given in the Scriptures. But even though the verses above describe rather than define faith, they make clear what faith is in the life of the believer.

Faith is not positive thinking. It is not following a hunch. It is not a feeling of optimism. It is not hoping for the best. All of these may be well and good in their place, but they are not biblical faith. What is faith, then?

FAITH IS SUBSTANCE

"Faith is the substance of things hoped for." "Substance" means "solid ground." The English word gives the meaning of the Greek quite well. *Sub-stans* means there is something beneath us to stand upon. When we are living by faith, we are not walking on eggshells and Jell-O. We are standing upon the Solid Rock.

Sometimes the materialist will say, "Don't talk to me about faith. Talk about real things." He means, of course, the things that can be experienced with the five senses—the things we can see, smell, hear, taste, or touch.

But are these the only things that are real? Paul reminded us that "the things which are seen are temporal; but the things which are not seen are eternal" (2 Corinthians 4:18). Which is more real—that which is temporary or that which is eternal?

FAITH IS EVIDENCE

"Faith is . . . the evidence of things not seen." This means that faith is the *convincing proof* that God will keep His Word.

Evidence is the proof of unseen reality. There can be no evidence without the reality that gave rise to the evidence. It is so important that we understand this. If we do, we shall see the difference between real and synthetic faith.

There is a counterfeit faith today that is really nothing more than positive thinking couched in religious terms. The prophets of this synthetic faith explain it by saying, "God is able to do anything. Therefore, if you have enough faith, He will do anything you want. All you have to do is *name it and claim it.*"

That sounds good, but it bears little resemblance to biblical faith. We do not "name it and claim it." We cannot legitimately claim it until *God* has named it. Faith is actually our response to a revelation of God's will by His Word and His Spirit. "So then faith cometh by hearing, and hearing by the word of God" (Romans 10:17).

Believing does not make it so. "Just have faith" is silly advice if there's no object to the faith. Faith does not bring anything into existence. Faith is the evidence of things that are already in the heart and mind of God.

I cannot truly believe until a thing is settled. Anything else is but positive thinking or a wishful desire. Faith is the evidence in my heart that God has spoken.

The Dynamics of Faith

Faith is the most dynamic force in the world because it releases the hand of omnipotence. Hebrews 11:6 gives us insight into the mighty power of faith: "Without faith it is impossible to please him: for he that cometh to God must believe that he is, and that he is a rewarder of them that diligently seek him." There are three major thoughts in this verse we need to consider.

LACK OF FAITH DISPLEASES GOD

"Without faith it is impossible to please him." A lack of faith—that is, unbelief—greatly displeases God. Unbelief is a vile and wicked sin. Really, there is no greater sin. It is the parent sin. Unbelief is the sin out of which all other sins grow, the one sin that keeps a person out of heaven. Jesus said:

> For God sent not his Son into the world to condemn the world; but that the world through him might be saved. He that believeth on him is not condemned: but he that believeth not is condemned already, because he hath not believed in the name of the only begotten Son of God. (John 3:17-18)

The sin of unbelief is so terrible because of what it says about the character of God. Suppose you are introduced to a group as a speaker. The master of ceremonies says many nice things about you but then adds, "There is one thing I must tell you about our speaker—you cannot believe what he says."

It would not matter then how many nice things he had said. When he said you could not be believed, he cut the tap-root of your character.

It matters not how many nice things you may say about God if you do not believe Him. What difference does it make how we speak of the greatness of God or of His love when we refuse to believe He is worthy of our faith? "He that believeth not God hath made him a liar" (1 John 5:10). What a sobering thought.

Someone may protest that he cannot believe because he has genuine intellectual problems. "It is not my fault if I cannot believe," he says.

But it *is* his fault. Unbelief is a moral sin, not an intellectual problem. It starts in the heart, not in the head. It may show up in the head, but that is only a symptom of what is in the heart. "Take heed, brethren, lest there be in any of you an evil heart of unbelief, in departing from the living God" (Hebrews 3:12).

A man who held an important position in the space industry at Cape Canaveral once came to see me concerning his wife. She was suicidal, and he wanted me to counsel with her. I said I would if he would come with her. He agreed to come.

In my study the wife poured out her story of a broken heart. She wept as she spoke of her husband's cruelty, infidelity, drunkenness, and gambling. I turned to him and asked, "Sir, are you a Christian?" Mind you, I was not asking for information but was turning the conversation toward Christ.

He threw back his head and laughed scornfully. "No, I am an atheist," he said.

"Well," I responded, "an atheist is one who knows there is no God. Do you know all there is to know?"

"Of course not," he shot back.

"Would it be generous to say you know half of all there is to know?"

"Yes, that would be very generous," he muttered.

"Then if you only know half of all there is to know, wouldn't you have to admit the possibility that God may exist in the body of the knowledge you do not have?" I asked.

"I never thought of that," he said. "Well, I am not an atheist then. I am an agnostic."

I said, "Now we are getting somewhere. Agnosticism means you don't know." (I didn't tell him that the Latin equivalent for agnostic is ignoramus!) "An agnostic is a doubter."

"Well, that is what I am, and a big one."

"I don't care what size as much as what kind. There are two kinds of doubters, you know—honest and dishonest. The honest doubter doesn't know, but he wants to know. The dishonest doubter doesn't know because he doesn't want to know. He can't find God for the same reason a thief can't find a policeman. Which kind of doubter are you?" I asked him.

His face softened. "I never really thought about it. I guess I never really wanted to know," he said.

"Did you know that there is a promise to the honest doubter in God's Word?" I asked. I then read to him these words of Jesus, who was speaking to the doubters of His day: "My doctrine is not mine, but his that sent me. If any man will do his will, he shall know of the doctrine, whether it be of God, or whether I speak of myself" (John 7:16-17).

I continued, "In plain English, this says that if a man surrenders his will completely, God will reveal Himself to that man." My friend was getting interested.

I then asked him, "Would you be willing to sign a statement like this: 'God, I don't know whether You exist or not, but I want to know. And because I want to know, I will make an honest investigation. And because it is an honest investigation, I will follow the results of that investigation wherever they lead me, regardless of the cost.'"

After a time of soul-searching, he responded, "Yes, I would be willing to sign a statement like that. I will do it. How do I go about making such an investigation?"

We shared further together, and I got him started reading the Gospel of John with the commitment that he really wanted to know the truth and would follow any truth revealed to him regardless of the personal cost or consequences.

In a matter of weeks he came back to my study, got on his knees, and gave his heart to Christ! In a letter I received from him years later he said, "Dear friend, thank you for being willing to spend time with this general in the devil's army." He was then an active and vibrant lay leader in another state.

Where was this man's real problem? It was not in his head as he first thought but in his heart. When he surrendered his will, faith followed. Unbelief reveals a wicked heart.

BY FAITH WE GIVE GOD PLEASURE

"He that cometh to God must believe that he is." If unbelief displeases God, faith obviously pleases Him. We should have no greater aim in life than to please God. For if we please God, it really doesn't matter whom else we displease. Conversely, if we displease God, it really doesn't matter whom we please. But there is no pleasing God without believing Him.

Why is this so? Why is God so pleased with faith? Why didn't He just create us so that we would automatically believe in Him? Why doesn't He do something to prove Himself to us?

Have no doubts about it. If God wanted to prove Himself, He would have no difficulty doing so. He could roll back the heavens and make Himself known with a display of His grandeur, might, and glory. There would not be one unbeliever left upon the earth. However, such displays would render faith unnecessary.

One day God will reveal Himself in just that way. It will not be to save men, however, but to judge them. At that time, every knee will bow and every tongue will confess, but it will be a fearful and awful day.

In this day and age God refuses to reveal Himself in that manner because He wants us to respond to Him by faith.

The reason God demands faith is that faith is a moral response to His character. Faith gives God the honor that is due His name.

Let me illustrate. A rich person may have many so-called friends, but in the back of his mind he may be wondering, "Do these people love me for who I am or for what I have?" No one wants to be used without being loved.

Likewise, God wants us to love Him not for what He can do, but for who He is. So God refuses to bribe or overwhelm us to make us follow Him.

This helps us understand why Jesus came into the world as He did. He came to reveal the *character* of God, not to display the *grandeur* of God. When He came to this earth, He left all of the splendor and glory and majesty that was inherently His in heaven.

Isaiah said of Jesus in His incarnation, "He hath no form nor comeliness; and when we shall see him, there is no beauty that we should desire him" (Isaiah 53:2).

This means that Jesus did not ride out of heaven in a jeweled chariot, wearing regal robes and a diadem on His brow. Rather, He was born in a smelly stable with cow dung on the floor. He was reared in an obscure village as a carpenter's son. He lived a life of poverty and humility.

It is true that He performed miracles, but not to gain followers. His miracles were works of mercy and revelations of truth, not cheap tricks or public-relations stunts. Often He would say after a miracle, "Do not tell anyone about this."

Jesus knew the mind-set of the miracle-mongers, those who wanted Him to give them a sign from heaven so they could believe. These were the ones who followed Him for a while after He had fed the 5,000. But when He preached to them about real commitment, they left Him.

Yet, there were others who loved and followed Jesus sincerely. They did not follow Him primarily for what He did or for what He had, but rather for who He was. They responded by faith to His character and person. A true heart responds to God by faith like a healthy eye responds to light and a healthy ear responds to sound.

The reason, therefore, that God honors faith is that faith honors Him. Faith is a moral response to the character of God. Therefore, above all things it is faith that gives God pleasure.

THROUGH FAITH GOD GIVES US TREASURE

Finally, Hebrews 11:6 tells us that those who believe God find Him to be "a rewarder of them that diligently seek him." Our God longs to show Himself mighty on behalf of people who trust Him. Faith is the key to meeting our needs, whatever they may be. Let me list a few of the needs that faith can supply:

Salvation. "Therefore being justified by faith, we have peace with God through our Lord Jesus Christ" (Romans 5:1).

The fullness of the Spirit. ". . . that the blessing of Abraham might come on the Gentiles through Jesus Christ; that we might receive the promise of the Spirit through faith" (Galatians 3:14).

Victory over the world. "This is the victory that overcometh the world, even our faith" (1 John 5:4).

Victory over Satan. "Above all, taking the shield of faith, wherewith ye shall be able to quench all the fiery darts of the wicked" (Ephesians 6:16).

Answered prayer. "Therefore I say unto you, What things soever ye desire, when ye pray, believe that ye receive them, and ye shall have them" (Mark 11:24).

There is an imagined story of a scene in heaven. Some angels approach the throne and say, "Father, there is a mortal on earth asking for a blessing. What is Your pleasure concerning his request?"

The Father asks, "What did he send his faith in?"

The angels answer, "He sent his faith in a thimble."

The Father responds, "Well, fill the thimble with blessings and send it back to him. According to his faith, be it unto him."

Again the angels come and say, "Father, another mortal is asking blessings of Thee."

Again the Father inquires, "And what did he send his faith in?"

The angels respond, "He sent his faith in a huge barrel."

With a smile the Father says, "Fill the barrel with blessings and send it back to him. According to his faith, be it unto him."

By faith we give God pleasure, and through faith God gives us treasure.

The Development of Faith

How do we develop this kind of faith? The writer of Hebrews gave us an entire chapter on what others accomplished by faith. Then he spoke to *us*:

> Wherefore seeing we also are compassed about with so great a cloud of witnesses, let us lay aside every weight, and the sin which doth so easily beset us, and let us run with patience the race that is set before us, looking unto Jesus the author and finisher of our faith; who for the joy that was set before him endured the cross, despising the shame, and is set down at the right hand of the throne of God. (Hebrews 12:1-2)

The idea is that these heroes of the faith are now in the heavenly grandstand, while we are in the arena as spiritual athletes running the race of faith.

There are some simple rules given in these verses that tell us how to develop a dynamic faith:

Saturate your heart and mind with the Word of God. Notice the word "wherefore" in verse 1. It refers us to what has already been said—in this case, the entire eleventh chapter of Hebrews, which is devoted to the subject of faith and contains references to almost all of the Old Testament. The point is that the Bible is a book that will develop your faith. Remember Romans 10:17—"So then faith cometh by hearing, and hearing by the word of God."

The Bible may need explaining, but it is first and foremost a book to be believed, not explained. The Bible may be admired, but the promises of the Bible are not so much mottoes to be hung on the wall as they are checks to be cashed at the bank of heaven.

Would you have faith? Love the Bible, study it, memorize it, meditate on it, and obey it, and you will find faith welling up in your heart.

Repent of all known sin. Verse 1 goes on to say, "Let us lay aside every weight, and the sin which doth so easily beset us."

An athlete is foolish if he endeavors to run with excess baggage or anything that would cause him to stumble. The phrase "easily beset" has the meaning of cleverly placing something around an object. Sin can cleverly place itself around us, so as to cause us to stumble in the race of faith.

Remember that unbelief comes from an evil heart. If you are having difficulty believing God, it may be that unconfessed sin is tripping you up.

In the Bible God often mentions grace and peace together, but grace always comes before peace, for that is God's order. We cannot know His peace until we have experienced His grace.

Likewise, God mentions repentance and faith in that same sequence. If you are having difficulty with faith, you should try repentance. It always comes first. Faith and sin are mutually exclusive.

Use the faith you already have. We are told to "run with

patience the race that is set before us." I like the word *run* because it indicates what faith is. Faith is active, not static. It is more than mere belief. Faith is belief with legs on it.

The athlete learns to run by running. Reading books about running is not enough. Lectures on running will not suffice. The athlete must get out on the track and begin to learn. Use the weak faith you have, and it will become stronger faith.

To change the figure of speech, let me remind you that Jesus said faith is like a mustard seed. What's so great about a mustard seed is that though it may be tiny, it has God-given life in it. It is meant not to be treasured but to be planted, so that it will produce so much more.

It has been well said that any fool can count the seeds in an apple, but only God can count the apples in a seed.

Take the faith you have now and put it into action. It will grow as you exercise it. It will produce as you plant it.

Keep your eyes on Jesus. We are told in Hebrews 12:2 to be "looking unto Jesus the author and finisher of our faith." Faith is the by-product of keeping one's eyes upon Jesus.

The word translated "looking" is *aphorao* in the Greek language. It means "to look away from all else unto a certain object." Take your eyes from self, Satan, and circumstances, and turn them to Jesus.

This word also speaks of our dependence and trust on Jesus. Suppose you had a financial need, and a wealthy friend said, "Look to me. I will take care of it." He would not mean that you were simply to look at him, but that you were to depend upon him.

Jesus is worthy of our trust. He alone is the Author and Finisher of our faith. Let His glory and beauty fill your heart right now. Look to Him for every need.

CHAPTER 12

◇

Blessed Assurance

How wonderful it is to be saved, to have the joy of sins forgiven. But there is something even more wonderful—and that is to *know* you are saved.

The assurance of salvation is one of God's greatest gifts to us as the people of His dwelling. Yet, we are told by many Christian leaders and workers who deal with scores of people that the number one question believers have is, "How can I know I'm saved?" The lack of assurance is a great problem among God's people. Living without assurance is like driving with your parking brake on.

But there's no need for this, because God's Word says we can know beyond a shadow of a doubt that we are saved. We used to call it a "know-so" salvation, and I think that is still a great description of our salvation.

I was in a hospital once witnessing to a woman. She had not yet given her heart to the Lord Jesus Christ, and the doctor said she did not have long to live. I asked her if she knew the Lord Jesus, and she said no. I asked her, "Would you like to know Christ?"

She answered, "I surely would." So I took God's Word and showed her how she could trust Christ. Then I led her in a prayer, and she invited Jesus Christ into her heart to forgive her sins and to save her once and for all, now and forever.

Some of her loved ones were standing there in the hospital room. I thought they would rejoice, so I turned to her son-in-law and said, "Isn't it wonderful that she's been saved?"

"Oh," he said, "no one can know they're saved."

I replied, "But if a person will trust Christ, they *can* know they're saved."

He repeated his objection. "No, no one can know they're saved."

This young man was not an unbeliever—that is, he did not repudiate Christianity. He just had a doctrinal stance that would not allow him to accept the fact that a child of God can say, "Praise God, I *know* that I'm saved."

I pointed him to a verse of Scripture I want to consider with you in this chapter, 1 John 5:13. Notice these words very carefully: "These things have I written unto you that believe on the name of the Son of God; that ye may know that ye have eternal life."

Don't miss the point. The Apostle John does not say, "that ye may hope that ye have eternal life." Neither does he say that we can only think or surmise or wish that we have eternal life. It is as if God said, "I wrote an entire book of the Bible so that you might *know* you have eternal life." Why did God do this? Because of the vast importance the assurance of salvation has for us.

Settling the Issue of Eternity

Let me show you what I mean. If you do not know you are saved, if you do not know your future, your eternal destiny, you had better get it settled. This is an all-important issue. We are not talking about denominational preference. We are not talking about whether you like the choir music or not. We are talking about eternity.

Where you will spend eternity is so vitally important that I do not want you to have any doubt at all about your destiny. Actually, I have two purposes in this chapter. I want to, as Vance Havner used to say, "comfort the afflicted and afflict the comfortable."

That is, if you are genuinely saved, I pray that by the time you finish reading this chapter you will *know* you are saved. But if you are not saved and are merely clinging to some experience that happened thirty years ago and have no spiritual reality in the present, then you need to feel uncomfortable about the issue of your salvation.

As we will see later on in this chapter, the Bible never points one back to a past experience for the assurance of his salvation. Belief and assurance are always in the present tense.

Before we go any further, I want to set 1 John 5:13 in its larger context:

> Who is he that overcometh the world, but he that believeth that Jesus is the Son of God? This is he that came by water and blood, even Jesus Christ; not by water only, but by water and blood. And it is the Spirit that beareth witness, because the Spirit is truth. For there are three that bear record in heaven, the Father, the Word, and the Holy Ghost: and these three are one. And there are three that bear witness in earth, the spirit, and the water, and the blood: and these three agree in one. If we receive the witness of men, the witness of God is greater: for this is the witness of God which he hath testified of his Son. He that believeth on

> the Son of God hath the witness in himself: he that believeth not God hath made him a liar; because he believeth not the record that God gave of his Son. And this is the record, that God hath given to us eternal life, and this life is in his Son. He that hath the Son hath life; and he that hath not the Son of God hath not life. These things have I written unto you that believe on the name of the Son of God; that ye may know that ye have eternal life, and that ye may believe on the name of the Son of God. (vv. 5-13)

The word "*know*" means "absolute assurance." If verse 13 means anything, it means you can know you are saved. It *is* possible to be saved and know it, but we have to recognize that it is also possible to be saved and doubt it. If doubt were not possible, John would not have needed to assure us that we can have a know-so salvation. He is writing to people who might have doubt in order that they might have assurance.

Can a person be saved and have doubts? Yes. Is doubt good? No. Doubt is to your spirit what pain is to your body. Pain is a warning, a signal that something is wrong. If you have doubts, and if you truly are a born-again child of God, those doubts are a signal that something is amiss.

All Christians have doubts from time to time. A woman once told Dwight L. Moody she had been saved for twenty-five years and never had a doubt.

Moody replied, "I doubt you're saved."

What did Moody mean by that? Well, it would be like your saying to me, "Adrian, I've been married twenty-five years and have never had an argument with my spouse."

I would say to you, "I doubt you're married."

I am not saying that arguing with your spouse is good—not at all. And I am not saying that doubting your Lord is good—not at all. There is no need to be a doubting Christian when you can be a shouting Christian. I want to help you remove doubt and have the certainty, the assurance, of your salvation.

As a matter of fact, if you will read through the book of 1 John and circle the word *know,* you will be amazed at how many times the apostle uses that word. It is an epistle of assurance.

How to Know You're Saved

Let me tell you how I know that Adrian Rogers knows he is saved. It is not because of any confidence I have in myself, but I do know I am saved, and I bless God that I know I am saved. I want to show you from God's Word how you can have that same assurance.

A PRESENT FAITH IN THE SON OF GOD

If I would have the assurance of my salvation, there must be a present, "right-now" faith in Jesus.

The key here is in 1 John 5:10: "He that believeth on the Son of God hath the witness in himself." Then verse 13: "These things have I written unto you that believe on the name of the Son of God."

The word I want to underline is "believe," because in the Bible the words *believe* and *commit* are the same word. You can see this in John 2:23-24, where the Bible says concerning Jesus, "Many believed in his name, when they saw the miracles which he did. But Jesus did not commit himself unto them."

The people said they believed in Jesus, but He did not

believe in them. He knew they were just miracle-mongers, not true believers. You see, true biblical faith is not just an intellectual exercise. You do not believe *about* Jesus—you believe *in* Jesus. You commit yourself to Him.

Let me illustrate. When I board an airplane, I commit myself to it. I do not just believe the airplane can fly. I do not just believe there's a good pilot at the controls. I get on that airplane and commit myself to it.

I want you to notice something very important here that has a great deal to do with the assurance of your salvation. The Bible does not say, "He that has believed," but "He that believes." The Bible does not speak of faith in the past tense. It is always present tense.

Have you ever asked someone, "Are you saved?"

"Yes, I'm saved," comes back the answer.

"Tell me about it."

"Well, I remember back when I was a nine-year-old child, I walked down the aisle and gave my hand to my pastor and my heart to Jesus Christ. I may not be living for God right now, I'll admit, but I know I'm saved because I remember what I did when I was nine. I remember believing on Jesus Christ."

It may surprise you to know that the Bible never encourages you to use an experience as proof of your salvation. The Bible never points back to some time when you believed on Jesus Christ.

I hear people say, "If you cannot name the time and place when you received Christ, you're not saved." That sounds good, but there's just one thing wrong with it—you won't find it in the Bible. The Bible never says you can know you are saved by what you remember in the past. Faith is always present tense.

If you want to know whether you are saved, ask yourself if you are believing in Jesus Christ right now. Are you committed to Him? Are you trusting Him today?

Please do not misunderstand. I am not saying the time you received Christ is not important. Unless you did that, you are not saved. Praise God for the day and the hour of your salvation. But that is not where assurance comes from. The acid test is, are you now believing in Jesus Christ? Are you trusting in Him at this moment with all of your heart and soul?

When I fly from Memphis to Dallas, for example, it's not important that I recall the moment we crossed the Texas state line. The proof that we flew into Texas is that I am now on the ground at DFW airport. Those who came to Texas by car may know when they crossed the state line, but the proof that I crossed the state line is that I am now sitting at the airport in Dallas.

Correspondingly, the assurance that I am saved comes not from the fact that I did trust Christ, but that I am now trusting Christ. I am now at this very moment trusting my eternal destiny to the One who gave all for me.

Why should you not have this blessed assurance? Does the claim for assurance sound arrogant? It is not arrogance or self-confidence but rather God-confidence that brings assurance. True assurance is in the full and finished work of Calvary. If even the smallest part depends upon me, I have no ground for assurance.

A youngster once came forward at church to present himself as a candidate for baptism. As the leaders questioned him about his salvation to make sure he understood what it meant to trust Christ, the boy assured them he was saved, explaining, "I did my part, and God did His part."

"What do you mean by that?" came back the question.

"I did the sinning, and God did the saving," he replied.

A BASIS FOR MY BELIEF

A second necessity if I am to have the assurance of my salvation is this: there must be a firm basis for my belief. If indeed I must be trusting Christ now, how do I know the object of my faith is reliable and authentic?

What is it that Christians believe? And why do we believe? Are we just gullible? Are we believing in fairy tales, or is there a basis for our belief? Why do we believe what we believe? The Apostle John gives us three wonderful bases or roots for our belief:

The Work of Christ

You will find this great assurance in 1 John 5:6: "This is he that came by water and blood, even Jesus Christ; not by water only, but by water and blood." The Bible tells us that when the Lord Jesus Christ was crucified they ran a spear into His side, and out came water and blood (John 19:33-34). Jesus died the excruciating, painful death of crucifixion, and out of His wounded side flowed water and blood.

We are saved by blood and sanctified by water. When a person entered the Old Testament tabernacle—which we have already seen was a picture of the presence of God (that is, the Lord Jesus Christ)—the first thing he encountered was the bronze altar upon which the bloody sacrifices were made. Then there was a laver or great basin that the priest would wash in. So there was first the blood, and then the water.

That was all a picture of the work of Christ on the cross. The Bible says He came by the saving blood and the sanctifying water. His blood forgives us, and the sanctifying water keeps us clean. We sing about it all the time:

Let the water and the blood,
From thy wounded side which flowed,
Be of sin the double cure,
Save from wrath and make me pure.

One way you can know you are saved is that Jesus Christ, the Son of God, died to purchase your salvation. That is a historical fact. That is the saving work of Christ. All assurance must rest on that!

The Witness of the Spirit

Here is another way we can know we are saved. In 1 John 5:6b-8, John says:

> It is the Spirit that beareth witness, because the Spirit is truth. For there are three that bear record in heaven, the Father, the Word, and the Holy Ghost: and these three are one. And there are three that bear witness in earth, the spirit, and the water, and the blood: and these three agree in one.

In other words, the Holy Spirit takes the water and the blood and applies them to our hearts.

Now, notice the argument in verse 9: "If we receive the witness of men, the witness of God is greater: for this is the witness of God which he hath testified of his Son." The fact that Jesus Christ died on the cross, that He came by water and blood, is established in history.

But how is that made real to us? How do we know there was a man named Jesus Christ who was the sinless Son of

God? How do we know that God sent Him and that He actually died on that cross and took our sin upon Himself? We do not have to depend upon somebody's argument, because the Holy Spirit of God is here to make it all real in our hearts.

God gave us the work of Christ. But then to make the work of Christ (the water and the blood) real to us, He gave us the Spirit.

Here in 1 John 5:9 the word *"If"* may be translated "since"—"Since we receive the witness of men . . ." All of us believe the witness of men. Every time I fly I receive the witness of an airline about a person I have never met before—the pilot. I don't ask to see his credentials. That airline has its stamp of approval on the pilot; so I just get on the plane and never think twice about it. You do too, I am sure.

We do the same thing when we eat in a restaurant. How do you know the food is not poisoned? You exercise faith in the people who prepared it. Again, your doctor writes you a prescription you can't even read. You carry it down to the drugstore, your pharmacist fills it, and you go home and take a medicine the name of which you cannot pronounce and which was given to you by a man you hardly know. Why? Because we receive the witness of men.

John's argument is that we have the work of Christ and the witness of the Spirit, which are far greater and far more reliable than the witness of men. Don't tell me you can't believe. I do not believe that you can't believe. Do you know why? Because if you want to believe, the Holy Spirit will help you. No one can say, "I can't believe." God eliminates that excuse because people who receive the witness of men can receive the witness of God through the Holy Spirit.

I can preach truth, but only the Holy Spirit can impart

truth. This is why I soak every sermon in prayer before I preach it. The apostles said, "We are his witnesses of these things; and so is also the Holy Ghost, whom God hath given to them that obey him" (Acts 5:32). First of all, the Holy Spirit witnesses *to* us.

Then He witnesses *in* us, according to 1 John 5:10. Before I got saved, the Spirit witnessed to me. He told me that what Jesus Christ did is true. And now He witnesses in me. I have the witness in myself.

Suppose I am enjoying a piece of apple pie. You come to me and say, "There is no such thing as apple pie. I don't believe in apple pie. And if there is apple pie, it is no good."

Well, I want to tell you, in spite of all your arguments I have the witness within me! A Christian with a testimony is never at the mercy of an unbeliever with an argument because the Christian has the witness in himself.

I must be careful here. The witness of the Spirit is not some emotion. It is not feeling warm around the heart or wet around the lashes. It is deeper than our emotions. Our emotions are the shallowest part of our nature. Salvation is the deepest work of God. God does not do His deepest work in the shallowest part. The witness of the Spirit, therefore, is not emotion, but rather God the Holy Spirit in His own way whispering to me that I belong to Jesus.

This always reminds me of a delightful incident that once happened to a good friend of mine. He and his wife were driving through the Smoky Mountains, enjoying the scenery. It began to get dark, and he was low on gas. His wife asked him if they shouldn't be getting gas somewhere, but he assured her they had enough for now.

Well, as these things often happen, he kept driving,

thinking that surely he would find a gas station soon. But there were no stations, and by now he was in trouble. He prayed, "Lord, help me find a gas station." He knew that if he didn't, there would be murder in the mountains!

He came around a turn and saw a country gas station with one of those old glass pumps. My friend knocked on the door, and an old mountaineer came out to pump the gas. His head was down as he kept his eye on the nozzle of that ancient pump.

My friend was so relieved that he took a deep breath of mountain air and with a smile said, "It's great to be alive."

The old mountaineer never lifted his head but just replied, "I wouldn't know. I've never been no other way."

Well, my friend, I can tell you I *have* been some other way. I was dead in my sin, and it's great to be alive in Christ! I have the witness of the Spirit on the inside.

The Word of the Father

The Word of the Father is a third basis for my belief. It is "the record that God gave of His Son" (1 John 5:10b).

What is this "record"? It is God's Word, the Bible, which tells us that we have eternal life in the Lord Jesus Christ. Verse 12 makes this so plain. If you have the Son, you have life. That brings us back to verse 13, which is our spiritual birth certificate.

Here is the basis of our belief, the reason for our certainty. We are not just gullible fools. Jesus Christ died. He came by water and blood. The Holy Spirit of God says, "Yes, this is true. It's all attested by the Word of God."

To doubt the Bible is to call God a liar (v. 10). Someone may say, "Well, I'm trying to believe." Don't pride yourself in that.

Suppose I told you something, and you said, "Adrian, I'm trying to believe you."

I reply, "It's true."

"Well, I'm trying to believe you."

What you mean is, you are not certain whether I am telling the truth or not. But if you do not believe me, you have just cut the taproot of my character. If you refuse to believe God, you have made Him a liar. Either the Bible is His Word or it is not His Word. This is the root of our belief: the work of Christ, the witness of the Spirit, and the Word of the Father.

Thank God, we are not just gullible people. Our faith is not auto-suggestion. There's a reason for believing. We have the inerrant, infallible Word of God. We do not have to surmise on that. It has been tested through the ages.

It's so good to have the written Word rather than just emotions. Suppose I am in a courtroom, and the judge says to me, "Mr. Rogers, are you married?"

I say, "Yes, I am."

"Can you prove you're married?"

"Yes, I can, Your Honor. I was there in the church, and I saw Joyce coming down the aisle. My heart got all twitterpated, and I was so happy. Your Honor, it's the most wonderful feeling in the world to be married."

What will the judge say? "I'm happy you feel that way. But your emotions are not admissible as evidence in this court. Do you have any proof of your marriage?"

So I go down to the courthouse and get my marriage license, all properly signed and recorded, and I bring it to the judge. He says, "Okay, that's better."

I am glad I have something better than my emotions to assure me of my salvation. I have the Word of God.

A BELIEF THAT WILL SHOW IN BEHAVIOR

If I am to have the assurance of my salvation, I must first have a present belief in the Son of God. Second, there must be a basis for my belief. And third, what I believe must show in my behavior.

So it is fitting to ask, what has my salvation done in me? The English word *believe* comes from the two words "by live." What we truly believe, we live by. Is this all just an exercise in philosophy? Or has there been a change in my life? How do I know God is at home in my heart?

John is very, very practical here. He gives us theological truths, the bases of our belief. Then he shows us how these truths ought to show up in our behavior by giving us some primary tests. If you want to examine your heart and life, read on and see if you measure up.

The Commandment Test

This is the issue of who is Lord of your house. If you are a genuine Christian, then your house, your temple, is under new management:

> And hereby we do know that we know him, if we keep his commandments. He that saith, I know him, and keepeth not his commandments, is a liar, and the truth is not in him. But whoso keepeth his word, in him verily is the love of God perfected: hereby know we that we are in him. He that saith he abideth in him ought himself so to walk, even as he walked. (1 John 2:3-6)

John says your walk must match your talk or you are lying about your salvation. This is what I call afflicting the comfortable. If you are a genuine, born-again child of God, that is going to show in your life. You are going to be keeping the commandments of God. Now, you do not keep the commandments of God in order to be saved. You keep the commandments of God *because* you are saved.

This brings a problem, because not one of us has always kept all of God's commandments. Yet, the Bible says this is the way we can know that we are in Christ.

Sounds kind of frightening, doesn't it? But remember, John wants to give us assurance of our salvation, not send us out on a futile quest for perfection. It's all wrapped up in that word *keep*. This is a mariner's word, a sailor's word.

In that day, sailors did not sail by all of the modern instruments of navigation. They set their course by the stars. A sailor navigating by the stars was said to be "keeping" the stars. His intention was to sail by the stars. That was his desire and goal.

In the same way, God says we are to "keep" His commandments. The desire, the goal, the guide for our lives is to be the Word of God, the commandments of Jesus Christ. You cannot say you have been saved if your desire is not to live by the Word of God. You may get blown off course, or there may be a time when you will get confused. But the aim, the goal, of your life should be to keep the commandments of God. We are not saved by faith and works but by faith that works (James 2:22-26).

Ever since I gave my heart to Jesus, there has been a divine, deep, and radical change in me and a burning desire to live for God. Is that true in you? If not, you do not need assurance of your salvation. You need to get saved.

The question is not whether we ever sin. The difference is, before I got saved I was running *to* sin. Now I am running *from* it. The desire of my heart is to live by the Word of God. If that's not the desire of your heart, you had better go back and check up on your salvation again.

This is the commandment test. If you can willfully and knowingly sin against the will of God with no conviction, no compunction, and no remorse, you need to get saved. Some may say, "I professed Christ once and was saved. I know I'm just an old backslider now, but I'm still saved and going to heaven."

Think again, my friend. If you can live sinfully—high, wide, and handsome—and it doesn't break your heart, if there is no conviction, no remorse over sin, you do not know the God of the Bible. Is Jesus the Lord of your house?

The Companion Test

Another test by which we can judge the fruit of our behavior is the companion test. "We know that we have passed from death unto life, because we love the brethren" (1 John 3:14).

When I am saved, I want to be *right* with my brother and I want to *be* with my brother. Someone will say, "Well, I'm saved, but I have no desire to go to church. I have no use for the people of God." However, if you have no desire to be with the saints down here, you have little hope of being with them up there. John says if you love Jesus—if He is not only the *Lord* of your house but the *love* of your house—you are going to love what Jesus loves. And Jesus loves the church.

Did you know that the word *saint* is seldom used in the Bible? It's almost always *saints*, plural—your brothers and sisters in Christ. Jesus takes this very seriously. When you despise the church, you despise Jesus. When Paul was on his way to Damascus to persecute Christians, Jesus asked him, "Saul, Saul, why persecutest thou me?" (Acts 9:4).

Paul could have said, "Whoever you are, I am not persecuting you. I am persecuting the church." But the inference is obvious: to persecute the church is to persecute Jesus. And to love the church is to love Jesus.

Billy Sunday used to say, "It's true that going to church will not make you a Christian, any more than going into a garage will make you an automobile." But when you realize you have been bought by the blood of Christ, when the Spirit of God comes to indwell you and you receive a new nature, when your desire is to keep God's commandments, then you are going to love the people of God. Is your house a headquarters for hate, or is Jesus who indwells you manifesting His love for the church?

Remember that keeping the commandments and loving our brothers do not save us, but they are evidences of our faith. They are evidences, not requirements, and yet they are part of the normal Christian's life. If they are not present, either you are lost or you are terribly backslidden and have no reason for assurance.

If you have genuine doubt about whether you are saved, ask God now to come into your heart and save you. Trust Him, and He will do it.

If that doesn't give you assurance, your problem may be somewhere else. There may be a broken relationship or a broken commandment that must be put right. May God give you a blessed assurance as Christ dwells in your heart by faith.

CHAPTER THIRTEEN

God's House Is Not a Hotel

I suggested in chapter 12 that as wonderful as it is to be saved, it is even more wonderful to *know* that you are saved.

But did you know there is something more wonderful still? It is even more wonderful to know that you are saved *forever*. This is the security of the believer. Assurance tells me how to know I have salvation, security tells me that once I have it, I can never lose it.

Jesus has made known to us a very thrilling truth, which is this: when God moves into the human heart, He moves in to stay. Jesus said of the Holy Spirit, "I will pray the Father, and he shall give you another Comforter, that he may abide with you for ever" (John 14:16).

The word "abide" may be translated "continue," "dwell," "endure," "remain," or "stand." God has come to settle down in us. My friend Ron Dunn put it well when he said, "My heart is not a hotel with check-out time at twelve noon on Sunday."

God's abiding presence is what theologians call the eternal security of the believer. This is a truth that ought to bring strength and joy to your heart, and I cannot think of a better note on which to conclude our study of the indwelling presence of Christ.

When I speak of His abiding presence—the eternal security of the believer in Christ—I want to make something clear. I am not speaking about the security of those who merely profess to be saved. There are many *professors* of salvation who are not *possessors* of salvation. Outwardly they may look, act, and talk like Christians, but they have never been redeemed.

Jesus spoke an emphatic word of warning concerning these pretenders who have never been born again: "Many will say to me in that day, Lord, Lord, have we not prophesied in thy name? and in thy name have cast out devils? and in thy name done many wonderful works? And then will I profess unto them, I never knew you: depart from me, ye that work iniquity" (Matthew 7:22-23).

Note the phrase that Jesus used: "I never knew you." We have all seen people who make a false start and then fall away and even deny the faith they once professed. They did not lose their salvation because they never had it.

Jesus said, "I never knew you." I do not know who first coined this little statement, but it says it well: "The faith that fizzles before the finish had a flaw from the first."

I call these people who start out fine and then fade away "Alka-Seltzer Christians." You drop them in water, they fizzle a little bit, but then they disappear.

The Apostle John made reference to people like this when he said, "They went out from us, but they were not of us; for if they had been of us, they would no doubt have continued with us: but they went out, that they might be made manifest that they were not all of us" (1 John 2:19).

Notice that they had never been added to the body of Christ through the new birth.

But those who are truly saved have God's promise that He will never leave them. Think with me about seven wonderful reasons why someone who has been made a partaker of the divine nature can never ever again be a lost soul.

The Perseverance of the Spirit

This is a wonderful truth expressed by the Apostle Paul: "Being confident of this very thing, that he which hath begun a good work in you will perform it until the day of Jesus Christ" (Philippians 1:6).

Who is it that has begun this "good work" in us, and who is going to carry it on to completion? The Holy Spirit, of course. And this verse says that what He has begun, He will finish.

Have you ever started something you couldn't finish? I think this is a trait common to human nature. I heard of a youngster named Billy who said to his dad, "Daddy, Jimmy says that his dad has a list of men he can whip, and your name is the first one on the list."

So Billy's daddy went and confronted Jimmy's daddy. "My son says you have a list of men you can whip, and my name is first on the list. Is that right?"

"Yes, that's right."

"Well, you can't do it! What are you going to do about that?" Billy's dad said.

"Then I guess I'll just have to take your name off the list," said Jimmy's dad.

It is not a trait of omnipotence, however, to start things that it cannot finish. When God saved us, our names were recorded in heaven; and God will never take our names off the list because He was not able to finish what He began.

Just think what the Holy Spirit does in our salvation. He is the *Convicter*, the One who shows us our sins and convinces us of our guilt.

He is also the *Converter*, the One who works the marvelous work of grace in our hearts so that we are "born of the Spirit" (John 3:8).

And since the Spirit is the Convicter and the Converter, He is also the *Completer*. He will finish what He has begun. He will not abandon you as some half-completed relic.

The Perfection of the Sacrifice

When Jesus died on the cross, He offered a perfect sacrifice that made us perfect forever. "For by one offering he hath perfected for ever them that are sanctified" (Hebrews 10:14).

In Old Testament times, when a sacrifice for sin was made, it was never perfect or complete. Those priests had to come time and again with bloody sacrifices to those smoking altars, because those sacrifices were only shadows and prophecies of that perfect sacrifice to come.

> For the law having a shadow of good things to come, and not the very image of the things, can never with those sacrifices which they offered year by year continually make the comers thereunto perfect. For then would they not have ceased to be offered? because that the worshippers once purged should have had no more conscience of sins. But in those sacrifices there is a remembrance again made of the sins every year. For it is not possible that the blood of bulls and of goats should take away sins. (Hebrews 10:1-4)

All those sacrifices did was to roll the sins of the people forward one more year. But when Jesus shed His rich, royal blood on that cross, everything was paid in full. And because of that sacrifice, we are "perfected for ever." We don't get just a fresh start or a new chance but an eternal perfection.

Think with me for a moment. If it were possible for one to lose his salvation (which, of course, it isn't), then for that person to be saved a second time Jesus would have to die a second time. But what He did at Calvary was good for eternal salvation. It was one offering, and it was forever.

This is why if you search the Scriptures through, you will never find mention of anyone ever being saved twice. Our salvation is once for all, and if it is not "once saved, always saved," it would have to be "twice lost, always lost." How I thank God that when Jesus died for me, He perfected me forever.

The Position of the Saved

When we are saved, not only does Christ come to live in us, but we also take our position in Him. "Therefore if any man be in Christ, he is a new creature: old things are passed away; behold, all things are become new" (2 Corinthians 5:17).

This verse clearly states our position "in Christ." That means, among other things, that we are actually a part of His mystical body.

For me ever to be separated from Him and be eternally lost would also mean that a part of Jesus was eternally lost. I have been made a part of His very body. Christ is the invisible part of the visible Christian. And a Christian is the visible part of the invisible Christ. We are in Him, and He is in us.

Peter showed us that our position in Christ is illustrated

by Noah's position in the ark (see 1 Peter 3:18-22). When that ark was finished, a perfect way of escape from the wrath of God had been provided. That's because the ark was covered "within and without with pitch" (Genesis 6:14). The Hebrew word for *pitch* is exactly the same word that is translated elsewhere as "atonement." Thank God for the atonement that keeps the waters of God's wrath from reaching His rescued ones!

Noah was not told to place pegs on the outside of the ark so he could hold on. That would have been ridiculous, and yet this is the kind of salvation some people think they have. They feel they will get to heaven if they can just hold out faithful to the end. But people who believe this have forgotten who is holding whom (John 10:28-29).

Imagine this scene: Noah is holding on to a slimy peg on the outside of the ark. His knuckles have turned white. He shouts above the roar of the storm to Mrs. Noah, "Honey, please pray for me that I'll hold out faithful to the end." Poor old Noah never would have made it.

Thank God it was not that way at all. God said to Noah, "Come thou and all thy house into the ark" (Genesis 7:1). God was already inside the ark inviting Noah to come in with Him! It was then that God shut and sealed the door.

Not only did God shut the water out, but at the same time He closed Noah in with Himself. Noah was as safe as the ark itself was safe, because he was in the ark. We are likewise in Christ. We will go down only if He goes down.

It seems to me that all Christians believe in some kind of security. Most believe their security will begin when they get to heaven. They picture themselves stepping over the threshold of the celestial city, heaving a sigh of relief, and saying, "I made it! I'm safe!"

But wait a moment! No one is safe just because he is in heaven. The Scripture teaches that the glorious angels fell from heaven. Security is not in a place but in a Person! His name is Jesus; He is our ark of safety.

You see, we have something that even angels do not have. I would rather be a saved sinner than an innocent angel. We are safe in Christ, and that is the only safety we have or need.

The Predestination of the Saint

> And we know that all things work together for good to them that love God, to them who are the called according to his purpose. For whom he did foreknow, he also did predestinate to be conformed to the image of his Son, that he might be the firstborn among many brethren. Moreover whom he did predestinate, them he also called: and whom he called, them he also justified: and whom he justified, them he also glorified. (Romans 8:28-30)

The child of God, according to this Scripture, has been foreknown in the mind of God since before the foundation of the world. Theologians have debated and dialogued about predestination for ages, and there have been some farfetched interpretations. Some feel that every event of our lives has been minutely programmed ahead of time, and there is nothing that we can do to change it.

The story is told of a little old lady who fell down the cellar stairs, got up, brushed herself off, and said, "I'm glad that's over with."

I don't believe in that kind of predestination. But I do believe that God will carry out His great, eternal purposes in the lives of every man and woman, boy, and girl who places his or her faith in Jesus Christ.

Whenever I fly from one city to another, my actions on the airplane are more or less of my own choosing. Yet the plane is headed to a predetermined destination. Humanly speaking, it is predestined to arrive in a certain city.

Now the airlines cannot always make it to their predetermined destinations. But what God predestines, He fulfills. I am predestined to be "conformed to the image of his Son," and all hell cannot stop it.

As a matter of fact, verse 30 speaks of me as having already been glorified. The verb is in the past tense. I do not have to wait until I die to see whether I am going to heaven.

In the council halls of eternity, I have already been glorified. In the heart and mind of God, it is already done. What has been settled in eternity cannot be undone in time; what has been decreed by heaven cannot be annulled by hell. Anyone predestined to be conformed to the image of God's Son is as secure as he could possibly be.

The Present Tense of Salvation

Eternal life means life that will never end. The believer has eternal life; he has life that is endless.

Consider this carefully. Eternal life does not begin for the Christian when he dies; it begins when he believes. "Verily, verily, I say unto you, He that heareth my word, and believeth on him that sent me, hath everlasting life, and shall not come into condemnation; but is passed from death unto life" (John 5:24).

This verse clearly tells me that I now have eternal life. If this is true, how could I ever cease to exist with God? How could I ever again be a lost soul?

If a man were a Christian for ten years and then became lost, all he would have had was "ten-year life." Whatever you have, if you ever lose it, it is not eternal. Thank God that the believer "is passed from death unto life," and the life he now has is "everlasting."

The Prayers of the Savior

Another reason for our security in the Lord Jesus Christ is the intercession of our dear Savior. The finished work of Jesus was His atonement on the cross. As He was dying in agony and blood, these words burst from His bruised lips: "It is finished" (John 19:30). And thank God it was! That was the perfect sacrifice of which we have already spoken.

But not only is there the finished work of the Savior—there is also His *unfinished* work. "Wherefore he is able also to save them to the uttermost that come unto God by him, seeing he ever liveth to make intercession for them" (Hebrews 7:25).

Christ is ever-living and ever-interceding. How He intercedes and prays for His own is seen in His great, high-priestly prayer in John 17. Notice the ones for whom Jesus is interceding: "I pray for them: I pray not for the world, but for them which thou hast given me; for they are thine" (v. 9). It is clear that He is praying for His own—the saints, His born-again ones.

And what is He praying for them? "I pray not that thou shouldest take them out of the world, but that thou shouldest keep them from the evil" (v. 15). He is praying for their keeping, for their eternal security.

We know that when Jesus prayed for their security, He was heard, for Jesus Himself said, "thou hearest me always" (John 11:42). Jesus never prayed a prayer that was not answered. So that clearly means that those for whom He has prayed will be securely kept.

Now here is the exciting part for us. He was not just praying for those early disciples—Peter, James, and John and their contemporaries. By faith Jesus looked down through the tunnel of time and prayed for you and for me also: "Neither pray I for these alone, but for them also which shall believe on me through their word" (v. 20). He might as well have inserted our names.

The intercessory work of Jesus is illustrated in the life of Peter. He was weak in the flesh, but he had a heart full of faith in Christ. Jesus, knowing Peter's weakness, predicted that he would deny Him three times.

But here is the comforting part. Jesus also said, "But I have prayed for thee, that thy faith fail not" (Luke 22:32). Though Peter stumbled, he did not utterly fall. He was weak, but Jesus had prayed for him; so his faith did not fail. The cowardly Peter became the apostle of Pentecost.

I might note here that Jesus never prayed such prayers for Judas. Peter had placed his faith in Christ, but Judas had never done so: "'But there are some of you that believe not.' For Jesus knew from the beginning who they were that believed not, and who should betray him" (John 6:64). "He spake of Judas Iscariot the son of Simon: for he it was that should betray him, being one of the twelve" (v. 71).

Judas never lost his salvation, for he had no salvation to lose. He never was a believer. That was the fundamental difference between Judas and Peter.

Judas may have looked better outwardly, but Peter had a heart of faith. And because he did, Jesus interceded for him. People like us, weak as we are, have a Savior who ever lives to make intercession for us. What a security we have.

The Power of God's Sovereignty

> Blessed be the God and Father of our Lord Jesus Christ, which according to his abundant mercy hath begotten us again unto a lively hope by the resurrection of Jesus Christ from the dead, to an inheritance incorruptible, and undefiled, and that fadeth not away, reserved in heaven for you, who are kept by the power of God through faith unto salvation ready to be revealed in the last time. (1 Peter 1:3-5)

We are kept by the power of God! What a comforting thought. Is there a loving parent anywhere who would not preserve his children from death or disaster if it were in his or her power to do so?

Yet, as parents we often fail because we do not have the power to perform our heart's desire. This is never true, however, with Almighty God. He has the power to keep His children.

In Romans 8 we have already seen that we are predestined for glory. But that great chapter goes on to teach that because we are *predestined* for glory, we are also *preserved* for glory.

No Fault Can Defile Us

I know that I am weak, but, thank God, in spite of my weakness and sin there is no one who can condemn me. In the face of the accuser comes the perfect answer—the upraised and pierced hand of my Intercessor.

> Who shall lay any thing to the charge of God's elect? It is God that justifieth. Who is he that condemneth? It is Christ that died, yea rather, that is risen again, who is

> even at the right hand of God, who also maketh intercession for us. (Romans 8:33-34)

No Foe Can Destroy Us

All the enemies of the Christian do not separate him from the Lord, but only draw him all the closer.

> For I am persuaded, that neither death, nor life, nor angels, nor principalities, nor powers, nor things present, nor things to come, nor height, nor depth, nor any other creature, shall be able to separate us from the love of God, which is in Christ Jesus our Lord. (Romans 8:38-39)

Romans 8 begins with *no condemnation* and ends with *no separation*. How I long that God's people would understand what a wonderful salvation they have in the Lord Jesus Christ. He moves into our hearts to stay.

I am aware that some call this teaching of the security of the believer a dangerous doctrine. But if it is true, it cannot possibly be dangerous. The reasoning of those who believe that there is a danger in teaching security is this: they fear that a Christian who feels he is secure will relax, let his guard down, and enter into a sinful lifestyle.

Sometimes it is explained like this: "If I believed in eternal security, then I would get saved and sin all I want to, since nothing I do could ever cause me to lose my salvation."

There are two fatal flaws in this line of reasoning. The first is that when a person says he wants to characteristically or habitually sin, he is giving evidence that he has never been saved at all.

Then again, there is a sense in which I sin all I want to.

As a matter of fact, I sin more than I want to, *because I don't want to.* God knows how often I fail. But from the time I said an everlasting yes to Jesus until this moment there has been in my heart a desire to life a holy life.

If you still want to sin, you need a new birth. And with the new birth, you will get a new "want."

Second, we need not think that security is a license to sin with impunity. The Heavenly Father will surely chastise His children if they are disobedient. "For whom the Lord loveth he chasteneth, and scourgeth every son whom he receiveth. If ye endure chastening, God dealeth with you as with sons; for what son is he whom the father chasteneth not?" (Hebrews 12:6-7).

That chastisement may take many forms. It may be the sense of broken fellowship, or perhaps the loss of joy. It may mean that our prayers do not get through. It may mean a loss of health or prosperity. But even in all of this, the Father is dealing with us in love. It is comforting to know that He loves us enough to chastise us.

It is also so very comforting to know that God has promised, "I will never leave thee, nor forsake thee" (Hebrews 13:5). If you are a believer in Jesus Christ, you do not have to hold on for dear life to Him. He is holding on to you!

Hear His wonderful promise to you: "I give unto [your name] eternal life; and [your name] shall never perish, neither shall any man pluck [your name] out of my hand. My Father, which gave [your name] me, is greater than all; and no man is able to pluck [your name] out of my Father's hand" (John 10:28-29).

Dear reader, this is all the security you will ever need, both now and forever. Amen!

Notes

CHAPTER ONE: WHERE ON EARTH DOES GOD LIVE?

1. Merrill F. Unger, *Unger's Bible Dictionary* (Chicago: Moody Press, 1986), p. 1065.
2. *Ibid.*, p. 1076.
3. Ian Thomas, *The Saving Life of Christ* (Grand Rapids, Mich.: Zondervan Publishing House, 1961), p. 19.

CHAPTER TWO: SUPERNATURALLY NATURAL, NATURALLY SUPERNATURAL

1. William Hendriksen, *Exposition of Colossians and Philemon, New Testament Commentary* (Grand Rapids, Mich.: Baker Book House, 1964), p. 164.
2. F. F. Bruce, *Ephesians and Colossians, The New International Commentary on the New Testament* (Grand Rapids, Mich.: Eerdmans, 1979), p. 285.

CHAPTER FOUR: WHEN GLORY FILLS THE HOUSE

1. "Colorful Sayings from Colorful Moody," *Christian History*, Issue 25 (Vol. 9, No. 1), p. 9.

CHAPTER SEVEN: LIKE A RIVER GLORIOUS

1. Robert W. Yarbrough, *John: Everyman's Bible Commentary* (Chicago: Moody Press, 1991), p. 83.
2. *Moody Monthly*, April 1975, p. 61.

CHAPTER NINE: KEEPING YOUR DOORS LOCKED

1. Debora Tkac, ed., *The Doctor's Book of Home Remedies* (Emmaus, Penn.: Rodale Press, 1991), p. 645.

CHAPTER TEN: A HOUSE OF PRAYER—NOT A DEN OF THIEVES

1. Alfred Plummer, *The Gospel According to St. Matthew* (Minneapolis: James Family Publishers, n.d.), p. 97.

Dr. Adrian Rogers, founder and president of Love Worth Finding Ministries, is heard over syndicated radio, television, and cable systems throughout North America and many parts of the world. For broadcast and other information, call 1-800-274-5683 or write:

Love Worth Finding Ministries
Box 38-300
Memphis, Tennessee 38183.

RONALD GOODMAN

A NOVEL

WHEN THE MOON IS PINK

ISBN: 978-0-578-65294-8
Library of Congress Control Number: 2020903467

Printed in the United States of America

Also by Ronald Goodman

NOVELS

How High Is a Robins's Nest?

Fly Home, Bluebird

Rebecca's Prairie

Cardboard Nation, Journey to the Edge

Inn of the Everlasting Vacancy

It's What She Wanted

Digging for Roots

NOVELLAS

A Place in the Shade

Crooked River Blues

Sophie's Candle

MEMOIR

Cornerman: Toe to Toe With Stage Four Cancer

"Do not call up that which you cannot put down."

—H.P. Lovecraft

For Mother Earth
May she cool off—soon

WHEN THE MOON IS PINK

Paper Dream

Eddie Edgeworth sits at the head of an alley with his backpack between him and a brick wall. It's the middle of January. He's in midtown Manhattan and feels like a squirrel trying to cross an Interstate. The alley afforded the best spot for getting out of the way before being trampled or run over. There's no snow on the ground, but the temperature is in the low 20s. His feet are cold, so is his butt, for his pants are thin and provide little insulation from the alley's concrete floor. He found a piece of cardboard in a dumpster and sat on it, but it isn't long before the cold finds its way to him once more. He's wearing two flannel shirts and a Miami Dolphins hoodie, so his upper body is decently warm. I should be in Florida right now, he thinks, hunkering over a paper cup of steaming coffee from McDonald's. He gingerly sips the coffee, not out of fear of burning his lips, but to make the coffee last longer. The brew and a biscuit cost him the last of his money.

Panhandling is always slow right after the holidays, and he is in an unfamiliar city where he doesn't know good spots from bad for holding his sign. Most people, at least those who are inclined to donate, have shot their wad and maxed out credit cards. Bringing the plastic down to earth out of the stratosphere will take some time. Handouts usually pick up again by early March when a hint of spring is in the air. Spenders began to feel more hopeful about their personal solvency, as though robins and early buds on trees will give new life to their wallets.

Eddie arrived in New York from Florida two months earlier. It was a bus ride from hell. Except for the companionship of his girlfriend, Sally, back home in Fort Lauderdale, he is a solitary man, and homeless 7 years. He's used to having his space; there is precious little of that on a bus. The worst of it was being stuck in a seat next to a young woman who kept talking about Jesus. She saw him boarding the bus with his backpack and sleeping bag. Homeless and panhandlers are perfect targets for those wishing to "witness" and share their faith with the poor, incompetent souls needing prayer and saved from themselves. Eddie learned long ago that it's useless to argue with them. Let them close their eyes and bay into the void with you if they must, accept their two dollars, then be done with them until the next one comes along, and they always do, sooner or later. Some are sincere enough in their own delusional way, Eddie figured. But he considered them myth addicted molesters, groping the human spirit without an invitation.

She was a punk rocker, or something like that, Eddie guessed. Her neck and arms were covered in tattoos. A ring was in her nose (to keep her from rooting?), two on her lips, and one each for her eyebrows. Her hair, cropped short, was dyed pitch black. Gothic, he heard. More of a horror look, he thought, a character straight out of a Stephen King novel. He was certainly a captive audience on the bus. The only relief he could get from her was to close his eyes and pretend to be asleep. Once, he even faked a snore. He wanted to just tell her to shut UP, but that might create a scene. He suspected that she might set Jesus aside for a moment and become violent. He could handle the witch, but didn't want to create a scene on the bus. She was pencil thin and sickly looking with characteristic facial blemishes of a meth user.

There was one response, though, that sometimes worked with the Jesus freaks, as they were called in the 60s and the hippie generation. He tried it on her: "Find someone else to feed your lonely, pathetic ego on." She remained in her seat, of course, for there were no others available. But he heard no more from her. She was either sufficiently insulted, or giving it some philosophical thought, Eddie figured. She got off in downstate New York. She left him a tract that read: Jesus is coming. He wadded it up and rested back in the seat.

His friends back in Fort Lauderdale call him Edgy. The nickname does have a certain appropriateness, for he was most always picking at his cuticles, or combing fingers through his hair. He has always been subject to low-grade anxiety, managing to find something to be silently anxious about, like where his next meal may come from, or when a cop is going to run him off a corner or median. "Flying a sign" is harder work that people might think, he and his friends would say. Drivers look at you like you're something they're afraid they might step in and track into the house. But Eddie disciplined himself not to be too quick to pass judgement on those staring at him through the windows of their cars. Just when he was on the verge of mumbling something ugly beneath his breath, down goes a window and out comes some cash, or at least something to eat.

Looking back over the years, he often tried to put a peg in what went wrong that reduced him to the life he was living. He served two tours in Iraq with the 1st Marine Division. He was fortunate not to have been wounded, though there were some close calls, one of which took off the arm of a fellow Marine with whom he was fighting house to house in Bagdad. Eddie didn't blame his homelessness on the war, but he was empathetic with those whose resiliency had been cracked or shattered by the horrors of the battlefield.

The older he got, the more difficult it became to find work. He was 59 years old now, and he didn't feel as good as he used to. Getting off the ground took more time than it once did; crawling out of his sleeping bag on cold mornings was harder, especially when there was nothing more to look forward to than a cup of coffee and biscuit at McDonald's, that is if he wasn't broke.

He was once strong as a mule, in his younger days, and worked like one for much of his life, mostly labor jobs, carrying brick for bricklayers, mixing mortar and wheelbarrowing it on the site. You name it. He'd done just about every backbreaking job in the books. He was well spoken, not deliberately; it just seemed to be a natural way of talking with him. Notwithstanding his homelessness, some supposed that he'd gotten a pretty good education under his belt back in the day. When asked, he told the truth: some high school.

He loved to read, though, and he was a regular at the library branch near where he camped in Fort Lauderdale not far from the beach. He read the best authors who knew how to write a good sentence, ones with a brain larger than a walnut, he would remind himself while searching for something new to read. He would steer away from authors who had written 90 books or more; formula crap, he thought. But like most homeless, he looked that way, for he always carried a somewhat overstuffed backpack. Strangers assumed that he was a drunk, or druggie; he was neither of those.

He had a homeless girlfriend. Though he wasn't a drinker, she was. Sally was quite a bit younger than him, 15 years his junior, but didn't seem to mind the age difference. Eddie was nice to her and she felt safe with him. Bother Sally, and Edgy will bust you up, his friends would warn newcomers on the street. Despite the hard miles on his face, Eddie was a handsome devil. The killer, some of his friends called him. "You guys are full of it," he would tell them, "I look like forty miles of bad road." They would laugh. He looked better than he felt. Eddie was good with words. He had a full head of hair with only a little grey at the temples, and most of his teeth, the front ones, anyway.

Eddie kept a journal for years. He would sometimes get lazy and make no entries for a while, a month or so, maybe, but he was always careful to write a date at the top of the page. Somewhere along the way, what he wrote took on more of a storytelling style, rather than things diary-like. He grew tired of personal observations about his own life, most of which was boring, for his daily routine varied little from one day to the next. How creative can one get in describing such a life as his?

Sitting around in the evenings, Eddie's friends would sometimes ask him to read from his journal. They noted a change in the direction of his entries. It's almost like you're writing a book, a novel maybe, they would say. Eddie would shrug his shoulders and smile. He was a modest man. But privately, when he was feeling better, well rested, and having enough to eat, he thought that maybe he was onto something with this new way of writing.

And so, he continued along those lines, more faithfully than in the past with his journal. He realized one morning at McDonald's that he'd told a story and come to the end of it. This isn't Hemmingway, he thought, thumbing through the handwritten pages on yellow legal pads, but it's not bad. Over the course of its writing, he spilled coffee on the manuscript, but it was readable. He wondered if he could sell it to a publisher. Off to the library he went. His first stop was at the reference desk. "Can you help me find something with book publishers?" he asked.

"Certainly, sir." He followed the young woman's switching fanny down the stacks to where the book in question was found. She handed it to him. He thanked her then found a seat at a table and opened the book. After perusing it for some time, he concluded that most of the publishers seemed to be in New York. There was a considerable list of literary agents as well, but he felt intimidated by the very word. Agents are for movie stars, NFL players, and the like, he thought.

Opening his backpack, he took out a legal pad and began writing down the names and addresses of New York publishers. I'll play hell finding all of these, he thought. He couldn't write them a letter. He had no return address. He couldn't call them. Each of their announcements said no unsolicited phone calls. (He lost his phone and couldn't afford another one just yet.) And no unsolicited manuscripts as well, the announcements continued.

He put the legal pad back in his backpack and returned the book of publishers to its place where the reference girl found it. He wondered what else he might need her to find for him so that he could trail along behind her once more. He couldn't come up with a legitimate reason for seeking her help again. Sally would have been jealous, had she been with him. He left the library and made his way to his favorite off-ramp where he extracted his cardboard sign and stood passively on the median. *Homeless. Anything Helps.* He never added Vet to his sign; he didn't want to play that card. His first "hit" was five bucks. He always felt better after the first one, even if it was only a dollar. Where there's smoke, there's fire. The next thing he needed to do was find out what a bus ticket to New York would cost. Sally would want to go with him, but he didn't care to subject her to the discomforts of life on the street in a strange city.

And so, it was in this way that Eddie Edgeworth, Edgy to his friends, came to be sitting where he sat on this cold January morning in New York City. Day by day he called upon the publishers written on his legal pad. And day by day he pretty much got the same answer: I'm sorry, sir, but we don't accept unsolicited manuscripts. And not one of them requested to even look at the first page.

Eddie didn't know how much more of this he could stand. Every joint in his body ached. He'd been hungry for days. A biscuit at MacDonald's was tasty enough, but he couldn't get much mileage out of it, especially with having to walk from one publisher to another when money for bus fare ran out. Dumpster diving was always an option, and he resorted to it, but found that someone had obviously gotten there ahead of him. By God this is no place to be homeless, he thought, when stepping over or around someone lying on a grate that produced some heat. He was good at finding places to spend the night, though, and his sleeping bag was warm.

Downing the last of his coffee, he crushed the cup and stuffed it into his backpack then turned his eyes once more to the building across the street: Lukenstein Publishing. He crossed the street earlier to see if there was anything on the door regarding when the office opened. He saw nothing. Looking at his watch, it was nine o'clock. He figured the place might open at ten.

At a few minutes till ten, he saw a woman approach the door and unlock it. She was older and quite heavy. Her hair was bluish, a dye job not mixing well with her body chemistry. Eddie dreaded facing her. He could almost hear the all too familiar words: I'm sorry, sir, but.... He thought that he would give her a little time once in her office, put on coffee, check messages, then he would strike with manuscript in hand.

Judging that the woman would have had time to become reasonably settled, Eddie made his way across the street and entered the building. A sign on the wall said that Lukenstein Publishing was located on the third floor. He figured that other private offices were in the building. He wasn't sure if the woman he saw entering the building was who he wanted to see; she could have gone to any of the other offices listed on the wall. He took the elevator, thankful that it was available. His knees were stiff from the cold.

Reaching the third floor, the elevator let him into a plush lobby. Photos of authors and their books were on the walls. On one hand he found it inspiring; on the other, depressing, given his shabby appearance and station in life. He strode across the lobby to a door with lettering on the glass that read, Ardith Lukenstein, CEO. He opened his backpack and extracted the folder containing his manuscript. He took a deep breath and released it slowly then opened the door just a bit and looked inside. He met the jaundiced eyes of Ardith Lukenstein, the woman he saw unlocking the door. "May I help you with something?" she said, setting her coffee cup down rather abruptly, as though immediately annoyed by her first visitor.

Strike one.

Eddie opened the door a little wider, just enough to allow him and his backpack to enter. The sleeping bag tied to the top could be a problem when squeezing through doorways. He hadn't tied it as snuggly to his pack as usual this morning; his hands wouldn't cooperate in the cold. When he tugged it past the doorframe, the bag came lose and tumbled to the floor. It didn't come unrolled, however, and he picked it up in his arms and answered the woman: "I—uh, I was wondering if you would be interested in publishing my book." Each of these cold turkey meetings with publishers left him a little less confident. He felt more and more that he was on a fool's errand. He unquestionably looked homeless and having the sleeping bag fly off his pack onto the fine carpeting made him feel even more awkward and out of sorts. This is worse than panhandling, he thought. He bucked up, though, and passed a hand through his disheveled hair that needed washing. He and his buddies back in Fort Lauderdale always said that if you dwell on how fucked up your life is, it will kill you.

These kinds of "over the transom" encounters were nothing new to Mrs. Lukenstein. She found unsolicited manuscripts taped to her door, partly stuffed under the door, and propped beneath the windshield wipers of her car. They rarely contained return postage. At any rate, she would pitch them into the trash. She knew of nothing more that she could do or say beyond NO UNSOLICTED MANUSCRIPTS. DO NOT CALL, in her announcements in one publication or another that listed services such as hers.

But this man, now standing in her office with a worn folder in his hands and a dirty backpack and sleeping bag touched her somehow, though not greatly, but just enough to give her pause about dismissing him out of hand, which was her usual custom. His handsome face was weathered, like so many homeless she saw on the streets of New York, and he looked terribly tired. She feared he might collapse in her office and she would be stuck with having to call an ambulance. She was a busy woman with a stack of manuscripts she requested from authors whom she thought may have some talent, enough, at least, to warrant having a look at their work, 99% of which she wouldn't consider publishing, as it usually turned out. She wanted to be rid of this sad soul standing before her, but she couldn't get the words to come out. He looked to where a coffee maker sat on a table beside a carton of donuts. "Would you care for some coffee and a donut?" she said at last, scarcely believing that she was prolonging this uninvited visit.

"Yes, thank you so much," Eddie said. He set his backpack and sleeping bag beside a chair then helped himself to coffee and donut then returned to the seat beside his belongings. He didn't like this woman. Her bluish hair gave her eyes a menacing look, and her tone of voice didn't come across as the most hospitable in the world. But this office somehow felt different than all the others he visited during the last two months. Well-dressed employees were somewhere, he supposed, scurrying about with papers in their hands, manuscripts from respectable authors who were probably well on their way to literary fame and fortune. And he was never offered coffee in the other offices, much less a donut. He took a bite of the donut then washed it down with coffee. The woman's facial expression seemed to have softened, her hair not so blue, as though she had gone offstage and changed for another role.

"What is your name, sir?" Mrs. Lukenstein said, clasping her hands before her on the desk.

"Eddie Edgeworth—my friends call me Edgy," he said, wondering why he stupidly added the nickname for someone who probably couldn't give a fiddler's damn about it.

She nodded and offered a perfunctory smile. She noted his manner of speaking, nothing fancy or pretentious, only that he completed his sentences—short ones, for the most part, like what Hemmingway learned while writing for *The Kansas City Star* as a young journalist—and didn't slur word endings. Then again, she thought, he may simply be petrified by his surroundings. "Where are you from, Mr. Edgeworth?"

"Florida. Fort Lauderdale, actually."

"I see. How long have you been in New York?"

"Two months." He took another bite of his donut and sampled the coffee once more. Starbucks, he thought. Good stuff, but he rarely bought a cup unless he'd been given one of their gift cards when panhandling. Gift cards were usually McDonald's. That was cool, for that's where he most always went for coffee and a biscuit. He could get a senior cup for eighty-five cents and all the refills he wanted. He remembered when it was only fifty cents. But it was good coffee, Arabica beans, and he didn't mind the price increase. He always saved one of the paper cups in his pack. When he was broke, he would present it at the counter and he would get a refill, no questions asked. They knew what he was doing, used to it from homeless in need of cup of coffee, the one bright spot for most of them when having to face another day on the street.

"Have you been around to other publishing houses?" Mrs. Lukenstein continued. She rose from her chair and refreshed her coffee and Eddie's as well.

"Yes."

"How many?"

"Dozens."

"And what did they tell you?"

"Always the same thing."

"Which was ... ?"

"We don't accept unsolicited manuscripts." He stuffed the remaining bite of his donut into this mouth. These are *good,* he thought.

"Have another one," Mrs. Lukenstein said, motioning toward the tray.

He rose and selected a glazed one this time.

"Is that your manuscript?" she asked nodding at the folder under his arm.

"Yes."

"May I see it?"

"What?" He wasn't sure he heard her right.

"May I see your manuscript?" she repeated.

"Yes, of course." Eddie licked icing from his fingers then wiped them on his pants. He handed the folder to the woman.

Mrs. Lukenstein cast a look at Eddie then opened the folder before her. "This is handwritten on legal pads."

Strike two.

"Yes," Eddie said.

"There are coffee stains."

Strike three.

"I'm sorry."

"Your handwriting is quite legible, however."

"Thank you." Eddie felt his knees beginning to quake.

She fell silent for what seemed an eternity to her visitor while she thumbed through pages, seeming to read some of them at length. Eddie didn't know what page she was on, but he thought he saw a faint if fleeting smile on her lips. Then again, it may be heartburn. His own heart was pounding so fast that he felt a little lightheaded. Finally, she looked up at him and said, "This should be typed."

Strike four.

"I don't have a way—"

"I understand," she said, breaking in. She closed the folder. Eddie expected her to hand it back to him. She didn't. "I love the title," she said. "How may I get in touch with you?"

"Excuse me," Eddie said, scarcely believing what he just heard."

"If I should want to get in touch with you, how may I do that?"

"I—uh, I don't have a mailing address, and I lost my phone," Eddie said, haltingly. This was no time or place for BS. Don't lie to the woman.

"You're homeless?"

"Yes."

Strike five.

She reached into a drawer of her desk and extracted a cell phone and charging cord. She rose from her chair and strode to where Eddie was sitting. "Keep this with you so that I'll have a way to get in touch with you. You needn't worry about airtime, just keep it charged," she added, handing him a charger for the phone. "Will you be returning to Florida?" she asked as Eddie came to his feet.

"Yes, if it's okay. It's too cold here for me."

Mrs. Lukenstein chuckled and said, "No problem. Just don't lose the phone."

Eddie picked up his backpack and sleeping bag. She walked him to the door. "By the way, do you have bus fare for returning to Florida?"

"Not at the moment."

"Hold on," she said, then going to her purse and returning with $300.00 cash. "This should get you something to eat besides donuts, and a bus ticket home."

"Thank you," Eddie said.

She shook his hand but said nothing more.

Eddie made his way to the elevator and exited on the ground floor. Outside the building, he sat down on the step. His knees were still quaking. He fought off tears, but they started coming in torrents. He tried to keep them dashed from his face so that passersby wouldn't note them. One man in a topcoat stopped and said, "Are you okay, sir?"

"No, but I will be," Eddie said, snuffing back tears and getting to his feet. There was a bus to catch, and plenty to tell Sally and his friends back home in Fort Lauderdale. He had noted a steak house across the street from the bus station. He might have a steak, you know, to celebrate, before he caught a bus. He wondered if the

$300 in his pocket was a kind of advance on sales, like real authors get. Well, first things first. He should have brought Sally along after all. She didn't have many teeth. But she could gum the hell out of a piece of steak, he figured. He'd buy her one when he got back home.

Prologue

The bailiff called the court to order when Judge David Henry exited his chambers and entered the courtroom. He strode to the bench and took his seat. He was a heavy-set, barrel-chested man carrying more weight than his doctor advised, for the judge's blood pressure wasn't what it once was when he'd been an offensive tackle for the Florida State Seminoles back in the day. His nickname was Caterpillar; opponents thought that was what it took to move him so that they could have a shot at sacking the quarterback. More than a few defensive linemen were flattened at the line of scrimmage only to see the ball carrier go past through a gaping hole. Goodbye, Malachi! Next stop, end zone!

In his late sixties now, he was the oldest member of the court. Just a wisp of hair remained on the top of his head, not enough to comb over. He wouldn't if he could, for he felt it much too vain and pretentious. Everyone knows what you're doing, he thought, when viewing men with combovers. The part just above the ear is a dead giveaway. For those men who didn't seem to have enough hair on the side of their head for combing over, he wondered if bringing it from their armpits might be next.

The judge's eyebrows were quite bushy, however. He trimmed them himself, often, but they seemed to grow back almost overnight. He sometimes thought they were trying to compensate for the lack of hair on his head, like men who have lost all the hair on the front part of their head then letting the back grow long, even into a ponytail. He liked the ponytails, though; something of a colonial look, he thought. He wouldn't mind growing one, but he didn't know if what little hair back there could manage it. At any rate, he figured he would look ridiculous during the process with just a little swatch of hair gathered at the back of his head and fastened with a rubber band. It would be a distraction in his courtroom, not a place of much humor.

His eyes were dark and beady, giving him a somewhat scary look that made newcomers to his court feel as though they may have entered an execution chamber. Ironically, the judge had a reputation of having the most pleasant demeanor of all the judges in the county, though he could be impatient and a little cross with arrogant attorneys whose nails were manicured and wore Italian shoes. These came mostly from Tallahassee, Atlanta or Miami. The judge would see them in his court from time to time representing big money cases. He was fair in his judgements. He understood and practiced justice tempered with mercy. He was generous in handing out probation—too, generous, some prosecutors thought. What's the point of prosecuting, some of them thought, if Judge Henry is going to let them all walk? He didn't let them *all* walk, and there were plenty of inmates who could attest to that.

After briefly examining files before him, the judge put a tissue to his nose; there was something in the courthouse that he was allergic to. He once asked the cleaning lady what sort of dusting spray was being used on his bench. It turned out not to be what set his nose to running. So, he always kept a box of tissue handy.

Judge Henry looked out onto the packed courtroom. Only a handful were here for their own summons; the remainder came to witness a young woman's case which had gained considerable attention in the press. He was not surprised at the size of the crowd; this wasn't the first time the defendant had been before him, and for the same violation. There's an adage in journalism: No face, no story. Isabella Cabrera's jarring beauty brought reporters out en masse. They came to Florida's big bend from Alabama, South Georgia, Jacksonville, Miami and elsewhere. The Associated Press was present. Flash cameras were not allowed in the courtroom. But the judge rather enjoyed the attention the woman brought to his court. It was a nice change from otherwise monotonous proceedings, bland things such as traffic tickets, barking dogs, and shoplifting.

"Ms. Isabella Cabrera," the judge said. Isabella and her attorney, George Davis rose and made their way to the front of the courtroom. Judge Henry smiled, though not widely, when the two came to a stop before him. God, how he would hate to sentence this troubled young woman to jail, he thought. But he wasn't sure there was another choice. If he reinstated her probation, the prosecutor would start howling—again. The prosecutor thought her to be dangerous; Judge Henry did not.

"Ms. Cabrera," the judge began, "two years ago, in April, you were in this courtroom for having discharged a firearm—quite a number of them—on St. George Island. The prosecutor wanted to charge you with armed, criminal action, but no evidence has been discovered, yet, that would support that very serious charge: Who—or, *what* you were shooting at has yet to be known. You were given probation. Some think that I'm too generous in handing out probation, and perhaps they are right, at times. Nevertheless, I thought it proper in your case, the most unusual, I might add, during my 30 years on the bench."

Isabella's attorney, George Davis, cleared his throat and glanced at his client. The judge's use of the word *unusual* was an understatement if ever I've heard one, Davis thought. He had been on shaky ground with his client from the start. One day he thought that she was a nut case, then he would flip flop the next day and buy into everything she told him. It's those damn big, dark eyes, and the Spanish lilt in her voice, he would say, scolding himself for being so gullible and unprofessional. But he wasn't inclined to recuse himself from her case. He wouldn't leave her twisting in the wind, even if she is crazy as a proverbial pet coon. He wasn't a public defender, and she didn't need one. She was known to be quite wealthy. He accepted her case for his usual and handsome retainer. He was considered the best criminal defense lawyer in four southern states.

The contents of his folder contained a last-ditch effort to keep her out of jail. Her charge teetered between a felony and misdemeanor. A misdemeanor could get her up to a year in jail. Felony? That would be up to the judge. She was something of a loner and character witnesses were scarce, only one of which he could present at her first court appearance a year earlier. She was born in the United States while her father and pregnant mother were visiting Florida. She possessed dual citizenship with Spain, the home of her late parents.

She was well liked on the island, but most everybody thought there was something wrong with her and didn't want to get tangled up in the current trouble. Davis had two fresh witnesses present this day, however, young brothers, 8 and 10 years old, who lived on the island. He did everything short of bribing the boys' parents in persuading them to bring their sons to testify. Any other judge but Henry, Davis, thought, and he wouldn't have bet a quarter on the success of the young boys' testimony. But he was going to go for it. There was nothing more in his jurisprudence arsenal for his client. He and the boys would unload a bomb for the end zone. Don't draw any flags, he reminded himself. It struck him as something of a playoff game. The loser goes home. But for Isabella, if might be jail. Seeing her lying on a cold, steel bunk was an image he couldn't hold for long.

"You've violated your probation," the judge continued, "in April, as it turned out, by discharging firearms—again, shotguns, to be exact—in what neighbors say was a horrific volley in the middle of the night. Law enforcement arrived on the scene and found no bodies, nothing but empty shotgun shells. The prosecution has suggested that you may have disposed of the bodies," the judge said, a faint smile forming at the corners of his mouth. "But no blood or other evidence of that sort has been found on the beach or near your house," the judge continued.

Some in the audience smiled, for the defendant hardly looked capable of removing bodies.

Isabella's attorney found no humor in this and thought the judge was getting a little ridiculous.

The prosecuting attorney, with what seemed a perpetual smirk on his face, shifted in his chair and picked a piece of lent from his suitcoat, examined his fingernails, then looked toward the defendant. Steve Appleton was the prosecutor, and Davis despised the ass kisser. He would send his own mother to the gallows if it put another win in his column. Not today, dude, Davis thought, glancing at the prosecutor.

"You have pled self-defense in both cases," the judge continued, passing a hand across his brow. "But this court has found no evidence to support your claim of having to fend off pirates converging upon your beach house. Not so much as a swashbuckling footprint has been found on the beach near your home on the night of the alleged encounters."

Soft laughter moved across the courtroom.

The judge paused and looked out across the room but didn't pick up his gavel. "I ordered a psychiatric evaluation" the judge continued. "You cleared it with flying colors. I might add, too, that you were found to be quite intelligent. That said, you are now before me once more, my dear. What am I to do? I have been most lenient. But

I'm running out of options."

"Your honor, I wish to call two witnesses to the stand," George Davis, Isabella's attorney said.

"Very well," the judge said. "You may regain your seat, Ms. Cabrera."

Davis turned to where Ricky and Stewart Jones were sitting with their parents. He motioned for them to come forward and take seats in the witness stand. Davis arranged for a large blackboard to be made available. It was wheeled into the courtroom.

Since both boys were under the age of 14, swearing them in wasn't required. After they were introduced, Davis asked them how long they had known Ms. Cabrera: "Five years, ever since she came to the island," the oldest boy said. He was obviously nervous, and picking at the cuticles of a finger.

"How did you become acquainted?" Davis asked.

"We walked along the beach with her, and she told us all about Spain," the youngest boy said. He seemed less nervous, probably not aware of the possible consequences of this proceeding.

"Did she ever tell you that she may be a distant relative of Queen Isabella of Spain?"

"No, but that would be really cool," the oldest boy said. He shot a look at Isabella, and she smiled back at him.

"Did she ever talk about pirates?" Davis asked.

"Objection, your honor," Steve Appleton, the prosecutor said while coming to his feet. "This is about unlawful discharging of firearms, at the very least, if not armed criminal action, not stories about pirates."

"Overruled. This court is trying to discover who or what Ms. Cabrera was shooting at," the judge said. "You may continue, Mr. Davis." The judge seemed to settle more comfortably in his chair. He liked the direction in which Davis was going.

"She never talked about pirates until—" the oldest boy said, then trailing off. He shot another look at Isabella. She smiled and nodded.

"Until when?" Davis pursued.

"Until … until I saw the ship."

A rumble of murmurs rolled across the courtroom. "Order in the court," the judge said, using his gavel.

"Objection! For God's sake, your honor," the prosecutor said, coming to his feet once more. "The defense is taking this into never, never land."

"Overruled. Sit down, Simp—Appleton. If never, never land is where we must go to get at the truth, then so be it. This court has gone to stranger places."

Soft laughter rolled across the courtroom.

"When did you see the ship?" Davis continued.

"It was spring," the oldest boy said.

"April, maybe?"

"Yeah."

"Did you see the ship in daytime or night?"

"Night. I woke up when I heard shooting."

"Could you see the moon?" Davis asked.

"Yes. I looked out the window. The moon was full and really pink."

"Objection. There's no such thing as a pink moon," the prosecutor said, coming slowly to his feet.

"Overruled. A full moon in April sometimes appears

to be quite pink under certain atmospheric conditions," the judge said.

"Do you and your brother share the same bedroom?" Davis asked.

"Yes."

"Did the sound of shooting wake him?"

"No. Hardly anything wakes him up."

Soft laughter across the courtroom.

"Did you try to wake him when you saw the ship?"

"Yeah, but he just groaned and rolled over in his bed."

More soft laughter across the courtroom. The judge smiled.

"When did you tell your brother what you saw?" Davis asked, feeling that a penalty flag was on the field; he wrongly supposed that both boys saw the ship.

"When we woke up in the morning."

"What did he think?" Davis asked

"Cool!"

"Objection. Hearsay, your honor," the prosecutor said, rising only halfway up from his chair this time.

"Sustained. Confine your questions, Mr. Davis, to what the older witness claims to have seen," the judge said. He was surprised that Davis, usually quite thorough, had left that stone unturned.

At this point, Davis approached the blackboard and positioned it so that the boys, the judge and audience as well could view it. "So, what did the ship look like?" Davis asked.

"It was really big, lots of sails, and holes all along the side," the oldest boy said. His brother was nodding in agreement.

"Objection! The younger witness witnessed nothing. Only what his brother told him the next morning. Hearsay."

"Sustained." The judge turned to the youngest boy and said, let your brother tell us what he says he has seen. You were asleep, young fellow."

"Yes, sir."

"Like holes where canon would be?" Davis continued with the older boy.

"Objection!" The prosecutor jumped to his feet. "Council is leading the witness." This boy is taking my case apart piece by piece, the prosecutor thought while regaining his seat. And the judge is buying into it.

"Overruled."

"Yes," the oldest boy said.

"Could you see any people on the ship?" Davis asked, pacing back and forth and feeling as though he were arguing before the Supreme Court. His witness was good, damn good. He was cruising and no longer picking at his cuticles.

"There was a bunch of 'em. Some were climbing up where the sails and stuff are."

Davis picked up a piece of chalk. He paused for long moments then said: "Did you see any flags flying?"

"Objection. No craft of this sort has been seen off the coast of Florida for two hundred years," the prosecutor said, barely rising from his seat. His voice was little more than a mumble.

"Overruled. Two hundred years doesn't preclude the possibility of another appearance of anything."

"Yeah," the oldest boy continued.

"Did the flag look something like this?" Davis said, putting chalk to the board and drawing a picture of a Jolly Roger with its skull and crossbones.

"Objection. Counsel is leading the witness," Appleton said, starting to rise from his chair then plopping back down. His case was lost, and he knew it. Davis and the kid had blown him out of the water.

"Sustained," the judge said. "Strike the image from the records." Many in the audience smiled, for they knew that the damage was done. Davis had gone for it on 4th down and made it. The end zone was drawing ever nearer.

"Yeah!" the boy blurted. "But they took it down real fast, like they didn't want anybody on shore to see it."

"I have no further questions," Davis said.

The prosecutor rose and approached the witness stand. His case was lost, but he would take a jab at the kid. "It sounds like you boys are very fond of Ms. Cabrera."

"Izzy is our friend," the oldest boy said.

"She seems like a very nice lady who can tell some really cool stories," the prosecutor continued with a smirk on his face. He thrust his hands into the pockets of his suitcoat and rocking back on his heels.

The oldest boy seemed to be on to this trick and didn't respond. He knew what the prosecutor was up to.

"You would do almost anything to keep her from going to jail, wouldn't you?"

The youngest boy teared up.

That's the last straw, the prosecutor thought. The

kid's tears just flushed my case down the toilet.

"Objection!" Davis said. "The prosecution is making a cruel inference with children. Of course, they wouldn't want to see their friend go to jail." Davis looked to Isabella and she was dabbing at tears.

"Sustained. Refrain from such suggestions," the judge said.

"I have no further question, your honor," the prosecutor said.

"You may step down and return to your seats," the judge said to the boys. When they were seated beside their parents, the judge said, "I'm an avid reader, but I don't read fantasy. I believe, however, that Ms. Cabrera and the witness have seen something. I'm ordering a squad of National Guardsmen to be present at Ms. Cabrera's beach house next April when the moon is full. And if it turns out that I've made a fool of myself and this court—well, I'll not be at all happy."

Chapter 1

Like a thousand rattlesnakes preparing to strike, a stiff December wind was shaking sea oats on north Florida's St. George Island. Tempting souvenirs; women like to cut a few stalks and put them in a vase. And children find anything that rattles interesting. Signs were posted, however, telling prospective pickers that it was a nono. Not the greatest deterrent; for some it only enhanced the perceived value of the oats. Just be more clandestine when purloining and promptly conceal them.

Eric Erickson turned the collar up on his barn coat as he strode away from the Chevy Suburban he leased when flying into Pensacola from Minneapolis and made his way onto the beach and among the sand dunes. He noted the sea oats rustling in the wind and stepped to a stalk of them and had a closer look. He wanted to snap off the stem of one but decided otherwise when glancing back at the sign prohibiting it.

The temperature was more on his mind; this wasn't quite the Florida he pictured when leaving Minnesota.

To mix a metaphor, it's cold as hell down here, he thought, hunching his shoulders and thrusting his hands into the coat's flannel lined pockets. I should have headed farther south, he muttered, trudging through the sand and circumventing a dune. But it was solitude and a little peace and quiet he sought, and this barrier island on Florida's Big Bend seemed to be what he wanted, even if he badly miscalculated how warm it might be. But it's not like I'll be sleeping on the beach, he thought. St. George Island is Florida's forgotten island, he read while researching the state in preparation for his trip. Just the place, he decided, with some things of his own to forget.

He had an appointment on the island, but there was an hour to kill. Before leaving Minneapolis, he called a realtor and arranged to rent one of the condos—or, beach house for a couple of weeks, through Christmas and New Year's, anyway. It wouldn't be like the holidays in Minnesota. But they wouldn't be the same without Sara. She died in a car crash in the spring, two years earlier. Each holiday season without her seemed to get worse. When does this pain end? he wondered. The great healer—time, wasn't working for him.

Sara was a youthful 45 years old, 7 years younger than himself. She taught English at the university. He was a forensic phycologist and an adjunct faculty member. He was on a year's leave of absence from the university as well as his private practice and planning to spend a couple weeks or so on the island. He and Sara vacationed in Destin, Florida, once. But going there again, without her, would call up memories he wouldn't care to face, like visiting the scene of a gruesome crime. So, he looked for a less populous spot and this place seemed to fit the bill. And, too, winter months should make it even more appealing, given its relative seclusion compared to South Florida. He could wear a sweater or windbreaker while walking the beach. A mug of hot coffee would sit well on a day such as this.

They hadn't married, he and Sara, but their relationship satisfied them both. Mutual trust and respect are what hold people together, they agreed, not matrimony. They were both socially liberal, progressive, they thought, for marriage was slowly falling out of vogue, they believed. And there were no children for whom one might need to explain the absence of wedding rings. A false sense of security. Promises all too easily broken. Just do the right thing by each other, they agreed. We don't need a piece of paper for that. If we quit loving each other, say goodbye and walk away. It's never quite that easy, of course, but they both got the point. They never quit, though, loving each other, ten good years before screaming tires and shattering glass ended it. God, how he missed her. Two years scarcely diminished the pain he felt at her loss. They were soul mates, buddies and lovers. It doesn't get any better than that.

Meeting with the realtor, Eric learned that no condo was available, but a beach house was. He thought that it might be preferable to a condo, given the added privacy it would afford. He rented it through New Year's. The owners lived in Topeka, and only came during spring and summer. The house faced the Gulf and was on stilts to protect it from storm surge during hurricane season.

Climate change is warming the planet, most everyone agreed nowadays, and could change hurricane season as well, which—historically—ended in November, pretty much. Less of less and more of more, climate scientists have been warning for some time. More extremes. They have known for a hundred years that carbon traps heat in earth's atmosphere. Eric was irritated when hearing deniers say that record keeping has only been going on since such and such a year. He liked to tell them that the earth has been keeping records for millions of years, and geologists know how to read them. Extracting and examining ice core from the Artic floor, for example, tells those educated in such things quite a lot about what has been taking place on our beloved planet, and for a very long time. Oh, well, never argue about politics, religion or—these days, climate change.

Eric unloaded the Suburban. He traveled light, only bringing clothes and a coffee maker should his temporary home not have one. A bottle of Johnny Walker Black Label was in one bag. The house was adequately furnished, nothing fancy, which was often the case with beach houses ... wet bathing suits, spilled margaritas, and the like. An open kitchen had everything needed for preparing a meal. Eric found the bottle of whisky in a duffel, water glass in a cupboard and ice in the fridge's freezer as well, and fixed himself a drink. He exited a sliding glass door and stepped out onto a deck that overlooked the beach. It was nearing dusk on this 2nd Saturday in December. It was cool, but there wasn't ten or more inches of snow like what was blanketing Minneapolis when he left.

Looking west down the beach he could see a sign that read, Oyster Cove, a restaurant and bar he noted while researching the island on the Internet before leaving home. He would shower and shave then go have something to eat. Oysters on the half shell? No thanks. He tried them when he and Sara visited Destin. He couldn't get them down, even with a little hot sauce and saltine. Sara loved them, however. What a woman! She would come in handy if the two of them were ever castaways on an uninhabited island. She could find all kinds of things to eat until rescued, if ever. Who would want to be rescued when stranded with a woman like her?

The restaurant was typical of a beach establishment: again, nothing fancy—as is the case with most beach houses, as well. The flooring was hardwood. Eight booths were along two walls. A half-dozen tables were arranged in the middle of the room. An assortment of fishing nets, buoys, tackle, and a couple of stuffed fish, the species of which Eric didn't know, provided nuance. The scent of burgers and fish wafted from an open order window on the west end of the room. A short bar hosted six stools with backs and armrests. Eric took a seat on one of them and awaited service. A waitress in Florida Gators sweats came from the kitchen: "What would you like, sir?"

Eric gazed at a menu written in chalk behind the bar. "I'll have the Blackened Grouper and a draft." He was a freshwater man. He didn't know a Grouper from a Carp, only that the former could be huge. He hoped the waitress wouldn't wheel the whole thing out of the kitchen on a wagon.

"Cole slaw and hushpuppies with it?" the waitress asked while she wrote the order.

"Sure."

Eric sampled the glass of beer that was provided. A few customers trickled in for supper, mostly folks living on the island year-round, he supposed, though some may have ventured over from the mainland. They were dressed casually in warm up suits and sneakers. One of them, a female took up a stool near Eric. She looked to be in her late 30s or early 40s. She was wearing a black, bulky knit sweater that hung on her thin shoulders. Workout pants with stripes down the sides seemed to be a size too large, as though she had gotten them at a thrift store. Perhaps she simply liked the comfort of loose clothing. Large, opulent eyes were dark as coal. Earlobe length hair was equally dark and didn't have the look of being colored; the lighting above the bar revealed a few strands of grey. A finely chiseled nose was turned up just a bit. Red lipstick was generously applied to a slightly pouting mouth. Eric's order came then the waitress turned to the woman. "What would you like, Izzy?"

"Burger, fries, and a long neck Bud," the woman said in a voice touched with something Hispanic. Given her dark hair and eyes, Eric judged her to have considerable Hispanic blood coursing through her lovely veins. There was a fragrance coming from her, expensive perfume judiciously applied ... so much for the thrift store. Beautiful women need less anointing; it distracts from their natural beauty, Eric mused while casting a furtive look at the woman. Anyway, that was his considered opinion.

Though he was no ladies' man, he was something of a student of the female among us. She noted his glance and said, "I haven't seen you here before."

"I arrived today."

"Visiting friends on the island?" she asked.

"No, it's just me."

"Where are you from?"

"Minnesota. Minneapolis, actually."

"Minnesota. Vikings up there," the woman said, taking her bottle of beer and sampling it while looking at Eric off the side of her face.

"I'm a Kansas City Chiefs fan," Eric said. "I do follow Twins baseball, though."

"I didn't mean football Vikings," the woman said, accepting her order of burger and fries. "Real Vikings. They were nothing more than pirates, you know."

"Yes, I suppose that's true," Eric said, setting his glass of beer down when his order arrived. He hoped this woman wasn't into ranting.

"What's your name?" she asked, happily leaving the subject of Vikings and pirates, Eric was pleased to note.

"Eric."

"That sounds like a pirate's name. I'm Isabella," she said, leaning toward him and extending a doll-like hand that became all but lost in his. "Everybody calls me Izzy around here. I really don't like it ... sounds too much like dizzy. But I live on the island all the time, so I don't make a big deal of it."

Back to pirates, Eric thought. "Isabella is a lovely name," he said, forking up one of the hushpuppies. "Spanish?"

"Yes. But I learned to speak good English as a child. Some in my family say that the philosopher George Santayana is a distant relative. He was Spanish and he spoke very beautiful English."

"Indeed, he did," Eric said. "And beautiful Spanish as well," I suspect.

"Yes," Isabella said. She fell silent and tended her burger and fries. Eric turned to his blackened Grouper which was served up on a plate, not a wagon. Except for a couple of glances at each other, there was no more conversation.

Eric finished his meal. He told the woman goodbye and said he might see her around. She smiled and nodded as he turned to pay his bill at the cash register. While making his way along the beach toward the house, he wondered—if he met her again—should he call her Izzy or Isabella. He preferred the latter. She was into pirates. He would probably hear more of them if they became better acquainted. He'd like to have another whiff of her perfume. Intoxicating. Sara liked Chanel Chance, much of the time, 3.4 ounces at fifty bucks or so a pop. She wore it well, though.

Chapter 2

As was his custom, Eric rose at first light. He chided himself for not finding a grocery store and buying a few things to eat and a can of coffee. This was not a place where one could live off the land—or sea, for that matter. At any rate, he hadn't brought along any fishing gear; light tackle for Minnesota lakes wouldn't cut it for bringing in a blue Marlin. And he would need some tips from Hemmingway's *The Old Man and the Sea,* though Santiago's shark ravished fish was nothing more than a skeleton when reaching shore. The home's owners left some canned goods behind. He wouldn't feel comfortable eating their food. He wondered what time the Oyster Cove opened. He needed a cup of coffee to get a couple cylinders firing. Sara's death reduced him to 4, he thought, so he hadn't much to work with on cold mornings. The older he got, the longer it took to get moving of a morning, whether summer or winter. He pulled on a sweatshirt and walked out onto the home's deck. The sun was just rising. Gulf waters were relatively calm while surf rolled into shore. Seagulls were in the air in search of breakfast.

Eric looked to the west. Past the dunes and stalks of sea oats, he could see a figure coming along the beach, perhaps fifty yards away. Another early riser. Walking the beach is something he would do later, he thought, when the sun was up and warming things. As the figure on the beach grew closer, Eric could see that it was a rather small woman. She was walking with purpose, as though on her way to an appointment and running a little late. She spotted him on the deck and waved. Eric thought now that it was Isabella, the woman he met at Oyster Cove. He hoped she wasn't hurrying to tell him that she'd seen a pirate. "Good morning," she said, as she approached the stairs leading to the deck. "I was hoping to see you on the beach," she added as she crested the stairs.

"Well, not just yet," Eric said.

"If you haven't had breakfast, I'd like for you to join me at my place. I'll fix us an omelet."

"Sounds good." The brisk walk along the beach flushed her cheeks, giving her a girlish look. He judged her to be no more than 5'2". His own six feet seemed to tower over her. She was wearing black yoga pants that clung to firm buttocks. Jose Cuervo was printed across the front of a matching black hoodie.

Eric locked the house. He and Isabella descended the deck stairs and took up her trail near the surf where there was firmer footing. "How long have you lived on the island?" Eric asked. Light breeze out of the north brought a faint, residual scent of the perfume she wore the night before. Mixed with the Gulf's salty air, it seemed even more intoxicating.

"Five years," Isabella returned. "My father owned a chain of jewelry stores in Madrid. When he died, my brother and I inherited the stores. My mother died a year earlier. My father didn't seem to care about anything after her death. I think he missed having her to verbally abuse."

An interesting bit of unsolicited personal history, Eric thought, casting a look at her. Though she was short, he had to work at keeping up with her. Women don't fool around when exercising. While walking an outside track at a YMCA not far from his home in Minneapolis, women were always lapping him. He learned to stay in the right lane. Here they come! Their Nikes to the floor!

"I didn't want to be in the jewelry business, neither did my brother, so we sold the stores," Isabella continued.

"How did you end up on St. George Island?" Eric asked as the two of them dodged incoming surf.

"I was actually born in Miami while my parents were visiting. My mother was pregnant with me at the time. I have dual citizenship. We visited Florida again when I was in school. I loved the beaches, but they were too crowded, kind of like most of ours near Madrid. After my father's estate was settled, I began looking into a more remote part of Florida. So, here I am. By the way, do you mind if I ask what your last name is?"

"Erickson."

"Eric Erickson.... Are there any pirates in your family, you know, way back?" Isabella asked, shooting a look at her walking partner.

"I don't know of any. My great grandparents immigrated from Norway."

"Jeeesus! Norway is *loaded* with Vikings. I mean that's where they're *at*."

"Well, not anymore," Eric said, a little startled by the intensity of the woman's response. "Anyway, Vikings weren't the only pirates around in those days. Spain had pirates, so did England, France, just about every country."

"Yes, of course," Isabella said. "Have you ever seen a real pirate ship?"

"I can't say that I have. How about you?"

"There's my house up ahead," she said, changing the subject abruptly.

Like many beach houses, Isabella's stood on stilts to protect it from storm surge. It didn't have the look of a recently constructed home. But salt air weathers any house quickly. The two of them mounted the flight of steps onto the deck. Isabella fetched a key from the pouch of her hoodie and unlocked a sliding glass door. Eric followed her inside. Though the interior wasn't lavishly furnished, most everything was Mediterranean, including pictures on the walls. Short knap, Kelly green carpeting that looked to be wool was wall to wall. A spiraling staircase led to a second floor. The kitchen was open. Eric's host invited him to take a seat at a dinette. "I'll get coffee going," she said, "then I'll fix our omelets." Copper and stainless-steel cookware hung from a rack near the stove. This woman is no peanut butter and jelly chef, Eric thought.

"Very nice," Eric said, casting about at his surroundings. The arrangement of the furnishings gave the impression that the items were chosen carefully, some if not all of which having belonged to her parents' home in Madrid, he reasoned. Shipping them from Spain would not have been cheap. But heirlooms are to be preserved whatever the cost.

"It's home," Isabella said. A bag of Juan Valdez coffee beans sat on the counter. She poured a measure into a grinder and set it to whirling. Eric was a hands man, at least that was the second thing he noticed. He thought a woman's hands with their tapered fingers and graceful movements one of the most beautiful parts of her anatomy, that is until she became angry. Then those lovely hands could become virtual hatchets.

When the coffee finished brewing, Isabella poured her guest a cup and asked if he cared for cream or sugar. He declined both and sampled the coffee. It was dark and rich. He thought that a parking lot could be sealed with it. But it was quite good. His four cylinders were humming right along.

"What do you like in your omelets?" Isabella asked while cracking eggs into a bowl.

"Anything but anchovies."

Isabella laughed. "I don't like them, either. Much too salty."

When the omelets were ready, she topped off their coffee cups and took a seat at the dinette. "Do you pray before a meal, anything like that?"

"No," Eric said.

"Neither do I," Isabella said, taking up her fork and

cutting into the omelet. “It’s not that I’m ungrateful for having enough to eat. But I think that it’s just talking to one’s self when praying. Do you agree?”

“Pretty much. I guess the point is not to take anything for granted. There’s a lot of hungry people in this world.”

“Yes,” Isabella said, then sampling her coffee.

After a few moments of silence while enjoying the omelets, Isabella said, “What kind of work do you do, Eric?”

“I’m a forensic psychologist.”

Isabella’s face sobered slightly.

“Are you married?” she asked.

“Sara was killed in a car crash two years ago.”

“I’m sorry.”

Eric didn’t respond. The empathy in Isabella’s voice and eyes touched him and he feared that his voice would break. He tested his coffee then said, “So, how about you?”

“Divorced—twice. I’m kind of embarrassed that I’ve done so badly in marriage.”

“It happens,” Eric said, “something like 3 out of 5 times, I’ve heard. Marriage may be a dying institution. More people are just hooking up.”

“Do you have any children?”

“No.”

“Me either,” Isabella said. “I wish I did. I love kids. My two husbands didn’t have enough spermies to knock me up.”

“It only takes one,” Eric said, chuckling.

“Yes, but it’s got to hit the egg at full speed. Otherwise it will bounce off and crash, maybe. Well, I don't know what happens to them. Do you?"

"No. I guess I never thought about it too much."

"Anyway, it would be nice to have one or two kids for when we grow old, you know, to help us when we get feeble. By the way, how old are you, Eric, if you don't mind me asking?"

"52."

"You're very handsome ... are you sure you're not related to pirates? Some of them were good looking devils, I've heard."

"As far as I know," Eric said, becoming puzzled with this woman's fixation on the subject.

"I have a selfish motive for inviting you to breakfast," she said.

"And what is that?"

"I don't drive. Would you take me into town so that I can get a Christmas tree?"

"I'd be happy to." He hoped she wouldn't grill him about pirates all the way there or ask him about his sperm count. He was okay, but Sara was infertile. They tried all the fertility stuff, but nothing worked.

"There's a place in Apalachicola that always have nice trees. I get the real ones. I like the fragrance of fir," she said, putting a fork to her omelet.

"I do too," Eric said. "They dry out quickly, though. I've heard of a company somewhere that sells the trees in pots. Customers can buy, or rent them, then bring them back after the holidays, or keep them watered at home for the next year."

"What a neat idea," Isabella said. "Christmas trees

bring back a bad memory for me, though," she said, taking up her coffee cup."

"How is that?"

"My father had a terrible temper. Once, when I was five years old, he flew into a rage at Christmas dinner and threw our turkey across the room and knocked over the Christmas tree."

"How awful," Eric said, clucking his tongue and shaking his head.

"It ruined our Christmas."

"I can well imagine."

"My mother and I cried. My father left the house. While he was gone, we stood the tree up and put the ornaments back on that had fallen off."

"What happened to the turkey?" Eric asked.

"Mom brushed the pine needles from it, put it back on the table, then she carved some for the two of us. My father came back after about an hour. He apologized, but the damage was done."

"What did he get mad about?" Eric asked, accepting a coffee refill.

"The mashed potatoes were kind of lumpy. He liked them really smooth."

"Hardly anything to fly into a rage about," Eric said, then finishing his omelet and putting a napkin to his mouth.

"I agree. My father was an excellent businessman, and our family was rather well off—filthy rich, actually. But he had a nasty disposition. He never laid a hand on any of us. But he was scary when he got mad about something, like a big jump in diamond prices for his stores. He once traveled to Africa and confronted diamond mine owners," Isabella said, chuckling."

"Did it do any good?"

"No. But he blew off some steam. Better over there then on us." Isabella laughed then the two of them began to clear away the breakfast dishes.

It was a short drive across the bay into Eastpoint, a community of less than 3,000. Occasional gusts of wind on the bridge required keeping both hands on the steering wheel. Gulls were being blown off course and squawked at the annoyance. It was 7 miles on to Apalachicola, considerably larger than Eastpoint, with a population just under 12,000. Isabella was a quiet rider. She said nothing while looking out onto the bay. She glanced at Eric from time to time, as though checking to see if he was enjoying the drive. He was indeed, especially in the company of this enchanting woman. And he was thinking that two weeks on the island wouldn't be nearly enough. He would need to see about leasing the Suburban for a longer period, and the beach house as well; neither should be a problem. Why return to Minneapolis for another three months of winter? This island could spoil a man, so could she, he thought, glancing at his passenger.

Upon reaching Apalachicola, Isabella directed Eric to the Christmas tree lot she preferred. Patrons were plentiful, but the selection was still excellent. An employee approached: "Hi, Isabella," the man said. That she was a regular customer was evident.

"Hi. This is my friend, Eric. He was good enough to bring me to get my tree."

The two men shook hands. "I set one aside for you. It's a really nice Douglas fir, seven feet."

They were led to where the reserved tree was sitting. "Oh, it's lovely," Isabella said. "Thank you so much for saving it for me!"

After the tree was paid for, it was placed on top of the Suburban and secured with baling twine. A well-dressed man wearing a Harris Tweed topcoat approached. "Hi, Isabella," the man said, smiling.

"Hello," Isabella returned. "This is my attorney, George Davis," she said, introducing Eric to him. "Mr. Davis managed to keep me out of jail," she added. The attorney smiled and lifted his eyebrows.

"It's nice to meet you," Eric said, taking the man's hand.

"Excellent choice," Davis said, looking at the tree on top of the Suburban.

"They always save me a nice one," Isabella said.

"Well, I want one for our office. Nice to see you again. And Happy Holidays."

"Happy Holidays to you," Isabella returned. When the man was gone, Isabella turned to Eric and said, "Would you mind taking me to a grocery store?"

"Show the way, I need a few things too," Eric said, sliding behind the steering wheel and turning the key in the ignition. He glanced at Isabella and wondered what she had done to nearly land her behind bars.

At a Piggly Wiggly, the two of them strolled the aisles with their carts. In the meat department, Isabella chose a frozen, Tom turkey. She turned to Eric and said, "I'd like to have you for Christmas dinner if you'll promise not to get mad and throw the turkey and knock over my Christmas tree."

"It's a deal," Eric said, chuckling.

She found a bottle of Merlot. "If you're not busy later, I'll fix us supper and we can have some wine and decorate my tree."

"Sounds like a plan," Eric said, putting a can of coffee in his cart. "May I bring something?"

"Just yourself."

Chapter 3

Returning to the island, the tree was unloaded and carried onto the home's deck. "How does supper at six o'clock sound?" Isabella said.

"Good."

"After we eat, maybe we can put my tree up. I'll have the decorations ready."

"I'm looking forward to it," Eric said, turning and walking to the Suburban. At the beach house, he took his groceries inside. He put on a pot of coffee and fixed a peanut butter and jelly sandwich. The day was proving to be a pleasant one, less wind and not so cold. He would finish his sandwich, look for a coffee mug in the cupboard, and go for a walk along the beach. He was curious, to say the least, about what Isabella did to nearly land her in jail. She hadn't commented on it while driving back to the island. He doubted that it was assault or shoplifting. She was too small for attacking anyone affectively, at least without a weapon; and her family was "filthy rich," she said. No need to steal. She and a brother inherited a fortune. Whatever her crime, it didn't appear to have been particularly serious, for she and her attorney were smiling during the short talk at the Christmas tree lot. One would certainly be happy and in good spirits after surviving a criminal charge, walking, as they say, presumably out of the courtroom into freedom once more. But being found not guilty or acquitted in a capital offense still left the defendant with a most somber demeanor, having narrowly escaped the end of one's life, at least virtually, in the event that a life sentence was handed down. Isabella didn't have the look of a felon. But then again, Jeffrey Dahmer didn't look like a cannibal.

It had been four years since Eric walked along a beach. He and Sara spent a week in July at Destine, Florida. The sand there was sugar white, brighter than what he was slogging through now. Visiting the beaches of Destine, alone, would have been unbearable. Still, he could imagine Sara beside him. She would have liked it here, he thought. She was easily pleased and entertained. Accommodating spirit born of an inner quietness. Even in difficult times, she could always see a light at the end of the tunnel. We'll just deal with it, she would say. Had the car crash not killed her instantly, merciful sometimes, she would have fought for her life as valiantly as any.

Triumph of the human spirit. A cliché, of course, but much loved by those who have surmounted seemingly impossible odds. Since Sara's death, Eric learned something about emotional suffering, so debilitating at times that he would wake of a morning and wish that he hadn't. And the manner in which she died only compounded the pain he felt. On one particular morning he struggled to even get out of bed. He did, however, and after putting on coffee, turned on the T.V.

A story came on that was a game changer for him. In another midwestern state, a young father walked into a police department office one winter morning in a small town and said that he had just drown his infant daughter in a pond. After learning the whereabouts of the pond, a police officer sped to the location and found the baby girl floating on her back. He quickly waded into the water and picked her up then rushed to shore. She wasn't breathing. She had mud and grass in her mouth and ears from having sunk to the bottom of the pond. Trained in first aid, of course, the officer cleared her lungs of water and administered CPR. She began breathing once more. He removed her wet clothes, took off his shirt and wrapped her in it then held her close to his body. She had fought her way to the surface of the pond, determined to live, and somehow managed to roll over and float on her back. She was suffering from hypothermia and wouldn't have lasted much longer in the icy water. An ambulance arrived and took her to a hospital. It was reported later that she was doing well. The officer, in tears during an interview, said that someone was absolutely looking after the child. One thing was certain: her father wasn't. Eric found that getting out of bed became easier for him.

At five o'clock, he showered and shaved then walked along the beach to Isabella's house. Mounting a dozen steps to the home's deck, he picked up the scent of food; something Hispanic, he thought. Enchiladas, perhaps.

Enchiladas it was with a side of refried beans and simple vegetable salad with cilantro dressing. His host poured wine then took a seat at the dinette. She proposed a toast: "Here's to Mother Earth—as we knew her."

When they clinked glasses, the words of the late cosmologist, Stephen Hawking came to Eric's mind. When asked what he thought of colonizing other planets, Hawking said, "We might as well. We're ruining this one." Eric supposed that climate change was what Isabella meant with her dystopian toast. He couldn't disagree.

"Thank you, again, Eric, for taking me to town to get my tree," Isabella said, laying a napkin in her lap and taking up her fork.

"You're quite welcome."

"I really don't know why I do a tree every year. It's just me to enjoy it, and an occasional person passing along the beach who see the lights through the window. There's a couple of young boys, brothers, who live on the island year-round. They like to walk the beach with me on Saturdays sometimes. They ask me all about Spain. I tell them as much as I know. They never seem to tire of it."

"Thank *you* for inviting me to dinner," Eric said, putting a fork to his salad. "I think the holidays aren't meant to be spent alone, but many do, sadly."

"Yes. When I was growing up in Madrid, my mother and I would take gifts to homeless people we found on the street during Christmas. We took them food items, warm gloves, socks, and a little money. It meant a lot to them. We did it every year. It hurt us when we learned that some of them died since the last Christmas. I can still see their faces. I always wondered what happened in their lives to bring them to such a state. Alcohol, drugs, mental illness, maybe. Some just give up, I think. They can't find a job, no place to live they can afford. Seeing their eyes, it's kind of like they are looking at you through the window of another world. They must feel so marginalized, even despised, by some. I saw a story on the evening news once where a homeless woman said that some people just *throw* their money at her. It hurt her feelings, like she was a dog being thrown scraps."

"Life is faster than it used to be," Eric said, picking up his glass of wine. "But I don't know what's to be said of us as human beings if we can't take a little time for someone struggling. It's like a merry-go-round out of control, throwing people off left and right. And everything is so expensive. It's been said that most people are just a couple of paychecks away from the street."

With dinner over, the tree was brought inside and placed in its stand. Lights and ornaments were in boxes sitting on a couch. Isabella liked the old-fashioned bubble lights. She plugged them in to see if they all were working; two weren't, but she found spares. There were a great many handmade ornaments, things she made while a schoolgirl. Despite her considerable wealth, this woman likes simple things, Eric thought, looking for a spot to hang a star cut from construction paper. It had some years on it, but carefully preserved.

When the tree was decorated, Isabella poured each of them another glass of wine. Eric noted a gun case standing in one corner of the room. "Some of my father's guns," Isabella said. "He was quite a hunter: birds, mostly, pheasant, quail, grouse. I kept half of them after he died. My brother took the other half." She ushered Eric across the room. She found a key hidden behind the case and unlocked it. They set their wine glasses on a small table beside the gun case. "This is a Famars AB Biatico & Salvinelli, Poseidon Deluxe, over and under, 20 gauge," she said, removing the gun from the case and handing it to Eric.

"Wow! Beautiful gun," Eric said, taking the gun and handling it carefully. "What would a gun like this cost?" he added, running a hand across the engravings.

"$29,500.00," Isabella said.

"Holy shit! Forgive the language."

Isabella smiled and took the gun from him. She returned it to the case and handed him another. "This is the A. Galazan, Pinless Sidelock, 28 gauge."

"How much?" Eric asked, taking the fine gun in hand.

"$59,500.00."

"Good God!"

"My father was a collector as well as a hunter," Isabella said.

She returned the gun to the case and handed Eric another one. "That one is the A-10 American Rose and Scroll, 12 gauge. A bit less expensive at $11,500.00," she said, handing Eric the gun. "This is a Beretta-S05 12 gauge. $25,000.00. It comes with extra barrels," she said, removing the gun from the case and exchanging guns with Eric. "One more," she said. This is a Browning Belgium Takedown, the one dad usually used when hunting. It's about $4,000 or so."

"Oh, a cheap one," Eric said.

Isabella laughed.

With guns all returned to the case, she locked it. She sat down on a nearby couch and Eric joined her "I'm curious about something," Eric said, picking up his wine glass and swirling the contents. "When you introduced me to your attorney in the parking lot at the tree lot, you said that he kept you from going to jail." Eric sampled his wine and cast a furtive look at Isabella and wondering if he might be getting too nosy. "Do you mind if I ask what it was that you did?"

Isabella sampled her own glass of wine, shifted on the couch and crossed her legs. "Discharging a firearm on the island."

"One of those shotguns?" Eric said, casting a look at the gun case.

"All of them. I have a case of shells for each."

"Were you like, you know, trying them out or something?"

"No. I was defending myself."

"Am I being nosy?" Eric asked.

"A little, but I don't mind. Are you in a hurry to go home?"

"No." Other than being with Sara, he couldn't image another place he would rather be.

"Two years ago," she began, "I had some visitors, unwelcomed visitors, as it turned out. It was in the month of April. I'd been having trouble sleeping all spring. On this particular night I was tossing and turning in my bed. It was exhausting! I looked at my clock on the nightstand. It was exactly midnight. So, I just got up and put on my robe and walked out onto the deck."

Eric shifted on the couch and turned a bit toward Isabella. This is going to get good, he thought. The Spanish lilt in her voice seemed to enhance the progress of the story. She once told him that the eloquent philosopher George Santayana was thought to be a distant relative. Believable, Eric thought, for Isabella could be quite eloquent as well.

"I don't like drinking alone, especially in the middle of the night, but I fixed myself a Pink Moscato Sangria," she continued. "Have you ever had one, Eric?"

"I don't think so, but it sounds interesting."

"The moon was full," she continued, "and it had a very pink hue. I guess that's what put the Sangria in my mind. I never saw a moon look like that."

"I once read about a pink moon in April, something about the atmospheric conditions. Quite rare, I think."

"Well, it was beautiful," Isabella said. "I gazed at it for the longest time until I saw something else."

"What?"

"I went back into the house and got my binoculars. Off to the east I could see that a sailing ship, a very large one with many sails, was making its way west and close to shore, too close, I would think."

"Probably a shallow draft for speed," Eric said.

"I never saw a ship like it in Spain or anywhere else, except in movies. I thought it strange that, though the Gulf was rather calm, the ship's sails were quite full. When it reached about mid-island, straight out from my house, the sails began to come down and the ship sat still in the water, though I saw no anchors being dropped."

"What do you think it was?" Eric asked.

"I knew what it was when I saw the Jolly Roger flying. They ran it down from the mast in a hurry, like they didn't want anyone to see it. I could see canon compartments all along the ship's side that was facing the shore. I thought they were going to open fire on my house!"

Eric laughed but cut it short when he noted that Isabella wasn't laughing.

"Some men lowered a dinghy, and several got aboard," she continued. "The one in the front was the captain, I guessed."

"It must have been scary," Eric said. He wondered if this woman was spending too much time alone.

"It wasn't so scary until the boat landed and the men looked straight at my house. That's when I went back inside, loaded all my shotguns and carried each of them onto the deck and propped them against the railing and waited. I don't know why I thought I needed *all* of them. My father was in the army and he talked of the need for overwhelming fire power. I didn't know what the pirates wanted, but by God they weren't going to get it, not from me. I went hunting with my father when I was grown, and he taught me how to shoot. I could throw up one of his shotguns and bring down any bird in flight. My father said I was better than him, and that's not something he would often say, if ever, to anyone about anything."

"Did they keep coming toward your house?" he asked, noting that his and Isabella's wine glass was empty. He hurriedly fetched the bottle and poured the remains into their glasses. He did love a story, and she was good at it.

"Thank you," Isabella said, accepting the wine. "Only one, the captain, I think, kept coming up the beach toward my house. The other men stayed with the dinghy. When the captain got within about 50 feet of my house, I picked up the Galazan 28 gauge, pointed it at him and called out, what do you want!? I spoke in Spanish, for the man looked to be Spanish. 'I just want to talk, senorita,' he said, answering in Spanish, a language in which I am quite fluent, of course. Talk from there, captain, or I'll blow your pirate ass back into the Gulf, I said."

Eric laughed. He doubted that she was bluffing.

"The captain roared with laughter and looked back at his men. 'Shoot all you want, love, neither canon nor sword can hurt the likes of us, not anymore'"

"Ghost?" Eric asked.

"Something like that, I guess," Isabella said. "I asked him, again, what he wanted: 'You are a descendent of our beloved Queen Isabella. She wants you on the other side.'"

Isabella paused and took a drink of her wine then continued:

"I got really scared—and mad. I'm not going anywhere with you motherfuckers! Forgive the language, Eric," Isabella said, putting a hand on his knee. "That's when I opened fire, one gun after the other. Ejected cartridges were flying all over the deck. You should have heard those babies popping off rounds! My father would have been proud. I had to spread my feet to keep from being knocked over by the recoil. My shoulder was sore the next day."

"Did they leave?" Eric asked.

"Yes. It appeared that I wounded or killed none of them. They returned to their boat. I could hear them laughing. When the dinghy reached the ship and the men climbed aboard, the sails and the Jolly Roger went aloft. I could hear more laughter when the ship turned and headed back east."

"Did anyone else see the ship sitting offshore?" Eric asked. He was a forensic phycologist, not an attorney, but a little something in the form of an eyewitness would make him feel better about the credibility of what he was hearing. He so hoped she wasn't screwy. He would love to at least develop a friendship with her, if not outright relationship.

"Ricky and Stewart Jones, two brothers who live on the island. They are 10 and 8 years old. Ricky, the oldest, said he woke up when he heard someone shooting farther down the beach. He looked out the window and saw the ship. He tried to wake his brother up."

"Did the younger boy see the ship?"

"No. His brother told him about it the next morning."

"Since the gunfire was of no harm to them, I wonder why they left?" Eric said.

"Maybe they just had a message to deliver."

Isabella was silent for long moments and took a drink of her wine. "It wasn't long before the sheriff and deputies showed up. I told them what happened. They searched the beach and couldn't find any footprints—or bodies, and nothing where the dinghy was pulled ashore.

I was arrested, but released on my own recognizance the next morning when the judge came in. I was given a court date. Judge David Henry gave me a year's probation. But he ordered a psychiatric evaluation."

"Did you ever see the ship again?" Eric asked.

"Yes, the next year, in April, when the moon was full."

"Was it pink, like before?"

"Yes."

"More gunfire?" Eric asked, tongue in cheek.

"Yes. It did nothing but make a lot of noise. But I had to do *something*. The captain kept coming this time. I gathered up my guns and ran into the house and locked the door. I could hear him laughing out on the deck. Then he just walked in, like the door wasn't there."

"What did he do?"

"He threw me onto the couch and felt me up. I didn't like it."

"No, I can't imagine that you would," Eric said. He found this story getting a bit too bizarre. But Isabella's eyes were direct, never shifting away, as is often the case when someone is lying, or at least unsure about whether they are getting the facts straight. Forensic phycologists are often called upon to determine what is truth and what is not. The problem is that liars can be very skilled. They know how to control body language which, in itself, amounts to quite a lot of guesswork and conjecture. The *interrogator* hopes to trip them up at some point with a blatant contradiction.

"I tried to fight him off," Isabella continued, "but my hands just went through him, like he wasn't there. I tried to kick him in his … but that didn't work, either. He kept laughing. His breath was like an open sewer. Disgusting!"

Isabella fell silent for a few moments. "Just when I thought I was about to be raped by a ghost—or whatever he was, he left without a word. Well, here came the sheriff and deputies, a state trooper as well, and a bunch of neighbors. I was arrested again. I wasn't released on my own recognizance this time. I had to appear before the judge. The prosecutor wanted to charge me with armed, criminal action, but he didn't have enough evidence."

"How did the evaluation go?" Eric asked.

"I passed with flying colors. The judge seemed kind of confused by the evaluation's findings. I think he may have decided ahead of time that I'm nuts. I was released from jail and my probation was reinstated. Do you think I'm nuts, Eric?"

"I'm no scientist," Eric began, circumventing Isabella's direct question about her sanity. "But I think that just because we can't see something with the naked eye doesn't mean it isn't there. For years some scientists were predicting a boson, subatomic particle. It's got to be there, they kept saying and believing. It was needed to account for how mass is formed. Then, the Large Hadron Collider near Geneva, Switzerland found it. It stunned the scientific world."

"Do you think I'm wacked?" Isabella asked again, rephrasing the question.

"I think that it's possible that ours is only one of many universes," Eric said, still not answering Isabella's question directly. "Who is to say that your pirates didn't sail in from another dimension?"

He might be simply patronizing a very disturbed woman, he thought. And he felt a sting of guilt for avoiding a direct answer.

"What's a boson particle?" Isabella asked, abandoning her sanity question.

"I'll explain it some other time."

"I should have bought *two* bottles of wine," Isabella said, finishing the little remaining in her glass.

"Indeed," Eric agreed, finishing his own. Curious, he thought, that while I've taken a leave of absence from my adjunct duties at the university as well as not accepting any calls for expert opinion in a court of law, I'm smack in the middle of the strangest case of my career, though not in a professional role. He never enjoyed sinking—or, ripping a whole in the sails of a defendant's ship with his *expert* opinions, at least those whose trouble wasn't something hideous. Sinking Isabella's shipload of pirates wasn't something he intended to do in any capacity. At this point, she was little more than an acquaintance. If it's a fantasy for her comfort level, enjoy, my dear. Just leave the shotguns in their cabinet. And, too, should he question the truth of what she was telling him, a fiery, Spanish temper—easily comparable to a proverbial Irish one—could find him on the wrong end of one of her 5-digit shotguns. He doubted that she would miss … talk from there or I'll blow your pirate ass into the Gulf, she told the captain. Whew! Keep your head on straight with this woman, Eric, and mind your manners, he told himself. She's not to be trifled with.

Chapter 4

When Eric returned to the beach house, he found a For Sale sign stuck in the sand. He called the realtor and asked if he was being evicted. "No," the realtor said. "The family is moving from Topeka to LA and won't be wanting the house any longer." Eric asked what was being asked for the house. He told the realtor that he might be interested. He would get back to her shortly. Unsettling when finding that a house one is renting has come up for sale, Eric thought. Every rental is for sale, if the price is right. Few landlords give a damn about where the current tenant might go next. Just get out when the place sells.

Sara was big on life insurance. Her policy was a hefty $500,000. He spent none of it. After getting on the Internet and researching some similar properties, it appeared that the house was priced to sell. The house was in good condition. He noted what appeared to be new guttering and planking on the deck. And it was wired for Internet. It seemed like a good investment. He might just spend the full year of his leave of absence on the island. His neighbors, not a great many of whom were present year-round, the realtor said, were rather private. He wanted to do some writing. This would be a good place to do it. And if Isabella turned out to be totally wacked, she might prove to be a good subject, that is if she agreed to be a case study. But he thought she wasn't the Ginny pig type, too proud and private. He must get his stock and trade off his mind and enjoy the woman's company for as long as it may last. Consider her a friend, not a subject or specimen ... *specimen,* for sure, a tribute to the female species and how lovely she can become. It seemed to him, though, that natural selection—Mother Nature, if you must, has a penchant for going overboard, and socially elitist: so much for some, so little for others. Why not spread the looks' wealth around a tad more? Well, beauty is only skin deep, after all. A breathtakingly beautiful woman may be an intractable witch, Eric concluded.

After signing papers and writing a check for the house, his next thought was what to do about the Suburban he rented when flying into Pensacola from Minneapolis. Perhaps the leasing company would cut him a deal for keeping the vehicle for a year. He would need to cross the bay into town now and then for some groceries. And, too, Isabella could probably use a lift from time to time, hopefully not for another court appearance.

He had good neighbors in Minneapolis, and they didn't mind keeping an eye on his house when he was gone. He'd give them a call to let them know of his plans to stay on the island during his leave of absence. It was a respectable address with little or no crime, so it wasn't like he would be asking them to stand guard. If the alarm goes off—which it never did except when he or Sara forgot to turn it off—call the cops. He would need to arrange for getting his mail forwarded, though he paid virtually all his bills online. Ah, yes, another wonder of the Internet age. He even quit taking a newspaper at his home. Why wade snow to fetch it from the driveway when one can get on the Internet and find all the news you want?

Eric awoke to the sound of sleet rattling on the windows. He got out of bed and pulled on a pair of sweats and a T shirt. He never cared much for bath robes. Sara bought him one for his 40th birthday. It was a silky thing, paisley print, maroon and purple. He really didn't like wearing it. It made him feel pretentious, a continental dude. All he lacked was a pipe. And he didn't smoke. But Sara liked the robe on him, so he wore it after showering and having coffee on weekend mornings. Romantically, she was a morning person, hormones up and zinging. Something about the robe turned her on, so he figured wearing it wasn't all bad. He'd wear burlap with Coop printed all over it if it was a ticket to bed with her. What a lover. Even if his cresting at the big 50 left him not quite up to it on rare occasions, she made him feel like it was nothing more than a fleeting anomaly. She was sympathetic with what is required of men in bed. She thought erection on demand nothing short of a miracle. God! How do guys do it? she would say. It's said, by people whose business it is to study such things, that women respond to touch and men to sight. The older a man gets, the more of an eyeful he needs to be aroused. Sara was "endowed" with no more than a handful of breasts, but one look at their uppy puppy nipples, as he called them, turned toward the sun, and tight, fussy V was usually enough to bring her man around.

Going to a window that looked out onto the deck and the Gulf, he clucked his tongue and thought, again, how badly he miscalculated what winter would be like in north Florida. The wind was howling and whipping sleet across the deck. He saw no gulls in the air. If they were smart, they flew farther south, he figured, precisely what he should have done. But this island was already growing on him, not to mention the senorita down the beach. He mustn't become a pest. Loneliness is hard to keep to oneself, he thought, when assessing his emotions on days when he was feeling out of sorts. It's the proverbial cat out of the bag, or a bird will tell it, a play on the Bible verse in Ecclesiastes. One wouldn't think that King Solomon could have been particularly lonely, given his many wives. It apparently wasn't all roses, however, for he said something to the effect that it's better to live in the corner of an attic than in a whole house with a contentious woman. Then again, the King might have been a royal pain in the neck, if not somewhere else and drove his girls up the Wailing Wall.

Not a good thing, loneliness. People who study longevity say that it can cut a person's life short by as much as 5 to 15 years. On days when he missed Sara the most, Eric thought he might have another week left, two at the most. It came as no surprise to him that often, when an older spouse dies, the one remaining doesn't last much longer. And there are those heart wrenching stories of them dying on the same day, and of so-called natural causes. So potent, and fragile, at times, the human spirit.

Turning from the window, he put on coffee then went for a shower. He bought canned biscuits, eggs and sausage at the store. It sounded good on such a morning as this. After breakfast, he would get his computer up and running, connect to the Internet and look up some pirate ships that might be similar to what Isabella claimed to have seen. Her story smacked of schizophrenia, or that of a pathological liar. Those who conducted the court ordered psychiatric evaluation may have misread her badly. Or she could have simply outsmarted the questions. Difficult to do but known to have happened. The Minnesota Multiphasic Personality Inventory (MMPI) is the most sophisticated test of its kind. But no test is utterly foolproof. They are written by humans, who are subject to error.

After breakfast, a fresh cup of coffee, and a look out the window to see if it was still sleeting—it wasn't, and the sky was beginning to partially clear—Eric turned on his laptop. Predictably, the first pirate ship to come up was the iconic Flying Dutchman of old. What a boat! Eric thought. It weighed 420 tons; 170 feet long; 46 cannons; and two, triple-barreled chase guns. It was one of the fastest ships on the seas in its day. She would strike fear into the hearts of all who spotted her. There was no outrunning or dodging such a ship, with one possible exception: The shallow draft, Portuguese Corvette could make

24 knots. She could come about fast and attack from the rear, like a Wolverine biting the butt of a Grizzly then stealing the meat while the bitten bear is looking elsewhere.

Mythically, the Flying Dutchman was a supernatural ghost ship given the sacred task of collecting all the souls who died at sea and ferrying them to the afterlife. According to legend and lore, the ship was given to Davy Jones by his love, the sea goddess Calypso, to perform this very work. And, of course, Davy would pick up a little booty along the way, gold bullion and other precious cargo, reluctantly handed over at the point of sword or cannon. Better to lighten a ship than to rest on the bottom of the Caribbean, only to be discovered—if ever—centuries later.

Eric doubted that it was the ghost of Davy Jones which allegedly came ashore at Isabella's beach house, for the phantom ship and its crew were sentenced to roaming the seas forever and to never again find a port. St. George Island was no port, certainly not for a ship of such size. How it remained stationary offshore without having dropped anchors, as Isabella noted, was interesting. And its sails were full when it arrived, though she said there was little or no wind at the midnight hour. She had an eye for detail, even when threatened. It's said that eyewitnesses, curiously enough, are among the poorest form of evidence. An odd phenomenon, seeing what we *choose* to see.

Eric remembered a murder case where a father was accused of murdering his wife and young children while in their beds. Working to establish a timeline, the prosecutor put forth a witness who said that, while working at a convenience store on the night of the murders, he saw the defendant at the store. A thoroughgoing defense attorney went to the said convenient store and checked the facts. The "witness" hadn't been working that night. That blew the prosecutor's case and the defendant was acquitted.

Sampling his coffee and musing about the subject before him, his thoughts were interrupted by a knock on the sliding glass door. It was Isabella. She was smiling with something in her hands wrapped in foil. He rose and opened to her. "My mother always said, 'Never go calling with your hands at your sides.' I baked some cinnamon rolls early this morning. I thought you might like one with your coffee," she said, stepping inside.

"Excellent," Eric said. "Would you like a cup?"

"Sure." She unwrapped the rolls and Eric poured her a cup of coffee. She cast a brief look at the Flying Dutchman on the laptop screen but made no comment. Eric thought it odd since the subject of pirates occupied so much of their conversation the night before. He wondered if her fixation on pirates could be episodic. With his right hand, he clandestinely scrolled the ship's image down and out of sight on the computer screen while Isabella placed the rolls on saucers she found in the cupboard, and forks as well in a drawer.

"Did you see the sleet this morning?" Isabella said, taking a seat at the dinette.

"I did. I woke up hearing it rattling on the windows. Are you sure this is Florida?"

"The last I heard," she said, chuckling and putting a

fork to her roll.

"The weather is getting more and more weird," Eric said.

"Yes. And climate change deniers are getting fewer and fewer."

"I'm afraid I was one of them, but not anymore," Eric said, cutting into his own roll. "The rate that the polar ice is melting is shocking. And if Greenland's ice sheet melts entirely, this island will be history."

"Yes," Isabella said, picking up her coffee cup." Miami's shoreline is already creeping inland."

"We'll probably be dead and gone before things get really ugly," Eric said. It's the next generations who will have to sweat it out, no pun intended."

When coffee and rolls were finished, Isabella rose to leave. She cast a look at the laptop screen. "So, I can expect you for Christmas dinner?"

"With bells on. And I'll bring *two* bottles of wine."

"I'm looking forward to it," Isabella said, giving Eric a hug, a close one, and not hurried. He could feel some of her ribs, and her breasts, not seeming to be large, were firm. She felt good, this woman. And he was ever-so-glad that he hadn't opted to go farther south, after all. Such fine twists of fate.

When his guest was gone, he watched her walking along the beach toward her house. The sun had returned, the gulls as well, and he donned a windbreaker and set out for the beach and a walk east. There wasn't much wind and surf rolled in gently, lapping the shore like a stolen kiss then receding with wet lips flecked with sand, he mused. Such primal romance. This island is turning me into a poet, he thought. I may have chosen the wrong line of business. He smiled at such fantasy, for he hadn't a poetic bone in his body ... wet lips flecked with *sand*? Some kiss! That beauty down the beach, he thought, looking west, has got me thinking that I'm more than I am, like loud pipes on a 40-horsepower car. Leaving his new self behind, he looked out onto the gulf and wondered what it would be like to see the Flying Dutchman making way and tacking toward the island.

A sadness swept over him and momentarily diminished the pleasure of this walk when the proposition that Isabella might in fact be mentally ill barged into his thoughts like a home intruder. It occurred to him that he himself wasn't entirely well, for Sara's death would scarcely leave him alone. He awakened more than once to the sound of screaming tires and shattering glass. Damn the drunken sonofabitch who broadsided her! He was in prison now for vehicular homicide. Closure? There is no closure, only justice, which closes nothing but a jail door. The pain and images may fade some with time—the venerable surgeon of broken hearts—but the terrible deed lurks in the shadows, always ready to pounce upon a suffering soul and bring it to tears once more.

Eric drew a deep breath and released it slowly. He stopped and picked up a piece of broken seashell, ran a thumb along the smooth interior then cast it into the surf. If his pain needs a new venue, this is the place for it, he thought. And there's a doctor on the island, practicing without a license, one might say. But he suspected that she has a prescription for him. He wondered what she might prescribe on Christmas Day. Come what may, he promised not to fly into a rage and throw the turkey across the room and knock over her Christmas tree as her ill-tempered father did when she was a child. They both laughed at such a scene, now. I'm not Freud, he thought, picking up another shell and biting on it to test its hardness, but such a scene obviously left an emotional scar on the child that she has carried into adulthood. Oh, the things we do to our children, he thought. And he wondered what kind of father he might have been if given the chance. He was certain, though, that he would have left the Christmas turkey on the table.

It's a kind of moral cowardice, he thought, taking one's frustrations out on those nearest to us, when they had nothing to do with the frustration. Go into the woods, kick a tree, break a limb. The tree won't mind, as far we know. What pain will it feel, beyond sending a few leaves down on an angry head?

Chapter 5

Eric wanted to get Isabella something for Christmas. She invited him to dinner twice and brought freshly baked cinnamon rolls to his house. He drove into Apalachicola and found a card and gift shop. Browsing the store, he chose a music box with a Christmas tree on top that turned with the music. It wasn't the most novel thing; he'd seen them many times. But the store wasn't Tiffany's. Given her fondness and care given for putting up a fresh tree each year, he thought that she might like it. An employee wrapped it for him.

Stopping off at a liquor store before returning to the island, he bought 2 bottles of Pinot Noir. He thought that he would take the gift to her on Christmas eve. They might want to open one of the bottles of wine and pick up their conversation where they left off, should she invite him to stay awhile. He didn't want to become a social vampire, showing up at her door every day or so. But she was a new acquaintance, a most hospitable one, and seemed to enjoy his company as much as he did hers.

And she hadn't spoken of other friends on the island, other than speaking or waving when encountering them along the beach, he supposed. She was anything but withdrawn. Pretty much keeping to herself on the island for five years couldn't help but leave her somewhat lonely, he thought—well, *hoped,* selfishly. One does have to look after one's own heart, you know. Root hog or die in this world, romantically speaking. Good things come to those who wait. But one can wait too long. He who hesitates is lost.

He considered himself rather ordinary looking. But there were probably few eligible men on the island or visiting it that would fit for her. I may have been a last resort, he thought. No problem. Eye of the beholder. Such mystery, what goes on in a woman's heart. Who can solve it? Who would want too? Certainly not me, Eric thought, lest he come out on the less desirable end of it.

It was nearing dusk on Christmas eve. Eric called Isabella and said that he wanted to bring her something. She had baked a Cornish hen and said that she would share it with him, an appetizer before Christmas dinner the next day.

Gathering up the bottles of wine and her gift, he left the house and made his way to a path among the sand dunes that would lead him to her home fifty yards away. His personal trail, he thought, winding its way and circumventing the dunes and chattering sea oats that seemed to speak to him, wishing a pleasant visit wherever it was that he was going.

"Good evening," Isabella said when he reached her home and knocked on the door. She ushered him inside. "Are you hungry?"

"I am. I brought you something. Put it under your tree and open it in the morning," he said, handing her the gift.

"Thank you so much," she said, taking the gift. "All I have for you is a good Christmas dinner."

"I couldn't ask for more." He set the bottles of wine on the dinette and removed his windbreaker.

Isabella served brown rice and a tossed salad with the Cornish hen. She carved the small bird then served it. Eric opened a bottle of wine and poured for both of them.

"Oyster Cove has a little Christmas Eve party every year. They have a band. I've never gone, didn't want to go alone. Would you care to go with me, Eric?"

"Sounds like fun," Eric said, picking up his glass of wine. "This is very good," he said, pointing his fork at the plate "You're an excellent cook."

"Thank you. My mother was a good cook. She taught me how to fix a lot of things. My father was not easy to please, so she became quite a culinary expert in ways to keep him from turning over the table if there was no turkey to throw across the room."

"Any more lumpy, mashed potatoes?" Eric asked, chuckling.

"No. It would have been the unforgivable sin."

"Wise woman." He wondered if her mother taught her anything else, like how to participate in things paranormal. As a forensic phycologist, he was sometimes called upon as an expert witness to give his opinion regarding motive in the commission of a crime. Once, he was asked his opinion on paranormal activity. He politely dismissed such notions. Now, he wasn't so sure. He hadn't *seen* the pirates that allegedly sailed into the Gulf and came ashore to her house. A young boy, however, claimed to have seen the ship sitting offshore. Isabella said the brothers were 10 and 8 years old. Both being under the age of 14, they wouldn't have been required to swear or affirm under oath. Their friendship with Isabella notwithstanding, he doubted that the boys would risk lying in a courtroom, especially with their parents presumably present. Then again, a child's imagination can be tricky ... seeing what they want to see.

With dinner finished, Isabella said that the band began playing at Oyster Cove around *7:30*. She suggested going a little early to get a good booth. She didn't like sitting at a table in the middle of the room. Eric suspected that he and his date would be persons of interest, so to speak, especially with her history of fighting off "pirates." She's probably used to being stared at, long before the pirate incidents, Eric figured. The world does love a beautiful face. He always thought that women are more observant than men, certainly in things of fashion. When women are seen wearing a new style of shoe, other women are all over it in a matter of days, it seems. Extremely competitive, women, more so than men in many ways. And they note the beauty of other women, perhaps not always out of envy. Just quietly marveling at such gifts and wondering what it would be like to look like her, with men—or women—all but throwing themselves at their feet. Not always what it's cracked up to be, though, being so beautiful. Eric recalled a remarkably pretty woman who worked at a McDonald's in Minneapolis. It was hard to tear one's eyes off her. Somewhere along the way of her young life, she began to realize how lovely she is. Fun for a while, being gawked at. But it got old. She didn't hold people's eyes for long—especially men's—when taking their order. She was particularly wary of older guys with their everlasting interest in "young stuff." She was happy to serve them burgers and fries, but that was all.

Folks had just begun to arrive when the two of them walked in the door. "Hi, Izzy," said a waitress passing by with a tray of drinks. They found a booth. Neither were hungry, or thirsty, for that matter, but figured they should at least order beer to be paying customers. And there was no cover charge for the band. When their drinks arrived, Isabella proposed a toast: "Here's to our friendship. May it blossom well." They clinked glasses and sampled the beer.

"By the way," Eric began, putting a napkin to his lips to sop the beer's foam, "the house I'm renting came up for sale, so I bought it."

"How wonderful!"

"The owners are moving from Topeka to L.A. and decided they wouldn't be wanting the house anymore."

"Well, then, I'm going to have you as a neighbor for longer than I might have thought," Isabella said, slowly turning her glass of beer on the tabletop.

"I took a year off from my duties with the adjunct

faculty at the university. I'll need to make a decision about that by this time next year."

"You're not sure you want to return?" Isabella said.

"I'm kind of burnt out on it."

"Does the loss of your wife have anything to do with it?" Isabella asked, having another drink of her beer.

"We weren't married. We both agreed that matrimony and a piece of paper doesn't guarantee anything. And, too, there weren't any children to ask where our wedding rings are."

"How long were you together before she was killed?" Isabella asked.

"10 years."

"Neither of my 2 marriages lasted anywhere close to that long."

"Where are they now, your exes?"

"Still in Spain, I guess. I got a letter from one of them a couple of years ago. He wanted to get back together. I said no. We had what we had. I've move on, I told him."

The band members were tuning their instruments. "Do you dance?" Isabella asked.

"Not all that well. I doubt that I could dance to Jingle Bells."

Isabella laughed then said, "I think the band is from South Georgia, so we'll probably have mostly country music."

"I could manage that, I think."

The band struck up a George Strait tune. "What do you think?" Isabella said.

"Let's go for it." The two of them made their way to the dance floor and joined 3 other couples. It was a down tempo song, *All My Exes Live in Texas,* and Eric put an arm around his partner's waist. As they swayed together, others joined them on the dance floor and began to form a line for line dancing. "I'm not sure I can do that," Eric said.

"It's easy," she said, pulling her partner into the line of dancers. "Just watch me."

It wasn't long before Eric got the hang of it. "You're very good," Isabella said.

"It's the old good teacher thing, you know," he said, keeping in step with his partner. He wondered what she would look like swirling with a castanet in each hand. He could be sitting at a table wearing a sombrero and doing tequila shots while her dark eyes met his. She seemed to like this gringo.

The room was filing up and most of their attention was on the lovely Spanish woman on the dancefloor. There was little question regarding who she was, Eric figured, for her alleged skirmish with pirates was known far and wide, though only a young boy claimed to have observed the ship sitting off the barrier island's coast the night pirates were said to have come ashore, on two occasions, no less, and during a full, April moon that was remarkably pink. This phenomenon was attested to by others, however, though only the oldest of the two brothers claimed to have seen the mysterious ship as it sailed by the light of such a moon. All hell broke loose when Isabella threw down and cleared leather with her shotguns—one after the other—resulting in a call to law enforcement. The rest is history, at least in terms of the court proceedings, which are anything but over, so long as her probation is in force.

What took many by complete surprise, however, was Judge David Henry's calling for a squad of Guardsmen to be present at Isabella's beach house in April, on a full moon to verify whether or not she was in fact being visited—even attacked by pirates, should they come again. Isabella wasn't without her fans, though most thought that she was probably paranoid schizophrenic, that is until the psychiatric evaluation came back clean as a proverbial hound's tooth. Well, Izzy is just different, most concluded. She keeps to herself most of the time. And she's harmless, unless you happen to be a pirate. I wouldn't advise walking the beach in front of her house and wearing a floppy hat with an Ostridge quill in it, a neighbor said. You may find yourself with a rear full of buckshot. You rile a Spanish woman and she would just as soon kill you as look at you. This assessment of Isabella was as far from the truth as one could get. But the Ostridge feather advice might be well taken, however.

That the judge ordering Guardsmen to be in place at her beach house in April when the moon would be full is something that Isabella hadn't told Eric. She figured that he was taking much if not all her story with a grain of salt and only being polite. He's a forensic phycologist and has probably heard it all, she figured. But he's lonely, still reeling with the tragic death of his partner, and he needs my company. She didn't mind, for she found him quite attractive in a rugged sort of way, even if he did have reddish blonde hair and a name sounding very Viking-like ... Eric Erickson, from Minnesota, and Norwegian ancestry. She might have steered clear of him, though, had he been sporting a beard. That would have been just a little too much.

After the Oyster Cove party, she would invite him back to her house for another glass of wine and tell him of the planned military presence at her house in April. His response would be interesting, she thought. Either she wouldn't hear from him again, or he would suspend judgement. Wait and see. She didn't want him to go. Getting him into bed might afford some insurance. A woman always needs a plan B in this world, she reminded herself. Bed, but not too soon. There was something classy about him. Men with class dislike sluts, her mother once told her when thinking that her daughter was getting an itch. If you must come on to them, do it slowly and with cunning. Make them think that they would be fools to resist you any longer. When the trap is sprung, enjoy, my dear.

In light of her father's disposition, Isabella wondered if her mother ever wished that she hadn't set such a trap, let alone spring it. But her father may have been a much different person as a younger man. The stress of the diamond business may have taken its toll on him over the years. And, too, familiarity does have a way of breeding contempt, sadly, when it might be the other way around. And it is the other way around when couples still hold hands after 50 years or more of being together.

Well, she wasn't going to set any traps for this man. She would allow their friendship to develop and mature ... her Lancôme La Vie Est Belle Eau de parfum was getting a little low, however. Perhaps she should order a fresh bottle....

Chapter 6

Christmas morning broke clear and warmer than what might be expected for the holiday, especially newcomers like Eric, born and raised in Minnesota. Not a problem he thought, stepping out onto the deck with a steaming cup of coffee in hand and wearing only his usual just out of bed attire: sweatpants and a T shirt. He thought of the poor souls in Minneapolis, those without garages, dashing to their cars to start them then dashing back into the house until the engine warmed enough to put out some heat. Many, though, used block heaters which they could plug in to keep the engine warm enough overnight to start in single digit temperatures above, or below zero. One woman in Maine said, "We don't eat up here in winter, we *stoke* ourselves." The same could be said for Minnesotans.

He and Isabella left the Oyster Cove party after an hour and a half. In addition to getting a little claustrophobic with the press of humanity in relatively small rooms, she said, Eric thought that she was growing increasingly annoyed with the attention she was getting. He agreed. Being her date, he too was the subject of a good many glances and stares.

One glass of beer each during the party is all they drank. Upon returning to her house, they poured wine and sat near the Christmas Tree. One of the bubble lights quit bubbling. She replaced it with a spare. She told Eric of the judge's decision to order a squad of Guardsmen to be at her house in April, when the moon is full, to witness the approach of the alleged pirate ship, if in fact that did occur. "What if there is cloud cover, or the moon isn't pink?" Eric asked.

"I don't know," Isabella said. At least he hadn't thrown up his hands and walked out, she thought. She was getting a sense that he believed her story.

"You know, of course, that we're talking paranormal here, don't you?" he said.

"Certainly. What other explanation could there be?"

"None that I'm aware of." He sampled his wine then said, "As a forensic phycologist I've been called as an expert witness at times, mostly to give my professional opinion on matters of criminal action and motive, evidence, those kinds of things."

"Do you think I'm a criminal?" Isabella asked.

"No. The only law that you've broken is discharging your shotguns on the island, albeit quite a bombardment, if I may put it that way," Eric said, chuckling. "No judge in this country would convict a person for legitimately defending themselves. Some, if not most states have a Stand Your Ground law."

"I was standing my ground alright," Isabella said. "I

had enough ammo to hold off an army. You should have seen the empty shotgun shells on my deck."

Eric paused for long moments, sampled his wine, then said, "Has anything ever happened like this before, you know, uninvited visitors, if I may put it that way?"

Isabella shifted her position on the chair and crossed her legs. Eric noted the body language. She had something to say that he thought was going to prove quite interesting.

"When I was six years old, my father flew into one of his tantrums, yelling, throwing things. My brother hadn't been born yet. I ran into my room and pushed the toybox against the door. It wouldn't have held my father back, of course, but I was just a child. As I told you once before, he never laid a hand on any of us. But his anger was so scary, we always wondered if he might."

This is headed someplace really weird, Eric thought. He wasn't sure how he would respond to it.

"He was the scariest I ever saw him," Isabella continued. "I wanted to leave the house and run away into the woods where he couldn't find me. But I was only six. Where would I go without my mother? So, I just sat on my bed, stared at the door, and prayed."

"And what was your prayer?" Eric asked.

"That someone would come to make me feel better and not so scared." She paused for long moments again. Then, "I don't know if I should tell you this. You will *really* think I'm nuts."

"Try me."

"Neither the door nor the toybox moved. But standing before me was Robin Hood, Little John, and Friar Tuck."

Eric felt the hair on his forearms and back of his neck rise. He felt a surge of regret at ever having gotten involved with this woman.

Isabella's eyes teared and she looked at Eric almost pleadingly, as though she feared he might simply get up and leave. He didn't. "Did they say anything?" he asked, feeling his pulse begin to quicken. He was playing into her mentally ill hands and he felt utterly helpless.

"Yes. 'Don't be afraid, my dear. We heard your call,' Robin Hood said. Little John—he was huge—nodded and smiled. Friar Tuck waved his staff and looked at the door, like he might use it if my father came barging in."

One of three things is going on with this woman, Eric thought, retrieving himself from near hysteria just moments ago. She may have paranormal powers to summon spirits of the dead; simply create, then call her creation to come forth; or, she is deeply delusional and a pathological liar, whom he deeply disliked. They never seemed to give a thought to how insulting their lying is to people who are listening to it, as though they are too stupid to know the difference. His belief system resisted what she was saying. But she was chipping away at it and the shell was beginning to crack.

"I heard our front door slam when my father left the house," she continued, "and all was quiet. 'Farewell, sweet Isabella,' Robin Hood said. Then they were gone."

"Did you tell your mother what you saw?"

"Yes."

"What did she say?"

"Nothing. She just stared at me. Then she took me into her arms."

Isabella tasted her wine then said, "So, this is probably the last straw for you, right? First it was the pirates, now the dudes from Sherwood Forest."

"I never bail out just because I don't understand something. Once, when I was called upon to give my opinion regarding an individual's motive for burning his own house—fortunately there were no injuries—I found myself in a quandary. The fellow was a brilliant historian, quiet wealthy, and obviously in no need of trying to collect insurance money."

"Why did he burn his house?" Isabella asked.

"He said a poltergeist haunted him day and night, claiming that he, the owner had no right to the house, and that the house always belonged to the poltergeist."

Isabella laughed and sipped her wine.

"So, the owner said, I'll just *burn* the house. He read somewhere that poltergeists have a great fear of fire. Anyway, some family members were trying to get him declared incompetent—"

"To get his money, probably," Isabella said, breaking in.

"Exactly. That was my private opinion, though I didn't voice it in court."

"So, what happened?"

"A psychiatric evaluation was ordered, of course. And like yours, it came back clean. The case was dropped. The fellow built another home, I heard later, and no more visits from poltergeists."

"Did you give an opinion?"

"No. I simply told the judge that I couldn't comment."

"Ah, a happy ending," Isabella said.

"Yes. By the way, did you ever see Robin Hood, Little John, and Friar Tuck again?"

"No."

"Any other visitors?" Eric asked.

"Yes. But I'll tell you about it at another time."

They parted with a Christmas Eve kiss, and one that lingered, not a perfunctory peck. He was due for dinner around two o'clock the next day. He asked if he could come and help with the preparations, but she had everything well in hand. She would put the turkey on at daybreak.

When taking a leave of absence from the university as well as his private practice, his plan was to write a book regarding the criminal mind and its impact on society. Not a particularly novel thesis. Criminal minds are a boil on the butt of any society. What could his book add to that? Another boil? He grew bone-tired of floundering toward even a first paragraph. Now, after meeting Isabella Cabrera and hearing her remarkable stories, his own ship was no longer sitting dead in the water. She sent his sails aloft and he was coming about 360 degrees and heading in an entirely different direction. He thought of an adage in literature: Write what you know. A very broad statement, of course. For few if any writers know so much that they have no need to look something up in the form of research. Eric considered that he might be wading into waters too deep for him, not to mention wildly esoteric. And he might just as well kiss his position at the university goodbye should his new "academic" interest become known. A bastion of intellectual freedom, however, though few would consider paranormal research in the realm of things intellectual.

Admittedly, he was no astrophysicist or cosmologist. But he read them rather widely, like a teenager pouring over graphic novels. He found the theory of *Many Worlds* most intriguing. It was first introduced by the physicist Hugh Everett in 1957. Contrary to the rigidly deterministic Copenhagen interpretation, it asserts that the universal wavefunction is objectively real and does not collapse and implies that all possible outcomes of quantum measurements are physically realized in some "world" or universe.

It's believed that Albert Einstein developed his theory of relativity out of pure thought while working as a 26-year-old patent clerk. He put the "thoughts" into a paper that stunned and revolutionized science. Eric wondered, while donning a windbreaker for a walk along the beach, what Einstein would think of the possibility of a gifted mind today having the ability to create, or simply snatch an image from the hide of a parallel universe and bring it forth into our classical world, as scientist call it. After all, string theory and many worlds asserts that our universe is just one of many parallel universes sitting as close to each other as slices of bread in a loaf. It seems inconceivable to some scientist that those other universes would be without life, if not as we know it.

Such exciting things lie in the future for cosmology and our quest for how life got started on this planet, Eric mused, stopping for a moment and looking out to sea. The wheels of research and discovery can turn painfully slow. He sometimes wished he was just being born so that he might have a better chance of being around for the great awakenings. But there have plenty already, and they never really end. It's like boxes of different sizes stacked into each other, one scientist said. You open one box, and there's another one inside, then another.... Just relish the wonders in your *own* lifetime, Eric concluded. Let the children of future generations marvel at what's discovered in theirs.

The temperature was seasonable for north Florida this 25th day of December, mid-fifties, Eric figured, though he hadn't turned on the news to catch the weather. There was enough breeze, however, to warrant a sweater. Having plenty of time to kill before dinner at Isabella's, he thought that he would have a nice long walk. His house was pretty much situated midway on this barrier island, 28 miles long. A couple of miles or so would do, though, then he would turn around and head back to the house.

After Isabella told him of her encounter with Robin Hood, Little John, and Friar Tuck, he asked her if she ever saw them again. She said no. He thought it curious that the alleged pirates ... *alleged*—she wouldn't care for that term—visited her on two occasions, albeit a year apart. Unlike the trio from Sherwood Forest, the pirates were quite menacing, so much so that she opened fire with her collection of shotguns.

Somewhere in the darker corridors of his mind he recalled the words of the horror writer, H.P. Lovecraft who wrote during the late 1800s and early 1900s: "Do not call up that which you cannot put down." Isabella, in her freewheeling gift—if that is the case, and one may call it that—might have crossed a paranormal line somewhere. The pirates wouldn't go away. Whether or not they would return for a third visit in April was the great question of the hour. The outcome would, in fact, be the difference between jail or freedom, though Eric thought that she would spend no more than a night or so behind bars, should it come to that. A warning shot across her pretty bow.

After having walked for nearly a mile, Eric thought he saw a figure coming toward him. The individual was a hundred yards off, he guessed. As the person drew nearer, he could see that it was a man. He was dressed in black pants and coat and white shirt with a high collar around which was a tie, of sorts. The fellow walked with his back especially straight. His feet had a curious motion of not seeming to bend at the arch. His dark hair was receded nearly halfway back along the top of his head. It was thick, even curly on the sides. He wore a pointed, rather unkempt beard on his chin. Drawing ever closer, Eric thought the man had a striking resemblance to Charles Dickens. "Hello," the man said, coming to a stop. His accent was British.

"Good morning," Eric said.

"Such a lovely Christmas morning," the man said.

"It certainly is," Eric returned.

"A little snow, however, would be nice on this Christmas Day."

"Yes. But this is Florida ... you certainly favor Charles Dickens," Eric added, chuckling.

The man laughed then said, "Well, I suppose that's

because I am indeed Charles Dickens. And I'm off to wish a lovely woman Merry Christmas."

"Who might that be, Mr. Dickens?" Eric asked.

"The beautiful Isabella. She wished me a Merry Christmas just moments ago. So, I must be on my way to her house to wish her the same. Good day, sir, and a Very Merry Christmas to you."

"And a very Merry Christmas to you as well," Eric said.

This encounter was a new wrinkle, if in fact he hadn't been hallucinating. He wasn't a stranger to weird thoughts, like wondering if the waitress at Oyster Cove would somehow bring him a whole blackened Grouper on a wagon from the kitchen. This wasn't April; there was no moon to be seen, certainly not a pink one; and he rather doubted that Isabella was sitting on her deck with a Pink Moscato Sangria in hand. She would be much too busy with dinner preparations.

He was thinking now that the pirates were simply riding on the coattails of a pink moon that was no creation of theirs. Rather, it was a cosmic signal, a cue, if you will, that Isabella Cabrera was chosen to begin making known the unknown. Perhaps the gods had grown intolerably bored, Eric mused. They auditioned her when she was six years old, sending Robin Hood, Little John, and Friar Tuck to her room. She turned out to be just the cast member they were looking for. Yes, their leading lady, one could say. But not yet. We must let her mature, reach the prime of her life and beauty. Then the curtain will rise, and the show begin.

So, what's my role in this? Eric wondered while

watching Mr. Charles Dickens striding west along the beach in his peculiar manner of walking. Supporting cast member? Called to this place to morally support a woman who is ransacking our thinking about what can and cannot occur? If so, it struck him as no coincidence that the gods—for lack of a better term or description—chose a breathtakingly beautiful woman to carry out the task: She can hold anybody's attention for a desired length of time simply by the force of her appearance. How dare you withhold your undivided attention? say the gods. How dare you question the truthfulness of one so lovely? How dare you subject her to the humiliating experience of sitting before a shrink? She is saner than all of them put together.

Suspending his walk, Eric turned and began making his way back home. He was wondering if there might be additional guests for Christmas dinner at Isabella's house. Tiny Tim, perhaps, or Jacob Marley—without the chains. I'd like to have a few words with Mr. Ebenezer Scrooge, Eric thought. The stingy bastard. He didn't deserve a quality employee like Bob Cratchit. Well, all's well that ends well, according to *A Christmas Carol,* Eric thought.

Given that little sashay into Isabella's world, he wondered if he himself might benefit from a psychiatric evaluation, you know, to find out where I stand, kind of like getting a credit score from one's bank. Don't get scared now, man, he thought. You willingly walked into this overflowing river, the source of which isn't known, certainly not by you. You've got two choices: Swim or be swept downriver to who knows where. You could run, but you can't hide, not from this woman and what she is revealing to you. You wouldn't make it halfway across the bridge to the mainland before you turned around and came back. This is long haul stuff, dude. Get used to it. You're caught in a cosmic nexus, and no one has ever been able to eject themselves from one. If the gods show you a way out, it won't be anytime soon. You may believe that, Dr. Erickson.

Chapter 7

After shaving and having a shower, Eric dressed in navy blue Dockers and a white sweater. It was a few minutes before two o'clock when dinner would be ready at Isabella's. Exiting the house and descending deck stairs to the beach, he decided that he wouldn't bring up his encounter with Mr. Charles Dickens, that is, of course, if the venerable storyteller wasn't present.

Reaching Isabella's house, Eric paused at the stairs leading to the home's deck. Through the windows he could see only her moving about. If Dickens was there, he might be sitting, Eric thought, as he began mounting the stairs. Upon the deck, he strode to the sliding glass door and peered inside. Isabella saw him. She came and opened for him. "Merry Christmas," she said, smiling and ushering him inside.

"And a Merry Christmas to you as well," Eric said, casting about the room quickly.

"Looking for someone?" she asked with a smile playing at the corners of her mouth.

"Uh, no, I just never tire of how comfortable your home looks."

The scent of baking meat, bread, and pies having been prepared was in the air. A dish of candied sweet potatoes sat on a counter along with a pecan, pumpkin pie, and mound of steaming mashed potatoes. The stove's oven door was open where a turkey and dinner rolls were being kept warm. A bottle of Chardonnay sat nearby. The dinette was spread with a festive cloth for the occasion and plates and silverware were set. A red candle burned in the center of the table.

"I've looked forward to having Christmas dinner with someone besides myself. Last year I celebrated with a grilled cheese sandwich," Isabella said.

Eric laughed. "You've been busy" he said, casting about at the food. "It looks like we'll have considerably more than grilled cheese. Thank you for inviting me." He wondered if Dickens got a takeout order, a little something for his trip back to London.

"Please honor me by carving the turkey, Eric," Isabella said, finding an appropriate knife for the job.

"My pleasure." Eric took the knife and carved a half dozen slices of breast, as well as dark meat from the drumsticks.

"Let's do buffet style," Isabella said, opening the bottle of wine and setting it on the table. The two of them fetched their plates and began to fill them. Images of Christmas dinner in Minneapolis when he was a young man ran through his mind like Wallstreet ticker tape. The aromas and scents in this room were much the same. There were no steamed windows in the kitchen, however, as there would be in Minnesota on such a day.

Seated, Isabella poured wine and proposed a toast: "Here's to Tiny Tim. God bless us, every one!"

Eric drew a deep breath and released it slowly as wine glasses clinked together. "Yes. God bless us, every one!"

As dinner progressed, conversation was light. Isabella asked what Christmas was like in Minnesota.

"Snow, usually, and cold."

"Sleigh rides?"

"I'm sure, in the countryside. Lots of things going on at Mall of America, of course. They go all out. What about Spain?"

"It snows in some places, but hardly ever in Madrid. It gets cold, though, especially at night. Plaza Mayor has the famous Christmas market, Mercado de Navidad, where you can buy beautiful handmade gifts. There are tons of lights and festivals. By the way, I haven't opened the gift you gave me."

"Why not now?" Eric said.

Isabella fetched the gift from beneath the Christmas tree and took her seat at the table. She unwrapped it. "Oh, Eric, I love it!" She turned the key that started the music and set the tree to turning slowly. "Thank you so much."

"You're welcome. I hoped you would like it."

She set the gift on the table next to the candle.

"Do you miss Spain?" Eric asked, raising his wine glass to his lips.

"A little, especially at this time of year."

"Have you gone back?"

"Once, three years ago, during summer, to visit my brother. The economy was really bad then, kind of depressing. My brother has been careful with his inheritance, so he's okay."

Eric wondered if her brother could call the likes Charles Dickens to come forth at will. "Does your brother know about the visitors?" Eric asked, slicing off a piece of turkey breast.

"No. He's kind of a stick in the mud. He would think I'm crazy. Well, a lot of people do, including me, at times." She laughed and picked up her wine glass.

"The judge may not be one of them," Eric said. "Ordering Guardsmen to be here in April when the moon is full sounds like he might be on your side."

"Yes. But if the ship doesn't show up, he will be really pissed!"

Eric sampled the candied sweet potatoes and wondered what the judge would do.

"After the pirates came the first time, and I did all that shooting, and nobody could find any evidence that they had been here, I started thinking that maybe I am crazy and imagined it all. It's scary when you think that your mind may be going. I remember a woman in Madrid, a neighbor who woke up one morning in a psychiatric ward. She had no clue about what happened to get her there. She remembered nothing. It was the scariest thing she had ever known, she said."

"What happen?"

"She just lost it one night and tore up her house. When she woke up in the hospital the next morning, she was in her right mind, but terribly embarrassed."

"I can well imagine."

"As I told you, the psychiatric evaluation the judge ordered came back fine. But I wasn't so sure. I hadn't told the doctor about seeing Robin Hood, Little John, and Friar Tuck when I was six years old. So, I wanted a second opinion, you know, on my own. I mean, if we're crazy, we would want to know, right?"

"Best to know, especially if there's any treatment available."

Isabella rose and cut the pies and asked Eric which her preferred. "Pecan," he said.

Returning to the table with pie for each of them, she resumed where she left off: "So, I made an appointment with a shrink in Miami and took a bus."

"How did it go?"

"I talked for a while and I told him about the guys from Sherwood Forest. I don't know if he was listening to me because he kept looking sideways and down at a pimple on his nose."

Eric laughed and put his fork to the pecan pie.

"Anyway, when I ran out of things to tell him, he said, "Well, Ms. Cabrera, I'll put you on some medication and see how you do. I was so disappointed! This guy isn't Sigmund Freud or Carl Jung, I thought. That's when they showed up."

"Who?"

"Freud and Jung. They were suddenly just *there.* Freud looked at me and smiled. Jung clucked his tongue and shook his head but said nothing.

"What did your doctor say?"

"He threw his papers into his briefcase and ran from

the room."

Eric laughed and said, "Did you get a bill from him?"

"No. I wouldn't have paid it if I had."

"I wouldn't have blamed you," Eric said.

"So, now you must think that I'm really wacked," Isabella said, sampling her own pie.

"If you're wacked, so am I."

"What do you mean?"

"I met Charles Dickens on the beach this morning before coming here."

Chapter 8

The day after Christmas Eric got a call from the previous owners of the beach house. The realtor handled all the paperwork and the deal was complete. The owners left nothing behind of consequence, no mementos, photos and the like, and furnishings were sparse. They didn't care to come for anything, dishes, furniture, etc. What few items of clothing in the closets could be donated or whatever. They thanked Eric and wished him well. Enjoy, they said. If you've not met your neighbor yet, Ms. Isabella Cabrera, you'll find her quite charming. She has an interesting collection of custom-made shotguns. Though our family has never been on the Island in April, we've heard that she got into some sort of trouble with them one night, something about a full moon that was rather pink. Eric said that he heard something about that. He didn't enlarge on the subject, however.

Though his leave of absence included adjunct duties at the university as well as any calls for his expert opinion in court cases, he did have one appointment that he would keep. It was with the International Association of Forensic Phycologists meeting in Davos, Switzerland at the beginning of the New Year. He was to give the keynote address. His speech was prepared. It had been for a while with its abundance of compulsive tweaks. Now, it lay in pieces, in the trash—all of it. He was preparing a new one. And he thought that he would like a traveling companion. Isabella had seen little or no snow in her life. She might enjoy Switzerland. Hit the ski slopes, maybe. He assumed that her passport was still valid. His airfare and expenses were being picked up by the Association. Though he figured that Isabella could easily afford her own, he would offer to pay her way in exchange for her company. The Association met bi-annually, and he attended all of them, not out of any great interest in the programs, for the subject matter rarely differed from one meeting to the next. And most of the speakers could put an audience to sleep faster than a bad movie.

Eric knew that his radically revised speech, except for the usual, perfunctory remarks at its beginning, wouldn't sit well with most of his colleagues. So be it. It was high time they heard something other than their own glorious achievements of professional opinions about criminal actions and what motivates them. Greater men than himself knew such scorn from one quarter or another. Alfred Nobel fought for years in trying to get nitroglycerin licensed, battling fear and doubt regarding the stability of the substances, under any conditions; Charles Darwin delayed risking being ridiculed for his transmutation of species theory which, in the end, revolutionized the theory of evolution; and in the 1800s, when 1 in 4 women were dying after child birth, Ignaz Semmelweis met skepticism regarding his call for doctors to wash their hands before examinations or surgery. That sort of reluctance and ignorance is hard to imagine in our time, Eric thought. Some think that George Washington was pretty much bled to death by his doctors, supposing to be releasing impurities—if not a few evil spirits—from the body of our first president.

Forensic phycology is, after all, concerned with legal questions, motives, and ethics regarding, in large part, the commission of crimes, Eric reminded himself while mapping out the new speech in his mind before beginning its writing. Is it a crime, for example, to shoot ghosts—shoot *at* them, perhaps one should say, when in violation of a law or ordinance? Disturbing the peace? Whose peace, ghosts' or the living? Does a firearms prohibition supersede the need to defend oneself, even if the danger is only perceived? I should think not, Eric mused. Esoteric stuff, of course, not likely to be widely embraced—if at all—by the audience he will be addressing. Having his lovely "witness" present, even on stage with him, might soften—if not crack, their empirical shell, that is if they can properly divide their attention from her to speaker. A man could drown in those dark pools she has for eyes. He wondered what suggestion Mr. Darwin would have for how—or, why natural selection came up with those. Perhaps to see how many men she could send floundering toward shores where there are none. How cruel. Survival of the fittest. Indeed.

Those who properly understand the theory tell us that natural selection—the mechanism that drives evolution, is always trying to kill us with something, Eric continued, in his philosophizing. When one virus or disease is conquered, another version takes its place. Evolution cares about one thing and one thing only: "Improvement" of species, no matter how long it takes or what the cost in lives, human or otherwise. Having been raised as a Lutheran, something the Apostle Paul said in his letter to the Romans came to mind: "God is no respecter of persons." The same could certainly be said of evolution, Eric considered. Life is a crap shoot, from our limited viewpoint. Luck of the draw. Except for the grace of God, there go I? Unadulterated, ignorant and arrogant BS. Leave God out of it. Evolution is the culprit, if there must be one. But who or what set evolution in motion? Now there's a question and a half!

But what should I hope to accomplish by delivering such a speech? Eric thought. The first thing to consider in writing any speech—or, sermon, for that matter, is to understand the nature or mindset of the audience, which, in this case, he understood all too well. And he was going to attempt to reshape that mindset.

He better put on a pot of coffee—think drink, and apply his best analytical skills, such as they are. It's got to be more than 20 or 25 minutes of ranting and haranguing unbelievers. After all, he himself is but a recent convert. A seed. Yes, that's it, plant a seed. How shall I water it? There's the crux. It would help if there were some precedent for these appearances. He knew of no credible ones which would stand up in the light of day. Some say that the movie *Exorcists* was based on true incidents that occurred in St. Louis, Missouri. Well, I'm no paranormal investigator, Eric thought, so I must suspend judgement. And I haven't witnessed any of the phenomena Isabella allegedly produced.

There I go again with the *alleged* thing, he thought while pouring himself a cup of coffee. Get off the fence, man! Show the woman some respect! The court ordered her to undergo psychiatric evaluation. The bar was set brutally high and she cleared it with ease. She would make an Olympic high jumper proud.

The truth is I'll be dealing with mere hearsay, Eric thought, returning to the *dimension* in which he is living. That crowd won't buy it. They'll need something tangible, like Isabella bringing Isaac Newton onto the stage. Eric threw his head back and laughed. Wow! What a scene. Let's see, who else? Galileo Galilei. Einstein—Jesus! Whoa. Now there's a visitor. He could bring Mary Magdalene with him. Be careful with this one, lest you enrage the myth addicts and be labeled a blasphemer. It wouldn't be the Second Coming that evangelicals and their ilk are looking for. Then again, he might have some wisdom for our troubled planet, like how to slow if not stop global warming that threatens to send us all to hell without descending one step; and gun violence with the stench of sulphur drifting from one school, place of worship, and neighborhood to the next. If I were to guess, Eric thought, the carpenter from Nazareth would have two words: Greed for the former; hate for the latter.

First things first. Invite Isabella along for the trip to Davos and the snowy mountains of Switzerland. I think she will accept, Eric thought, testing his coffee. If there's anything women love more than rearranging furniture and coloring their hair, it's travel. Take her someplace where she's never been, and you may have an inside track to her affections.

Eric wondered if Isabella was on supervised probation, if so, that would be a problem with her leaving the country. But her case wasn't a felony—yet, and she hadn't spoken of a bond being required after she spent a night in jail. She was released on her own recognizance. At any rate, when he invited her to accompany him, he would inquire into the status of her probation, lest he be accused of escorting her out of the country which undoubtedly wouldn't fly with the judge.

He was to be in Davos on Friday, January 10. The meeting was to begin at *10:00 a.m.* His keynote address would kick things off. He had traveled out of the country on other occasions; Switzerland would be a first, however. A problem now, though, is that he planned to stay on St. George island through New Year's then return to Minneapolis and fly out of there to Zurich, then overland to Davos. He brought no proper clothes for a flight out of Florida. And his ticket would be waiting for him at Minneapolis-Saint Paul International. Should Isabella accept his invitation to accompany him, he wondered if she would mind flying to Minneapolis first so that he could gather suitable clothes for the trip. The meeting wasn't black tie and tails, but flip flops and sweats would be a little much, especially in Switzerland in January. Another one of these crazy Americans.

Phycologists have a reputation of being a little off center—some of them—if not outright screwy, suspected of entering the field in hopes of curing themselves:

"Physician, heal thyself." Eric didn't want to become a person of interest in that way. There's *something* wrong with all of us, he thought. But keep your foibles under wraps as much as possible.

After Christmas dinner, they talked of what they might do for New Year's Eve. Isabella said Oyster Cove would host a party, but she didn't care for loud, shoulder to shoulder gatherings and spewing champagne. She wondered if Eric would want to join her at her home for a quiet evening for bringing in the New Year. He would like that, he said, and they could drive into Apalachicola for a bottle of champagne. She had some music she could put on, an excellent string quartet. And she didn't dare discharge one of her shotguns at midnight. Let others bring in the New Year with a bang, hopefully far enough from her house so as not to suggest that it might be one of her guns, she said, laughing. Eric agreed. He figured that a few neighbors would have at least one ear turned toward her house when the clock struck twelve. And she obviously preferred the full monte, giving each of her fine guns a part in rapid succession. Though a shotgun's range is relatively short, neighbors instinctively tended to duck their heads, if not get on the floor or under a table, when their diminutive neighbor started pulling triggers. "Get down! Izzy's got her guns out!"

On the morning of New Year's Eve, Eric and Isabella drove into Apalachicola for a breakfast of bagels and coffee. Visiting the Piggly Wiggly grocery store, she put what was needed for tacos into her shopping cart, and a moderately priced bottle of champagne.

There was full sun this New Year's Eve and the temperature was forecast to reach the lower 60s. Returning to the island, they deposited groceries and champagne at her house then decided upon a walk along the beach. The perfect time, Eric thought, to invite her to accompany him to Davos: "I've been asked to give a keynote address to the International Association of Forensic Phycologists in Davos, Switzerland."

"Wow!" Isabella said, turning to him and smiling. "When?"

"Just after New Year's, January 10th, actually."

"Less than two weeks," Isabella said.

"Yes, and I'd like for you to go with me."

Isabella stopped and turned to him. "I'd *love* to go."

"The Association is paying my airfare and expenses. I want to pay for yours."

"That won't be necessary," Isabella said as they resumed their leisurely walk. "I haven't been anywhere since visiting my brother in Spain three years ago. And I've got more money than God," she added, chuckling.

"The only hitch is that we need to fly to Minneapolis so that I can get some proper clothes. Then we'll fly out of Minneapolis-Saint Paul International. We'll land in Zurich, then take overland transportation to Davos."

"I've never been to Minnesota—well, Switzerland either, for that matter."

"You'll need warm clothes."

"Would we have time to do some shopping? I'd love to see the Mall of America."

"I don't see why not. The first thing we need to do, though, is tickets for Minneapolis for the two of us, and try to get you on the same plane with me to Zurich. My ticket will be waiting at the airport."

"God, this is so exciting!"

"Is your passport good to go?"

"I'll need to get it renewed for traveling to Switzerland."

"We can do that when we get to Minneapolis. In the meantime, we'll need to get on my computer and make arrangements. I think we should fly into Minneapolis the day after New Year's. We can hang out at my house until it's time to catch our plane to Zurich. By the way, are you on supervised probation?"

"No. I just need to make sure that I'm here for the full moon in April. I don't think the judge much cares where I go, so long as I leave my guns behind," Isabella said. She laughed and took Eric's arm.

"I wonder what the odds are for another pink moon," Eric said.

"Let's ask the bookies in Las Vegas. It could be a record, you know, three in a row. I can't wait to see the look on the Guardsman's faces if the ship comes into view. It's an amazing sight, Eric, seeing those sails set against the full moon, and pink as a Valentine."

Eric woke to the warmth of Isabella's body snuggled next to him. The faint sent of her perfume was a lingering reminder of their first night of love making. Empty champagne glasses sat on a nightstand. Her lavender panties and bra were in a nearby chair. The bra dangled from the back of the chair, panties on an armrest, as though the two items were hastily removed and slung. While in each other's arms, they heard fireworks going off at midnight. The two lovers remained in bed with fireworks of their own. A good thing, the noise outside, Eric thought, for when Isabella arched her back and came off the bed in a proverbial screaming orgasm, she might have been heard as far away as Oyster Cove where revelers were bringing in the New Year.

Love making, for the first time, changes the chemistry of a relationship. Not always for the better, one might add. But if it was good, the lovers meet each other's eyes in a pleasantly different way the next morning. Nothing could be more intimate than what they shared: Naked feasting upon their partner's body and soul; a mutual giving up of what arguably lies as close to the core of one's being as any act known to human beings; to violate might easily be considered a kind of crime against humanity, deserving a Nuremberg of its own.

The flight out of Pensacola for Minneapolis left on time. Eric was able to get Isabella successfully booked on his plane to Zurich, even in a seat next to him, with a little online persuading. I'll see what I can do, Dr. Erickson, the agent said. I'll get back to you. And she did with good news. Eric virtually never added Dr. to a conversation, though it did appear on his credit cards. It seemed to have gotten him a little needed edge on this occasion. Perhaps the agent thought the good doctor might me escorting a patient overseas for specialized treatment, Eric mused. It was he who had gotten *specialized* treatment.

John Steinbeck once said that making love to a woman purifies a man. Exactly what Steinbeck meant by that, Eric wasn't sure. Wholeness, perhaps. He did know, however, that he was feeling ever so well as he glanced at Isabella sitting beside him while their plane flew over the nation's heartland with its sights set on the snowy landscape of Minnesota and its 10,000 lakes.

"I can see the Mississippi and Missouri Rivers," Isabella said from her seat by a window as the plane flew over the east central part of the Show-Me State.

Eric leaned into her and peered out the window. He nodded and smiled. "Muddy Mississippi. The Missouri is only 33 miles shorter," Eric said. "Some say it gets the muddiest when the Missouri flows into it."

Passing over the confluence where the two great rivers joined for their journey to the Gulf, Isabella said, "I can see the Gateway Arch!"

The plane lowered its altitude some, making for a better view of the rivers, though not necessarily for that purpose. "That's Hannibal, over there," Eric said. Isabella rested back in her seat. She drew a deep breath and released it slowly.

Settling back into his own seat, Eric noticed a man coming from the rear of the plane, having used the restroom, he figured. A striking resemblance to Mark Twain, Eric thought. His eyebrows were grey and bushy. A walrus mustache and rather wild head of hair were also grey. He was dressed in white. Coming abreast of Eric and Isabella's seats, the man stopped and said, "Good afternoon, Ms. Isabella." His voice was rather high-pitched and broken.

Isabella nodded and said just above her breath, so as not to be heard by other passengers, "And a good afternoon to you, Mr. Clemens." The man then proceeded along the aisle. Eric shot a look at Isabella who returned her attention to the plane's window. She reached and lay her left hand on his. No one else seemed to have noticed the fellow.

Upon deboarding their flight at Minneapolis-Saint Paul International, Eric and his traveling companion collected their sparse baggage then strode to where a car would be leased for a few days ahead of their departure for Zurich. In addition to getting to his home, Eric wanted to show Isabella around the twin cities. And, too, she wanted to see Mall of America and do some shopping for appropriate clothes for visiting Switzerland.

It was a twenty-minute drive to Eric's house. On the way, they stopped off at a library branch and got Isabella's passport updated. The city was blanketed in several inches of snow. The streets were clear, however; this town knows how to deal with great amounts of snow. "Does it do this every year?" Isabella asked while peering out the car's window.

"Pretty much," Eric said. "We can get a January thaw sometimes, but it's short lived. We're right back in the freezer. The winters are long, here. It's a far cry from the shores of the Mediterranean, or St. George Island, for that matter."

"I don't think I would like that," Isabella said.

"Many of our older folk don't either, so they head south until spring."

"Snowbirds."

"Right. I guess I was one of them this year, sort of, since north Florida is where I landed. Most of the others will head farther south, Miami, maybe, Corpus Christi, Brownsville, Texas, or west to Phoenix and the desert."

"I'm glad you landed where you did," Isabella said, putting a hand on Eric's arm.

"The best mistake I ever made. I think we better stop at a grocery store for a few things," he added. "I left the fridge all but bare."

"This is where I usually shop, closest to home," Eric said, pulling into the parking lot of a Lunds & Byerlys. Inside the store, he put eggs and bacon in his cart, bread, half gallon of milk, and a couple of frozen pizzas. "Let's get some things from the deli so that we don't have to do a lot of cooking and dishwashing," he said.

Arriving at his home, Eric pulled into the driveway. "Very nice," Isabella said. The house was two-storied brick with white shutters. Plentiful windows were paned. A fireplace chimney rose above cedar shakes. The home sat on a large lot with a half dozen mature maple trees, now skeletal, divided between the front and back yard. Eric got out of the car and strode to the garage door. He punched in a code that ran the garage door up. He returned to the car and pulled inside the garage beside a BMW. Unloading groceries and their baggage, he ushered his guest into the house. "So civilized," Isabella said, casting about at the interior.

"It's comfortable," Eric said, passing through café doors to the kitchen and setting groceries on a counter. Most of the furniture was French Provincial. Finely patterned and colorful area rugs lay upon the living and dining room hardwood floors. Carpeted staircase with white railing led to a second floor. The walls were papered in off white with floral trim near the ceiling and above floor molding. A few pictures of northern landscapes and abstract paintings hung on the walls.

A photo of Sara sat on a writing desk. "She's lovely," Isabella said, noting the photo and guessing who it was.

"Yes. A terrible tragedy. She left us much too soon."

After a lunch of pizza, Eric suggested that they visit Mall of America where Isabella wanted to do some shopping for their trip. She was truly stunned by the size of the mall. "I've never seen anything like this!" The mall was crowded, as usual, and after strolling about for an hour and visiting one shop or another where she purchased a couple of sweaters, muk luks boots, and a parka, she said that she was ready to leave. Eric suggested another stop: The Walker Art Center, one of the most visited modern and contemporary art museums in the United States. Their guide noted that the museum hosted the first exhibits by Joseph Cornell, Frank Gehry, Julie Mehretu, O'Keeffe, and Warhol.

"Minneapolis has more independent bookstores than fleas on a dog's back," Eric said as they left the museum. "Wild Rumpus over on 43rd Street is my favorite. We might want something to read on the plane. It's a 10-hour flight to Zurich, then about 2 more overland to Davos.

"I'm so looking forward to it," Isabella said.

Chapter 9

Skies were clear over Zurich when the 787 landed. The two Americans collected their bags. A man was standing near with a sign that read, Dr. Eric Erickson. "I'm your man," Eric said, approaching the fellow.

The man looked at a notepad in his hand then said, "Ms. Isabella Cabrera, I presume." He spoke in English with a heavy German accent.

"Yes."

"Welcome to Switzerland and Zurich."

"Thank you, sir," Isabella said.

The driver had a baggage cart with him, and he loaded Eric and Isabella's baggage. "I have refreshments awaiting you," he said as they made their way from the terminal. The temperature was in the 40s, but full sun was pleasant. Eric expected to see a van waiting. Rather it was a limousine.

"Wow, Dr. Erickson," Isabella said softly, glancing at her traveling companion.

"I wasn't expecting this," he said as the two of them

entered the limos' plush interior. After the Association hears my keynote address, he thought, we'll probably have to *hitchhike* back here to catch our flight for home.

He told Isabella of his request for her to be seated with him on the platform. She had no problem with it, better than being jammed in with the crowd, given her penchant for discomfort in large crowds. But he hadn't shared the radical change of plans regarding the speech. She might experience some early anxiety. He would unload it on her—as well as the audience—cold turkey when the meeting got under way. She wouldn't exactly be a captive audience, seated behind him on the platform, but he doubted that she would get up and leave; some in the audience might do just that, he thought. It will be something like opening night of a play, he mused, feeling a little pre-speech jitters: How many will leave before the play is over? Had his speech been printed and circulated, he probably wouldn't be here at all; his invitation to speak would have surely been withdrawn, he figured. He doubted, however, that any tomatoes or eggs would be thrown his way. This crowd would be much too polite for that—he hoped.

He remembered reading a story about a bluegrass band—not a terribly good one, presumably—deciding to tour on the coattails of an Oscar nominated film set in the Ozarks. The movie was well received, the bluegrass band was not in a certain city where fencing was erected to shield the band from flying objects, soda and beer cans, who knows what else.

"There are sandwiches, coffee, and cookies," the driver said, taking his seat behind the wheel. "Please feel free to enjoy." With that, the limo whispered from the terminal parking lot with its sights set on the Alpine city of Davos where a keynote address like no other would soon be delivered the next day.

Helping themselves to ham and Swiss cheese sandwiches and coffee, Eric said, "I've never delivered a speech to a large audience. I'm getting some stage fright, and I'm not onstage yet."

"You'll do fine," Isabella said. "You're very articulate and well spoken. I can hardly wait to hear the speech. I won't have to talk, will I?"

"No. I'll introduce you as my friend at some point. Just smile."

"How many will be there?"

"Several hundred, probably, if not more, and from all over the world."

"God! Thank you for having me sit on the stage with you. Will I be, you know, kind of behind you?"

"Not exactly. Everybody will be staring at you," Eric said, playfully with tongue in cheek.

Isabella elbowed him.

"By the way, I saw Charles Dickens on the beach, and Mark Twain during our flight."

Isabella shifted on the seat while she unwrapped her sandwich. "You didn't tell me."

"No, but you knew, didn't you?"

"Yes."

"How?"

"I hear a door opening when it happens, that's all I know. I try not to think of weird things like that, but I can't seem to help it sometimes."

"It appeared that you and I were the only ones on the plane who saw Mr. Clemens."

"Yes. Just us."

"How?"

"You're sounding like an Indian in an old western," Isabella said, laughing then checking the interior of her sandwich. "I'm able to decide who sees them."

"How?" Eric said.

"Eric! Quit saying *how*. Some tribe member may find it offensive." Isabella laughed and shot a look at the driver on the other side of the glass that separated him from passengers. She selected one of the cookies, a jam filled Spitzbuben. "I've had these before," she said, biting into the cooking. "Try one, Eric, they're delicious."

Eric sampled one. "Yes, they are good. So, how—sorry, when did this sort of thing start happening?"

"Who knows?"

"Stop saying who. You sound like an owl," Eric said. "One might hear you and find it offensive."

Isabella laughed. Then, "Whoooo!" She continued with her answer: "When Robin Hood, Little John, and Friar Tuck came to my room when I was little, I was thinking that I wanted to run away to a big forest where my father couldn't find me."

"Sherwood Forest was the trigger that brought the visitors to your room?"

"Who knows?" Isabella laughed, casting a playful look at Eric.

"So, are you a Great Horned owl, or the Barn type?"

"Who knows."

"Okay, enough," Eric said, laughing. "You're a grown

woman now. Surely you have some theory."

"I guess I do, maybe. It seems to happen when I need entertaining or want to please someone."

"I can't imagine that the pirates were entertaining," Eric said.

"Certainly not for me."

"By the way, did I ever ask you what a pink moon has to do with pirates?"

"No. I've thought about it a lot. I fixed myself a Pink Moscato Sangria that night in April when I saw the full moon rise. It was kind of like my drink. That's when the ship came sailing from nowhere."

"Have you ever heard of a black Russian drink?"

"Yes. Vodka and coffee liqueur."

"Right. Don't order one while we're here," Eric said with tongue in cheek.

"Not to worry. I don't like vodka," Isabella said. She laughed and reached for another cookie. "I love these. I'll have to find the recipe."

The limo arrived in Davos midafternoon. Reservations were waiting at Hotel Edelweiss. A porter collected Eric and Isabella's bags and they followed him to the elevator which delivered them to the third floor and their room. Eric tipped the porter and thanked him for his help.

Windows faced the snow-covered Alps. Skiers were on the slopes, dark figures from this distance, looking like thrill-seeking penguins. "I don't think I want to do that," Isabella said. "The last thing I need is a broken leg on this trip."

"Same here," Eric said. "I'm not the most athletic

dude in the world. Let's rest for a while then walk around town. Maybe have an early dinner and some Swiss cuisine."

"That sounds safe enough," Isabella said. She took off her shoes and lay on the bed.

Eric opened his briefcase and extracted the keynote speech then took a seat by a window. He was a compulsive tweaker, and this speech was tweaked within an inch of its life. Having taken a writing course as an undergraduate, a professor once said, "Don't wool a piece of writing to death. Things that aren't wrong begin looking that way. At some point you must pronounce Pharaoh's benediction on the thing: Let it be written, let it be done."

"What are you going to say?" Isabella asked from her spot on the bed. She fluffed her pillow then added a second one to elevate her head.

"Well, since much of forensic phycology is about ethics, motive, and crime scenes, I'll talk some about those, of course. Then I'll throw in something new and fresh."

"Like what?"

"Just some things I've come to believe, of late."

Eric perused each page of the speech. He looked over to where Isabella was lying on the bed. She was asleep. He would let her rest for a couple of hours then wake her at five o'clock. Putting his speech away, he settled into the chair and gazed out the window. Light snow was coming down in a mostly clear sky, blown downwind from its lofty source. He thought of how high snow could drift in Minnesota, a world away now. Kids pulling sleds in the neighborhoods, heading for a favorite slope for entertainment that cost nothing but cold hands and feet by the time they headed for home. His old *Western Flyer* hung from a rafter in the garage. The runners were rusty and lettering faded.

Eric figured that the temperature was falling outside. Isabella's purchase of muk luks and a parka was wise. Small women with little body fat need more protection from the cold, he guessed. But she could produce plenty of body heat in bed, he mused, looking over at her sleeping form. Whether or not his speech went over well, the audience would have a treat, nonetheless, with her on the stage. She could hold her own with any Swiss beauty in this country.

Pulling his briefcase to him, he opened it, then closed it. Don't wool the thing to death, man! he thought. It is what it is. Don't get scared now. It's a little too late. He wished, though, that he'd been called upon to deliver a keynote address to SETI and its search for extraterrestrial life. A more receptive audience. If not SETI, then some paranormal group. Yes, that would have been the ticket. They would embrace him with open arms, welcoming him into their otherworldly midst. Instead, he would be standing before a packed auditorium of forensic phycologists who would, in the end, probably, think that one of their colleagues has gone off the rails. And one whom they invited to give a keynote address! Well, it'll be us against them, girl, he thought, cutting again to Isabella, still sleeping soundly.

He suddenly felt a curious sting of guilt at having brought her along. He was probably subjecting her to the same ridicule that he himself might endure. Misery loves company. She was plucky, though, and up to whatever insults that may be hurled. Should that be the case, insults, the audience better be glad she hadn't brought along her shotguns. He smiled and dozed in the comfortable chair.

Eric woke to the sound of Isabella's voice. "Come lie down with me, baby." She led him sleepily to the bed where she turned down the covers and began to get undressed. She's got more in mind than a napping partner, he thought, while unbuttoning his shirt. The Alpine air agrees with her.

Chapter 10

Their lovemaking, "evening on the town," and strolling in and out of shops calmed Eric's pre-speech jitters. In a cozy café, ever so Swiss in its décor and menu, they enjoyed a traditional dinner of leeks with potatoes and plump, crimson sausage. Wine and cheese for appetizer set the tone for an enjoyable meal.

Eric was to deliver his keynote address at *10:00 a.m.* He and Isabella arrived at the auditorium 45 minutes early. She was wearing a stunning, black dress that went to her ankles. Though she wasn't a woman who could exhibit a great deal of cleavage, she cunningly managed a bit with the dress cut just low enough for that purpose. Her subtly applied perfume was the finishing touch. Eric wore grey slacks and herringbone sport coat and burgundy tie.

Upon entering the hall, the two of them checked in with an usher. They were given name tags. Being the keynote speaker, Eric was advised that he and Isabella could mount the platform approximately ten minutes before the program would start. There were three chairs: Eric and Isabella would occupy two of them; Master of Ceremony would be in the other.

Mingling among the crowd in the foyer, Eric spoke with colleagues whom he knew. He introduced his date. The tragic death of his mate two years earlier was well known across the Association. They all wondered, of course, who Isabella was. The couple were holding hands, so it was clear that she was probably more than a secretary.

"It's show time," Eric said, looking at his watch. "Let's do it." The two of them entered the hall and made their way down the center aisle toward the platform and podium.

Eric smiled and nodded to familiar faces as he passed. "My God, where did he get her?" one woman whispered while leaning into her husband.

"Heaven, I would think," replied her husband.

"I could rake your eyes off with a stick, Henry," his wife said. "Put them back in your head."

Reaching the platform, Eric and Isabella mounted the steps and took seats next to the Master of Ceremony. He and Eric shook hands. Eric introduced Isabella. She extended a hand to the MC.

At ten o'clock sharp, the MC rose and welcomed everyone to the meeting. After a few pleasantries regarding the great city of Davos, the MC introduced Eric: "We are privileged to have as our keynote speaker, Dr. Eric Erickson."

The audience applauded.

"The lovely woman sitting next to him is Ms. Isabella

Cabrera, a friend who has accompanied Dr. Erickson to Davos. He asked that she might be allowed to sit with him on the platform, for moral support."

Laughter and applause from the audience.

Isabella smiled and took Eric's hand.

"And now, without further ado, I give you Dr. Erickson."

"Go get 'em," Isabella said, releasing Eric's hand as he rose to the applause and approached the podium with his vanilla folder containing his speech.

Extracting his speech from the folder and laying it before him on the podium, he cleared his throat, had a drink of water provided, and began: "It is indeed an honor to be giving the keynote address to this esteemed gathering of colleagues. As I look out onto the audience, I am humbled when seeing those who have won the Nobel Prize for their pioneering research."

Eric paused for another drink of water; nerves rendered his throat dry.

"Settle down, boy, you're doing fine," Isabella said beneath her breath.

"This past year has been an interesting one for the work of forensic phycologists," he continued. "Our work in discovering motive as well as uncovering evidence has solved a number of cold murder cases, bringing at least a little satisfaction, if not closure for families whose loved ones were unaccounted for, some for many years."

Applause.

"My own work seems to have been lodged more and more in motives behind crimes that have been committed. Treacherous waters, motive, for one cannot see into another person's head to know, for sure, if they are telling the truth regarding why they were moved to do what they have done."

Isabella shifted in her chair. Where is he going with this? she wondered.

"In our courts of law, judges are sometimes in a quandary regarding intent, which can determine the difference between first, second degree murder, or manslaughter, especially if one wasn't at the scene of the crime, or present in the early moments of its development. Yes, having been an eyewitness is most helpful, that is if the witness is a credible individual, not given to lying, or simply stretching the truth."

I think I know now where he's headed, Isabella thought, and I'm not sure it will fly with this crowd.

"Seeing is believing is an old cliché," Eric continued. "But what if one doesn't see, and the witness is an individual of sterling character, then what?"

Damnit, Eric, be careful! Isabella thought. You're not speaking to a group of ghost chasers. You're about to unload something onto these people that is way out of their line of work. She suppressed a laugh. It's no wonder, she thought, that he hadn't shared the nature of his speech ahead of time.

Eric forged ahead: "Let me give you an example. But first, how many of you have seen a pink, full moon in April?"

"Oh, hell," Isabella mumbled.

Several raised their hand.

"I haven't, but I know someone who has, and more than once. Let me tell you a story about a pink moon."

"What does our work have to do with a pink moon?" one man whispered to the fellow sitting next to him."

"Damned if I know," the man returned. "I guess we're about to find out."

Eric turned slightly to look at Isabella, then returned his attention to the audience and said, "Does the beautiful woman sitting behind me look like a criminal?"

Heads shook across the audience, some verbalized with no. Eric looked back at Isabella. Her face was flushed. She managed a smile, however.

"In the month of April, a little over two years ago, my friend and traveling companion was arrested in Florida, on St. George Island where she owns a beach house."

Heads in the audience were turning, people looking quizzically at each other.

"What was her crime?" Eric continued. "Discharging a firearm—several of them—on the island."

Soft chuckling rolled across the audience. Eric looked back at Isabella. She lifted her eyebrows and smiled, as if to say, give 'em both barrels, baby.

"You are wondering, of course, who—or, *what* was she shooting at. The answer: Pirates. A three masted ship sailed into view under a full the moon—quite pink, I might add—with the intention of abducting Ms. Cabrera."

Murmurs rolled across the audience. Women put a hand to their mouth and shook their heads slowly.

"The ship quickly lowered the Jolly Roger, as well as the sails, then a party, one of whom was the captain, presumably, came ashore in a dinghy. Seeing that the men's eyes were on her beach house, my friend promptly gathered her four shotguns—the finest collection I have ever seen, left to her by her late father—loaded them, and awaited the uninvited visitors."

Many in the audience were settling more comfortably in their seats, as though preparing to watch a good movie. Isabella marveled at Eric's memory in recalling all that she told him.

"We need some popcorn," one man whispered to his wife, "this is getting good."

"When the dinghy landed," Eric continued, "only the captain strode toward Isabella's house. That's when she raised the A. Galazan, Pinless Sidelock 28 gauge and ask the captain what he wanted. 'I just want to talk, senorita,' the captain said, coming to a stop on the beach in front of her house. Talk from there, Isabella told him, or I'll blow your pirate ass into the Gulf."

The audience roared with laughter. Isabella's eyes moistened at the boldness in which Eric was relating this story. His stage fright was gone and he was rolling.

"You are a relative of our beloved Queen Isabella," the captain said. "She wants you to be with her on the other side." 'I'm not going anywhere with you mother—' Isabella said. Eric deleted the expletive ending.

Thunderous laughter rolled across the audience once more.

When the audience quieted, Eric resumed: 'Shoot all you want, love,' the captain said, 'neither cannon nor sword can hurt the likes of us anymore.' "Isabella said she got really scared, and mad. That's when she opened fire, one shotgun after the other. The captain returned to his men, unharmed. She could hear him and his men laughing as they rowed the dinghy back to their ship. Well, she got some more visitors close on the heels of the pirates: The Sheriff. Neighbors said it sounded like all hell was breaking loose with the shotgun blasts. She told the Sheriff that she was defending herself against pirates. Given the horrific gunfire, the Sheriff supposed that bodies might be found lying on the beach, or at least a little blood; neither was found. Isabella was arrested for discharging firearms on the island. She was released on her own recognizance the next morning."

The chemistry in the audience began to visibly change when things smacking of paranormal were introduced. A handful rose and left the auditorium. Undaunted, Eric pressed on: "She was put on unsupervised probation. The next year, during the month of April when the moon was full—and pink, the ship and pirates returned. Isabella was waiting. Though she knew from experience that her guns couldn't harm them, she opened fire nonetheless, thinking, perhaps that the roar of the guns might deter them. It didn't. She ran into her house and locked the door. The captain entered, simply passing through the door as though it wasn't there."

Another handful in the audience walked out. The MC rose from his chair beside Isabella and strode to the podium. He spoke softly near Eric's ear. Eric shook his head and continued: "What did the captain do? He threw me onto the couch and felt me up, Isabella said. She tried to fight him off, but her hands simply passed through him."

The MC rose from his chair again when another handful in the audience left the hall. He spoke softly once more to Eric who ignored the advice: "Well, off to jail again for my friend," Eric continued. "The judge ordered a psychiatric evaluation. She cleared it with flying colors. Did anybody else see the pirate's ship? you may ask. Yes. Two young boys, 10 and 8 years old live on the island. The oldest of the two testified in court that he saw the ship sitting offshore."

A few more in the audience rose to leave but sat back down upon hearing of the witness.

"The problem, however, was that an ongoing investigation could find no evidence of any such visitors having come ashore on either of those nights. They found no marks in the sand where a dinghy might have been pulled ashore, nor tracks that swashbucklers would have left in the sand near Isabella's house. The judge was in a quandary. The woman before him came across as remarkably sane and truthful. So, to get to the truth once and for all, he ordered a squad of Guardsmen to be present at her beach house in the month of April when the moon is full and, supposedly, pink. And that all will transpire this coming spring in America, of course, and on Florida's St. George Island."

Eric paused for long moments, had a drink of water, then cut back to Isabella who sat sedately.

"What am I asking of you, my colleagues?" Eric resumed, casting about at the audience. "It is this: Do not underestimate the power and gifts that may be present in a creative mind. One more story, a brief one, and I will leave you: Having purchased a beach house of my own, not far from Isabella on the island this past December, I went for a walk along the beach. It was Christmas Day. I saw a figure coming toward me, perhaps a hundred yards off. He was dressed rather oddly, I thought, in black coat and pants and a white shirt with high collar and tie, of sorts. As he drew nearer, I could see that he wore a pointed, unkempt beard on his chin. He walked very straight-backed with an unusual motion with his feet, as though they weren't bending at the arch. As we reached each other, he stopped before me and said hello. I returned the greeting then said, you have a remarkable resemblance to Charles Dickens. 'Well, I suppose that's because I am indeed Charles Dickens and I'm on my way to wish the lovely Isabella a very Merry Christmas.' With that, he stepped around me then said, 'and a very Merry Christmas to you, sir.' And to you, as well, I returned."

At this point, it seemed that most of the audience was coming to its feet to leave, many of them looking at their watches and shaking their heads. Eric looked back at Isabella. Her face was flushed in anger. How dare you be so rude to Eric, she thought.

Eric returned his attention to the audience when he heard gasps roll across the hall. Standing to his left, no more than a few paces away, was Mr. Charles Dickens. Had he entered from a wing his appearance might have evoked laughter. He simply materialized before everyone's eyes. There was such a tumult that those who left the auditorium earlier and lingering in the foyer to discuss the strangest keynote address they ever heard, rushed back in. They saw Mr. Dickens, who said nothing, only looking out across the hall. He smiled at Isabella.

"Try these on for size, folks," Isabella said sarcastically beneath her breath. Enter Sigmund Freud; Albert Einstein; Wolfgang Amadeus Mozart; Robin Hood, Little John and Friar Tuck—'nice to see you again,' Robin Hood said to Isabella. 'You're not a little girl, anymore,' he added.

Eric moved to where Isabella was sitting.

"Let's see ... two more," Isabella said, putting a finger to her lips. Enter Jesus and Mary Magdalene.

At his point the noise in the auditorium dropped dramatically. They could only stare. Jesus bent down and fastened a strap on Mary's sandal then turned to Isabella and said, "Nice trick. Can you walk on water as well?"

"Who knows? Thank you for coming."

"Our pleasure," Jesus said, then taking Mary's hand.

In what seemed like an eternity to the MC as well as auditorium management in general, the visitors began to disappear, one by one, and each waving goodbye. When they were gone, Eric took Isabella by an arm. "Let's get out of here," he said. "We'll try to find a back door."

There were no empty seats in the auditorium, for virtually all who left returned and everyone was on their feet and dumbstruck. What they saw would long be spoken of, especially among those of paranormal persuasion: Vindicated at last, and not by one of their own, until now.

Chapter 11

Eric and Isabella's flight home by-passed Minneapolis and landed at Tallahassee where they caught a shuttle flight to Pensacola. Eric's leased vehicle awaited them for the drive to St. George Island. They wondered how long it would be before news of the events in Davos found the state, not to mention the island. They were certain that global newswire would be all over it by now.

Reaching the island, the two of them held their breath, half expecting to see people thronged on the beach near Isabella's house. All was quiet, however. That would probably change, they figured. And it did, though not to the extent one might have thought. The reason being is that many suspected it was simply more false news, so prevalent these days when it was increasingly difficult to discern truth from falsehood. Ironically, some advertisers whose adds were on the same bogus page were all too happy to pay the liars, and rather handsomely.

Judge David Henry, who presided over Isabella's

case and put her on probation, heard of the story coming out of Davos, Switzerland. He was the first individual to deal with the alleged phenomena, in a legal capacity. Her second visit to his courtroom was for violating probation by opening fire on the island once more. Self-defense in fending off pirates, she pled. Her attorney made a respectable enough case to put at least a kernel of doubt as to whether the whole affair was nothing but fantasy coming from the mind of a disturbed woman. To deepen his quandary, she cleared a psychiatric evaluation without a hitch. This is one of the brightest, sanest individuals I've ever dealt with, the doctor concluded in a written report to the judge.

What to do? Order a squad of Guardsmen to be present at her beach house when the moon is full in the month of April. The moon was pink on both occasions, the defendant claimed. What are the odds of atmospheric conditions being right three times in a row for producing the pink moon? No one would hazard a guess. In the meantime, something else most unexpected was developing with Ms. Isabella Cabrera.

The Ides of March brought steadily warming temperatures to St. George Island. Eric and Isabella's friendship grew steadily, and they thought that they had fallen in love. But her demeanor was somber of late, uncharacteristic for a woman in love, and who was always ready with a smile and some idea of how to enjoy each day.

In the second week in March, she asked Eric if he

would drive her to Tallahassee for her annual checkup. There's a history of breast cancer in her family, she said, so she though it wise to get regular exams. In the past, she had taken a taxi to the state's capital.

It was approximately 80 miles to Tallahassee, a little over an hour's drive. Eric pulled the Suburban in front of her gynecologist's office. He said that he would wait outside for her.

The exam was surprisingly short, Eric thought, when Isabella returned after a mere 20 minutes. "So, how did it go?" he asked.

"All is well for another year," she said.

She was a quiet rider who seemed to enjoy gazing out the window no matter what the scenery. "Well, I guess this beautiful weather will bring more folks to the island," Eric said, hoping to open up a little conversation. Isabella only nodded.

Reaching the island, Isabella said, "I have some nice ham. Let's have lunch on the deck and enjoy the sun."

"Sounds like a plan," Eric said. He was glad that she suggested lunch, for he didn't want to return to his house just yet. Something wasn't right, but he wouldn't pry. When she was ready, he hoped she would tell him what was wrong.

With sandwiches and sweet tea in hand, the two of them took seats at a table on the deck. Eric called it right about more visitors to the beach, even though it was Monday. Folks were walking along the shore east and west, but not a great many. "That's something I've always loved about this island," Isabella said, sampling her sandwich, "it never gets wall to wall people even on summer weekends. And vehicles aren't allowed on the beach."

"It does have that appeal," Eric said, sampling his tea.

A family of five strolled along the beach in front of the house. The mother carried an infant in her arms while two other children trailed along behind, stopping now and then to examine a seashell. The father saw Isabella and Eric on the deck and waved.

Eric took a bite of his sandwich then chased it with tea. The glass stopped abruptly halfway between his mouth and the table when Isabella said, "Do you think I'm too old to be a mother?"

Temporally lost for words, Eric said at last, "Certainly not. A lot of women your age become mothers. Why do you ask?"

"Because I'm pregnant."

Eric was about to set his glass of tea on the table when Isabella dropped the bombshell. He turned the glass over and quickly put his napkin to the spill. "Did I hear you right?"

"Yes. Let me put it another way: You knocked me up." As her heart pounded, she searched Eric's face for a response.

Eric couldn't get words to come out. His eyes moistened. That was the only answer Isabella needed. Tears began to roll down her cheeks. Eric got up from his chair and came around behind her. He put his arms around her with his head next to hers. "Do you think I'm too old to be a father?"

"Certainly not. A lot of men your age become fathers," she said, mimicking his words to her. "There's something else," she said, snuffing back tears."

"Shoot—no pun intended."

"The doctor heard my heartbeat."

"That's good to know," Eric said, chuckling.

"He heard something else?"

"Like what?"

"Two more heartbeats."

"Clearing his throat, Eric said, "I—uh, I suppose a lot of men my age become fathers of twins, right?"

"I'm sure of it," Isabella said, taking one of Eric's hands and kissing it.

Chapter 12

April and its full moon were fast approaching; a kind of "D-Day," legally speaking, that would resolve Isabella's claims, one way or the other. It was the opinion of many, however, that her credibility was already established, and satisfactorily. What took place in Davos was being attested to by some of the most respected scientists on the planet: "This isn't just a phycological issue, but a matter of astrophysics and quantum mechanics as well. This five-foot-two, one hundred and thirty-five-pound woman, now carrying twins in her womb, possesses a trigger—no pun intended—can develop images in a cosmological darkroom. It's all there, everything and everyone that ever was. And she can *summon* them, seemingly at will."

"That's insane!" cried the skeptics.

"Stay tuned," returned the followers of the likes of Stephen Hawking, Carl Sagan, and Peter Higgs, though those scientific luminaries wouldn't necessarily buy in to these current theories of their groupies, one would guess.

There was a problem, though, that no one had an answer for: Why won't the pirates go away? Why have they returned for two consecutive years to menace Isabella? All the other *visitors* were benign and presented no danger. Queen Isabella of Spain wants you to join her on the other side, the captain said. Her response that night of the full, pink moon is well documented.

Eric and Isabella, now growing increasingly great with child—two of them—hashed over this problem nearly day and night as April crept ever closer. "For lack of a better term, we will call them ghosts," Isabella said. "What is it that ghosts dislike or fear most?" she asked Eric as they sat on her deck one balmy evening.

"They seem to prefer darkness," Eric said.

"Yes. And no more than the moon's glow. Why?"

"A fear of bright light," Eric suggested.

"Exactly," Isabella returned, "lest their evil deeds be seen in the light of day. What if we stationed a large search light near my house? And, if the pirates show up, we turn the light on them full force."

"It might be worth a try," Eric said. "We know that they only laugh at gunfire."

"Let's get on the Internet and see where we could rent such a light," Isabella said.

In addition to ordering a squad of National Guard personnel to be present at Isabella's beach house on the 15th of April when a full moon was to appear, Judge David Henry also ordered a quarantine, of sorts, for the island on that night. Homeowners wouldn't be required to leave—no mandatory evacuation—but they were encouraged to stay in their homes and away from Isabella's house when the clock struck twelve at midnight. Who could say what danger may be present if the pirate ship appeared offshore once more?

According to Isabella's account, this would be the scoundrel's 3rd visit, if in fact they did come back. It was her they wanted, and they left empty handed on both previous occasions. They might be considerably more aggressive this time. A full-fledged attack upon the island, perhaps.

Media would be banned from the island this night, for they could not be trusted, the judge thought, to remain hidden if events began to transpire in a way that was suggested by Isabella's story. It was a safety issue. This ban was a recent order by the judge when he learned that media from a dozen or more countries converged upon tiny Apalachicola and Eastpoint, 7 miles apart, with a combined population of less than 15,000. Neither town could accommodate such a horde. Those without a proper roof and bed slept on sidewalks, behind stores, in people's back yards—those who would allow it—like homeless souls, for the state closed the island to traffic, siting environmental and ecosystem risks. Come midnight on the 15th, however, media would find their way to Eastpoint and the bridge connecting the island with the mainland. It was from this vantage that they hoped to observer the mysterious ship, and the iconic pink moon, should either appear.

The economic upside was significant, however, and business was booming for local merchants. Every country represented saw to it that their reporters and staff had plenty of American dollars, and they spent them liberally. Media had been arriving daily for two weeks. Store owners and restaurants were caught off guard. But they were soon on the phone and Internet placing orders for food and goods. UPS, Federal Express, and delivery trucks of every size rolled non-stop toward Florida's Big Bend. One panicking grocery store owner was on the phone: "Bring me bread, lunchmeat, peanut butter, potato chips, cookies—anything that humans eat!"

"Need beer?" the purveyor asked.

"Semi load!"

A searchlight that Isabella suggested for possibly dissuading the pirate ghosts was found in Panama City. It was to be delivered on the 14th of April, a day ahead of the supposed event. Isabella's attorney, George Davis spoke to the judge regarding the idea: "It's worth a try," the judge said. "Her safety is paramount. I understand, too," he added, "that she is pregnant."

"Yes, and with twins," Davis said. The judged raised his bushy eyebrows and smiled.

A seven-day forecast predicted cloud cover for the 15th day of April along Florida's Big Bend and west to Panama City. "The moon will still be present, of course," Eric assured Isabella who was growing uneasy. "Anyway, these seven-day predictions often change," he added. "The forecasts are usually pretty good for three days, after that it gets dicey. The Jetstream has a mind of its own."

"I'm swearing off alcohol with these two babies in my belly," Isabella said, "so I'll not be fixing a Pink Moscato Sangria."

"Fix one for me," Eric said. "I've never had one."

"The pirates may try to abduct *you,*" Isabella said, laughing.

"I doubt that Queen Isabella would be interested in me," Eric said.

"Well, she can't have you," Isabella said, taking his hand. "I'm not going to raise these alone," she added, placing a free hand on her increasingly enlarged stomach.

"What do you think," Eric said, bending and putting an ear to her stomach, "boys or girls?"

"When this is all over, we'll get another ultrasound," Isabella said. "We could have one of each."

Chapter 13

At *8:00 a.m.*—0800 military time—a squad of National Guard arrived on the island. There were 7 men, 2 women, plus the squad leader, a corporal. The searchlight that Isabella ordered arrived the day before. "Will we be looking for aircraft as well?" joked the corporal.

"No," Eric said, laughing. "We have a plan."

The corporal was satisfied with that. He returned to his squad where there was muffled laughter.

The seven-day forecast of cloud cover was unfortunately holding up by early afternoon. But there was a chance for *some* clearing by late evening. What wouldn't change, of course, was a full moon for this 15th day of April. Whether or not it would be seen, was anybody's guess; pink, would be another question as well.

With binoculars to her eyes, Isabella could see that media were gathering on the bridge that connected the island with the mainland. "Have a look," she said, handing the glasses to Eric.

"Wow! There's hundreds of them, I would guess."

"I hope they're not disappointed," Isabella said, taking the glasses and having another look. I'll be the laughingstock of the whole country, if not the world," she added, still keeping the glasses to her eyes. "Will you visit me in jail, honey?"

"Yes. I'll bring you anything you want," Eric said. Given what was now well documented regarding what took place in Davos, no one thought that jail was in the cards should the pirates not show. Judge David Henry simply wanted to see this through. And it was rumored that he was somewhere on the island even now.

The Guard personnel were armed, of course, and Eric reminded them that there was to be no gunfire. It wouldn't do any good. They shot glances at each other. It was clear to Eric that most of them thought this the dumbest mission ever. But it was fun, for now, even if they ended up being the butt of every joke about having been called upon to be a part of this.

Dusk was falling on the island. The Guard members were stretched out in the sand around Isabella's house. Some dozed, others chatted about what was supposed to happen come midnight.

Isabella was looking exhausted, Eric thought, and he suggested that she lie down and have a nap. She was reluctant but gave in and lay down on a couch. "I'll wake you in plenty of time," he assured her.

Eric put on a pot of coffee and when it was ready, he circulated among the Guard members and offered coffee to any who wanted it. Most did. They fetched tin cups from their packs and he poured for them. He returned to the house and brewed another pot.

Eric gazed at Isabella's sleeping figure. The pregnancy was maker her even more beautiful. Her face was radiant. She's really getting big, he thought. Twins is an awful lot of cargo for such a small woman. But she seemed up to it, even when dealing with bouts of morning—and, evening sickness. Someone once said that if men had babies, there would only be 1 child per family. So amazing, he thought, a woman's ability to bring forth children. All a man needs to do is have the time of his life fertilizing her eggs. We get off easy. It's like throwing down a little grass seed when the real work is for the one pushing a mower and trying to keep weeds out.

Eric woke Isabella at eleven o'clock. She gently scolded him for letting her sleep so long. You were exhausted, he reminded her. She went onto the deck and looked to the sky; cloud cover remained. Guard personnel were up and positioned behind sand dunes nearest to the house. "There she is," said one of the men to a comrade.

"Pregnant with twins, they say," returned the friend.

"The pirates—if there are any—will play hell gettin' past us," said one. "We got your back, girl," he added.

"You got that right, dude," said a female, affixing a bayonet to her rifle, as though it might do some good. It wouldn't, but it made her more comfortable.

Isabella found the binoculars and panned the bridge connecting the island with the mainland. The bridge was lit up like Christmas Eve in Miami. "They've been ordered to turn off all flashlights and lanterns a few minutes before midnight," Eric said.

At five minutes before the appointed hour, the bridge grew dark as all flashlights and lanterns were turned off. The lights of the bridge were turned off as well. Isabella looked to the sky. A breeze was rising, and the overcast was breaking up slowly, revealing a faint, pinkish hue, like early dawn. Then the clouds parted, as though a great hand was pushing them aside. “There it is!” Isabella said. A gust of wind tossed her dark hair and she pushed it from her eyes.

“Wow! It’s pink as a Valentine!” Eric said.

“Look at the moon!” said a Guardsmen to the one next to him.

“Whoa! I’ve never seen a pink moon.”

But there was no ship in sight. “I should have made you a Pink Moscato Sangria,” Isabella said.

Five minutes passed, then ten, then fifteen. That’s when Isabella heard Ricky Jones, the oldest of the two Jones brothers call to her as he and his brother rounded the back of her house at a full run. “Izzy! There’s the ship!”

Isabella and Eric turned and looked north. This time the ship was tacking into the leeward side of the island. The full moon was casting light onto the bay and the ship. Her sails were full. Eric guessed that she was making 14 knots or better and plunging in the Gulf waters while her bow sent up spray and the Jolly Roger flapped in the breeze. The Guardsmen’s squad leader heard the boy and signaled to his squad. They quickly moved to positions at the rear of the house. “Jesus, Joseph, and Mary,” said one of the men as he scrambled with his gear.

Eric moved to the search light and cranked a wheel

that turned it north. He removed a side panel that housed the gasoline generator. He started it then replaced the panel which muffled the sound. He moved to where Isabella was standing at the base of a sand dune.

He could only imagine the excitement on the bridge while media and other spectators, no doubt, watched in awe as the three-masted ship continued into the bay. When the boat came abreast of Isabella's house, it settled into the water and sat still. Her canvas was lowered while shipmates clung to the masts. The Jolly Roger remained aloft this time, however. A dinghy was lowered, and several men boarded it. The captain stood in the bow as the men began to row toward shore. "Here comes the bastard," Isabella said, easing against Eric and drawing the two boys to her.

Eric left Isabella's side and returned to where the search light stood. He waited for the dinghy to come ashore. He looked about him at the Guardsmen. They were wide-eyed and silent. Some were mumbling beneath their breath.

Reaching shore, the men disembarked and pulled the boat onto the sand a few feet. The captain turned and looked toward Isabella's house. Neither he nor his men seemed to sense anything different from their last visit, only that they had approached from the island's leeward side. Leaving his men with the dinghy, the captain began walking toward the house 100 feet away. "Please stay here, boys," Isabella said softly as she started toward the approaching captain."

"Be careful, Izzy," the youngest boy said. Izabella only nodded and continued to walk slowly toward the captain."

"That's close enough, woman," Eric muttered from his position behind the light.

As though she had heard him, Isabella came to a stop 50 feet from the captain who also stopped. "Where's your gun, senorita?" the captain said with a cruel twist on his lips.

Isabella didn't answer. She just stared at the captain.

"Queen Isabella is still waiting for you," the captain said. "My, my, it looks like our lovely Isabella is with child," the captain added, gazing at her luridly.

Isabella said nothing. She waited for the captain to make a move toward her. When he did, she raised her hand in a prearranged signal for the search light. Eric hit the switch and the 4000-watt light came on. The captain threw up his hands and screamed. He stumbled backward, falling several times, then began crawling back to the dinghy where his men were screaming and covering their faces. Eric kept the light on them. With great difficulty, falling in and out of the boat, they managed to push it from the beach and began rowing toward the ship while Eric kept the light steadily on them. When they reached the ship, Eric panned the boat from stem to stern while pirates hastily sent sails aloft and brought the boat about and headed east. When the ship was out of sight, an applause went up among the Guardsmen. They could hear thunderous applause and whistles coming from the bridge where all the lights were back on. Eric turned the searchlight off and came to Isabella who was still standing on the beach. "I don't think we'll see them next year," she said.

"I think not," Eric agreed.

Isabella looked up at the pink moon. Isn't it lovely? I suppose this is the last time we will see it."

"Don't be so sure," someone standing behind them said. They turned to see Galileo Galilei with an eyeglass turned to the sky. "Most interesting, my dear. Most interesting indeed.

Judge David Henry dismissed the case against Isabella, of course. Things were crazy around St. George Island for much of the spring. But like stormy weather, things settled down as the dog days of summer approached. Isabella gave birth to healthy twin baby girls in August. They named them Victoria and Veronica, 2 Vs for victory. One of the girls had Eric's reddish, blonde hair. The other favored her mother with dark hair, finely chiseled nose turned up just a bit, and Spanish complexion.

Eric and Isabella were approached by a major publishing house that offered them a mid-seven-digit advance to write a book about all that had taken place on the island and in Davos. They accepted the offer. Eric resigned his adjunct position at the university and decided to take an indefinite leave of absence from his work as a forensic phycologist. He sold his home in Minneapolis and his beach house on St. George Island as well. Isabella's house was plenty big for the four of them.

While they were certain that they had seen the last of the pirates, other visitors, quite enjoyable, dropped by from time to time when Isabella was in a certain frame of mind. Ricky and Steward Jones liked to come to her house when Charles Dickens or Mark Twain were there.

Winnie the Pooh made an appearance now and then, to the delight of the twin girls. The Jones boys always wanted to know how Tiny Tim was doing. He's fit as fiddle. Fit as a fiddle, Dickens would say. And Twain, when asked about Tom and Huck: rafting the Mississippi, boys, lighting out for the territory.

Dreams for Two

Ardith Lukenstein stood at a window in her office on the third floor of Lukenstein Publishing. The view looked out onto midtown Manhattan. She had a coffee cup in her right hand and a hardcover book in her left. It was April. Though temperatures were unseasonably mild this day, and folks in shirtsleeves on the sidewalk down below, a proverbial March snowstorm had blanketed the city, the remains of which were pushed up in great mounds wherever there was room for them.

It was Saturday, and school children were climbing the mountains of snow and sliding back down on the seat of their pants or on pieces of cardboard; the relative short distance from top to bottom didn't lend itself for using sleds. Given the laughter among the children, one might have thought they were snowboarding in the Alps. This day of entertainment would cost them nothing but a wet bottom.

The city endured a long, bitterly cold winter, one that seemed to belie a warming planet, less a theory these days and more an increasingly accepted fact. But we're in for extremes on both ends of the spectrum, say climate scientists. Get ready for both. Well, they were right so far regarding heat waves, at least; there were record numbers of deaths caused by record temperatures in many places around the world.

Ardith tested her coffee and found it cold. She turned from the window and strode to a sink, dumped the coffee, refreshed the cup, then returned to her desk. She looked at the newly published book in her hand, a debut novel by 59-year-old Eddie Edgeworth. Whether or not he could produce another one would be a matter of wait and see. But this one was good, though she doubted that Harry Potter sales would be threatened. Ardith found it interesting that an author's first novel is often considered his or her best. She thought that maybe it was because the author was less cautious, and just let it rip.

The designers did a beautiful job on the cover with foil lettering, at Ardith's direction. I want a first-class cover, she told them. The author, homeless in Fort Lauderdale, Florida, arranged for a new photo of himself. He cleaned up pretty well, she thought, smiling. It was a head and shoulders shot. He was wearing a black sweater, and looked very author-like. He had gotten himself a mailbox; she sent him an author's copy of his new book. He was thrilled. He opened a bank account, too, at her insistence, so that royalty payments, scant as they might be, could be direct deposited.

She sent copies out for reviews two weeks earlier. They were slow coming in. Those that she received so far were somewhat disappointing. Then, again, Eddie

Edgeworth isn't a household name in the literary world. But she knew the publishing business, and the difference between a sleeper and a dog. Eddie's novel is the former, she believed. It isn't one of those stories that start out with a bang, she knew, but it gains momentum slowly, with care, and reaches a decent arch about midway. One never really knows what a new book will do, especially a debut novel, Ardith often told her authors.

The story gets a little fanciful for readers who want bare bones realism, but too much realism makes for a dull read, Ardith thought. If one wants to escape while reading a novel, go where your imagination can run wild. And throw in a smidgen of cheese, too. A slice of cheese makes a sandwich and *story* taste better. All your readers aren't highbrow intellectuals for whom emotion is a nasty word, Ardith told her newest authors. Give them some tears, too, now and then. She quoted Robert Frost: "No tears in the writer, no tears in the reader."

In the early going, Ardith touched base with Eddie every couple of weeks to let him know how the book is coming along in the process. She suggested a few editorial improvements, mostly mechanical things, like better paragraph arrangement, chapter breaks, and improved punctuation here and there. There were no changes of substance. The author has some talent, and she wasn't inclined to derail any of it. Eddie had no problem with the minor changes Ardith suggested.

She managed to get a couple of "praise" lines for the book's back cover. No big-name authors, but respectable ones. None of them said they'd been up all night reading it or couldn't put it down. But Ardith preferred the honest reviews over the flowery ones which were mostly patronizing, in her opinion, things like "Destined to be a modern classic"; "One of the great emerging writers of our generation." On and on they would go with such premature jargon.

Her favorite praise line for Eddie's book came from a reviewer in Kansas City: "If you stay with this book, you're in for a fun ride into another world." This was the only early review Ardith shared with Eddie. He liked it.

Spring and fall are the traditional times for launching new titles. Eddie's book was set to go on sale the first Tuesday in April. At some point, she would speak with him about doing a few book signings, probably in his home state of Florida, and test the local waters.

Eddie Edgeworth's new book—a small printing of 1,000 copies, for starters—went on sale in the first week of April as planned. Orders from booksellers were slow, predictably for a debut novel, one that hadn't gotten tons of pre-release hype. Eddie's book needed word of mouth—don't they all? and that wouldn't come overnight, barring a wow review from a big-name reviewer.

After learning of his book's release, Eddie called Ardith every few days to see how it was doing. It's selling some, she would tell him, though not how many, and she didn't always have those numbers at her fingertips. Sales were slow—godawful slow—but she wouldn't relate that to him, not yet.

Eddie visited a lot of Fort Lauderdale bookstores and

searched the shelves for his book. He found none. He thought of asking customer service to see if they could find the book on their computer, but decided against it: If it's not in their store, why would they give a damn? he thought. And his homeless appearance—backpack and all—wouldn't exactly put him in the best light as an author whose new book was worth taking up shelf space.

He wasn't given to much depression, except mild bouts when panhandling was poor and he and Sally were forced to dumpster dive, but he was depressed as hell now. And he hadn't felt well since returning from New York. He was experiencing occasional shortness of breath. Anxiety did that to him sometimes. There was plenty to be anxious about with his book going down the tubes.

Something was about to change, however. A freelance book reviewer on the Internet, who lived in Fort Lauderdale, did some investigating and learned that the author of a new book is a homeless vet, having served two tours in Iraq with the 1st Marine Division. The author had been on the street 7 years while writing it, and was still homeless. The reviewer hadn't read the book. He bought it, though, and found it to be a pretty good read. Americans—the world, for that matter—love the underdog and redemption. He wrote an honest, moving review of the book. The story went viral.

When Ardith Lukenstein saw the review, she tried to reach Eddie by phone, but no answer. Two days later, orders for the book started pouring in from Florida bookstores. It was all hands on deck at Lukenstein Publishing. This was the beginning of a big one, for she knew the signs. Readers were hungry for just such a feel-good bombshell like this. She placed an order for 50,000 copies that would be shipped directly from printer to booksellers. Eddie's book wasn't what one would call great writing or a literary masterpiece. But it was a fun story that wouldn't disappoint most readers, Ardith believed. And they would get their money's worth for the beautifully designed, $27 hardcover.

Word of mouth, as well as a host of new reviewers, was doing its magic for Eddie's book. Large orders came in from all over the deep south; then up the Atlantic seaboard; then a sharp U turn and cutting a wide swath across the nation's heartland with sights set on the West Coast. North to Alaska and Canada were next; then back to New England.

"Damnit, Eddie! Where are you?" Ardith said after trying over and over to get him on the phone. She was pumping royalties into his account on a weekly basis. Yet she heard nothing.

The book was kicking unadulterated butt up the New York Times Bestseller List, steamrolling every title in its way. When it hit #1, and on Amazon's list as well, Ardith told her staff to watch the store. She was taking a plane to Fort Lauderdale.

Her plane landed at Fort Lauderdale/Hollywood International in the early afternoon on a Friday. She rented a car then tried Eddie on the phone once more. Nothing. She doubted that she could learn anything from his mailbox at a UPS store. Private information. Anyway, how would they know where a homeless person might be living from one day to the next? She drove to his bank but couldn't learn anything other than his mailbox address. All they knew was that cash was spilling into his account like an out of control slot machine. What to do now? Find out where homeless hang out and ask around.

After two hours of driving and talking to one homeless person after the other, and giving each a few dollars for their trouble, she struck paydirt: "Yeah, I know Edgy," said a homeless man. "I haven't seen him for a while." He told Ardith where he last saw Eddie's camp. It was a grove of trees near the beach. Ardith drove to the location and learned that he was in the hospital. Edgy had a bad heart attack, a homeless man told her. After being told which hospital, she drove there and inquired into his room number. She found him in bed and on oxygen. His girlfriend, Sally was there. Ardith quietly introduced herself. "Why isn't he in the Intensive Care Unit?" Ardith whispered.

"He wouldn't let them put him there," Sally returned. "He said that he was dying beyond his means already."

Ardith smiled slightly, for she knew that Eddie was quoting Oscar Wilde when upon his own deathbed.

Eddie had lost weight since she saw him in January. His eyes were closed. She quietly pulled up a chair and sat down beside the bed near his head: "Eddie," she said softly.

"Call him Edgy," his girlfriend mouthed.

"Edgy, it's Ardith."

His eyes fluttered open and he turned his head to her. A faint smile came to his face. "Mrs. Lukenstein, what are you doing here?" His voice was weak and the effort of speaking those few words was difficult.

"I've been trying to get you on the phone for days."

"I lost the damn thing," he said. "I always do that."

His girlfriend, Sally, smiled and nodded. Though she didn't have many teeth, at least in the front, she was an attractive young woman. Her youthful face belied her homelessness and drinking. Resiliency.

Eddie struggled to get his breath then continued: "Before I started feeling really bad, I went around to a bunch of bookstores. My book wasn't on any of their shelves. I'm sorry I caused you so much trouble, Mrs. Lukenstein. I should never have gone to New York and bothered you."

"Why didn't you tell me that you're a veteran?" Ardith asked, taking one of Eddie's hands.

"I don't talk about that much."

"Have you checked your bank account lately?"

"No."

"You should. Your book took off took off like a Saturn rocket and didn't stop until it hit the top of the New York Times Bestseller List and Amazon's as well. You're fast becoming a famous and wealthy author."

Eddie's eyes filled with tears. "You're kidding," he said weakly.

Tears started rolling down his girlfriend's face and she took Eddie's hand.

Ardith withdrew a section of the Times and showed Eddie his book sitting at #1.

"Wow, we made it, baby," he said, looking at Sally and squeezing her hand.

"*You* made it, Edgy," she said, dashing at tears on her cheeks.

"Indeed, you did," Ardith said.

Sally left the room and Eddie asked Ardith to come closer so that he wouldn't have to raise his voice. He asked her to find an attorney to prepare a will. She said that her publishing house retained an Intellectual Property Attorney. Eddie requested cremation, the means by which most of his homeless friends were disposed of over the years. And he didn't want a funeral service. He wanted to leave his book's copyrights and royalties to Sally, 15 years his junior. "She's a good soul who has never had two nickels to rub together," Eddie said.

"I'll see to it," Ardith said. "And the money should be put in a trust so that nobody can bilk her out of it. She'll have a very comfortable income for the rest of her life."

"She's always wanted a little house near the beach," Eddie said. "Do you think she could have one?"

"My God, yes," Ardith said. Though she wasn't going to get into numbers here, she knew that Eddie's bank account hit high 6 digits a week ago and was climbing fast.

Ardith left Eddie's room and got on her cell phone. She told her publishing house attorney to prepare a will—immediately—and fax it to her before the day is out. Standing at a window, she saw a Staples store across the street. She told the attorney to fax it there. She gave him Eddie's instructions. And, too, he wanted the hospital bill paid in full.

Ardith left the hospital and crossed the street to Staples. She said she was expecting a fax from New York.

She gave them her cell phone number and asked them to call her as soon as the fax came in. It's a matter of life and death, she told them. And she meant it literally.

At eight o'clock that evening, Ardith got the call from Staples: her fax had arrived. After collecting the faxed will, she ran across the street to the hospital and walked as fast as she could down the hall toward Eddie's room. "Please don't be dead," she mumbled, breathing heavily, for she was a large woman. Entering Eddie's room, she found him in his bed. His eyes were closed. Sally was sitting near his head. Her eyes were swollen from crying. Ardith pulled a chair up to the bed and sat down near Eddie's head. "Edgy," she said. He opened his eyes slowly. "Thank God," Ardith mumbled. "I've got your will. You must sign it."

Eddie nodded. "Can we crank his bed up a little?" Ardith asked Sally.

"Yes," she said. She rose from her chair and found the handle for raising Eddie's head.

Ardith extracted the will from her purse. "You should read it," Ardith said.

"I can't," Eddie said. It was clear that he was too weak. "I trust you," he said. Ardith picked up a tray on a night stand and placed the will on it. She gave Eddie a pen and told him where to sign it. He did and handed the pen back to her. It wasn't as legible as his handwritten manuscript on legal pads with its coffee stains that he had first presented to her on that cold January morning in her office. But it was good enough.

"I directed our attorney to make it out as you requested," Ardith said, folding the will and returning it to her purse." Eddie smiled and nodded then closed his eyes. The will was properly deposited in the Broward County Courthouse.

Eddie Edgeworth died the next morning at *9:00 a.m.* Too many homeless days and nights had, in the end, taken its toll. Ardith and Sally were at his side when he drew his last breath. Ardith told the young woman what Eddie bequeathed to her. She broke down: "I ain't never had nothin' in my fuckin' life," she said, dashing at tears on her cheeks.

"You do now," Ardith said. "And you'll need to take care of yourself. I want to keep in touch with you. You were Eddie's best friend, and you knew him better than anyone. People will want to know more about him, what kind of man he was, how he lived on the street, that he was a Marine vet who served in Iraq, things like that. Would you be willing to help?"

"Yes. I'll do anything."

At Eddie's request, there was no funeral service. Sally and a few homeless friends gathered at the funeral home where he'd been cremated. They were his only family, as far as anyone knew, for no next of kin could be located. Sally said that he had never spoken of family members anywhere. The funeral director suggested a nice urn for Eddie's remains. Sally said he wouldn't want that. She was given his remains in a cardboard box. She clutched it close to her breast.

Eddie's book remained at #1 on the New York Times Bestseller for 18 weeks, then dropped to #2. After two years, it slipped to #3. During the holidays, however, it would elbow its way back to #1. It was translated into a dozen languages and more were being planned. It sold 6,000,000 copies, and counting, worldwide.

Eddie Edgeworth's girlfriend, Sally stopped drinking and never took it up again. She bought her a comfortable little house not far from the beach in Fort Lauderdale, and a car. She went shopping for a new wardrobe as well, and got some dental work done, for she wanted to look her best when talking to one group or another about bestselling author, Eddie Edgeworth—Edgy to his friends.

CPSIA information can be obtained
at www.ICGtesting.com
Printed in the USA
LVHW050957220620
658650LV00006B/597